1993

University of St. Francis
006.6 F899
Friedhoff

W9-ADC-182

3 0301 00053444 2

visualization

the **SECOND** computer revolution

VISUALIZATION

richard
mark
friedhoff
and william benzon

W. H. FREEMAN AND COMPANY
NEW YORK

LIBRARY
College of St. Francis
JOLIET, ILL

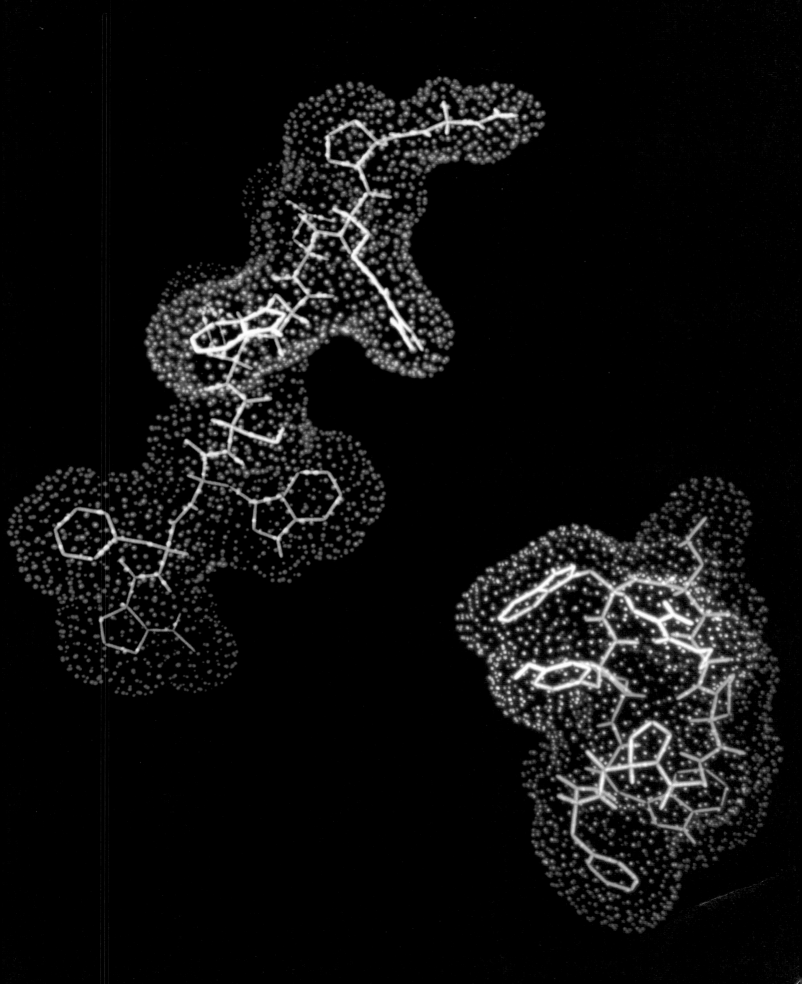

006.6
F899

FOR EDWIN H. LAND

Front cover: *Shuttle Stop Space Station* by Randy Bradley RPI/CICG © 1988. This image is a rendering of a three-dimensional scene that has been defined within the computer. Such three-dimensional modeling techniques have vast application in virtually every area of human endeavor.

Back cover: Top, Visualizing a bacteriophage, J. Jiménez and J. M. Carazo from Javier Jiménez et al. "Computer Graphic Display Method for Visualizing Three-Dimensional Biological Structures," *Science* vol. 232, May 30, 1986, pp 1113–1115. Copyright 1986 AAAS. Middle, Black hole density, Image courtesy Dr. Larry Smarr and Dr. John Hawley, National Center for Supercomputing Applications, Champaign, Illinois. Bottom, *Inside a Quark,* designed by Ned Greene, NYIT Computer Graphics Lab.

Pages 3, 5, 7: Image sequence showing template forcing of a molecule (see *Visual Experiments*).

Editor: Edith M. Pavese
Designer: Elissa Ichiyasu
Photo Editor: J. Susan Sherman

Paperbound edition published January 1991,
by W. H. Freeman and Company,
by arrangement with Harry N. Abrams, Inc.
Text copyright © 1989 Richard Mark Friedhoff
and William Benzon
Illustrations copyright © 1989 Harry N. Abrams, Inc.
Published in 1989 by Harry N. Abrams, Incorporated,
New York. A Times Mirror Company
All rights reserved.
No part of the contents of this book may be reproduced
without the written permission of the publisher
Printed and bound in Japan

147, 375

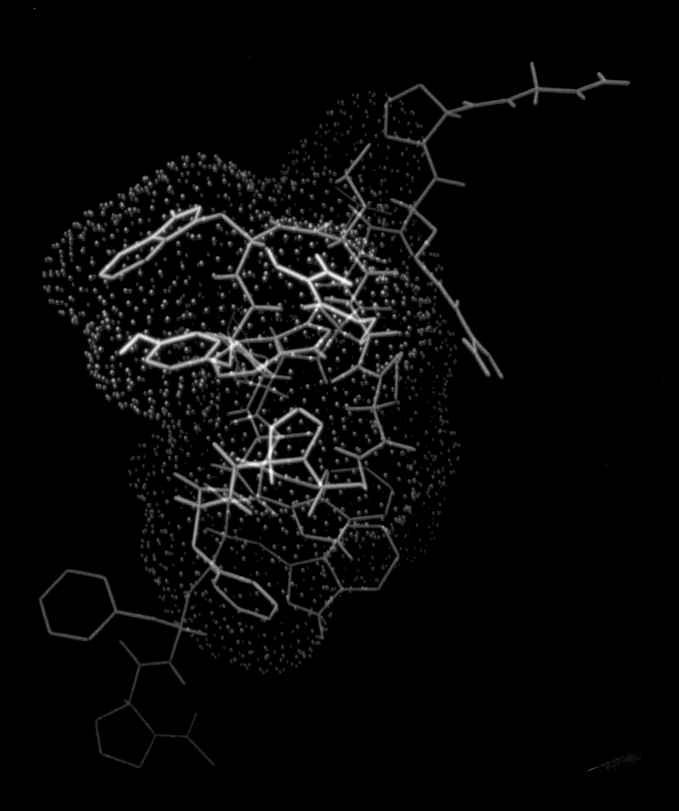

contents

FOREWORD BY RICHARD L. GREGORY 8
PREFACE BY RICHARD MARK FRIEDHOFF 10

introduction: visual thinking with computers 12

we create the world we see 18

images from energy 46

computer graphics 82

visual experiments 132

emergent technologies 172

ACKNOWLEDGMENTS 200
FURTHER READING 202
INDEX 204
CREDITS 214

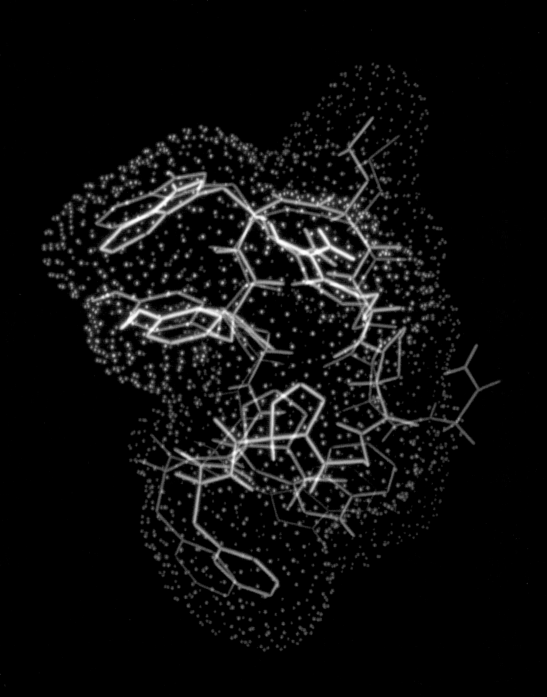

foreword

Picture-images have held magic power from cave paintings more than 20,000 years old to what are no doubt infant computer images of today born of technology less than twenty years ago. Creating pictures is a uniquely human ability. Like language, pictures can project into the past or imagined future and create new or even impossible worlds. But they work only for observers with knowledge and intelligence to create meaning from the pictures, as one creates meaning from the words of a language. So the key to understanding the power of pictures, or any symbols, lies in the human brain or the mind.

Richard Friedhoff distinguishes between preconscious and conscious visual processes, as most of the still only partly-understood processes of perception are hidden below our awareness. They must be discovered by experiments of the Brain Sciences, mainly cognitive psychology and physiology, with suggestions from the successes and failures of attempts to make machines capable of seeing.

The central point that this book makes is that the newly discovered *preconscious* processes of human vision can be tapped and used to powerful effect by computer images—especially by computer graphics to suggest ideas. Perhaps its most powerful form is interactive graphics, where the hand can control and change the image, much as though it is a solid object lying in the familiar space of the object world. But the possibilities exceed the normal hand-eye interaction with objects, for the computer may display *abstractions* and even impossible *fantasies*, which can never exist as real objects. It has been claimed that computer interaction allows visualization to take off from our familiar world of objects, even to further dimensions of space. So a computer generated four-dimensional hypercube, although at first a meaningless jumble of lines, becomes a richly meaningful object as it is explored by moving it around under the control of the viewer. A fascinating question is how powerful computer graphics will ultimately turn out to be for enhancing our visual awareness, and conceptual powers to understand and invent.

Richard Friedhoff points out, though, that computer graphics can be deceptive: "Where else is it possible to find a tree trunk that only has an outside surface? Fly into a mountain on a flight simulator and you might just disappear into 'unspace'—a place that has no characteristics at all....We can, if we wish, design algorithms to advance the capabilities of the computer beyond simply modeling light and surfaces. Computers are already used to simulate the forces binding molecules, the support structures of buildings, manufacturing processes, astrophysical systems, theoretical mathematics— and the list is growing. There is no foreseeable limit to the kinds of phenomena that can be modeled."

We used to think of machines as humble tools and weapons—slaves in our hands. Then as engineering came to develop superhuman strength and accuracy, virtually the only limits to the practically possible were set by limits of human imagination and ability to focus data and knowledge to create effective designs. Computers are accessible knowledge-bases and are becoming independent intelligences. But they have their own languages, and work on a different time scale of processing speed from us. Now, almost as prehistoric man communed and tried to control nature with paintings on cave walls, we control and invent and discover ourselves with machine-handled symbols communicating with pictures through our eyes.

There is much of interest and importance in *Visualization: The Second Computer Revolution* from something of the nature of perception and its physiological and psychological processes to the power of pictures generated by computers to transform realities and imaginings to our will—sometimes with startling results.

Richard L. Gregory
Bristol, England
May, 1989

preface

This volume began with a single interview, now nearly nine years ago. In 1980, while a graduate student at Yale University, I was a Fellow of the American Association for the Advancement of Science in Media and I had been assigned to work for the CBS News program *Walter Cronkite's Universe.* I had no idea that particular day, as I was flying to Cambridge, Massachusetts, to interview the legendary Edwin H. Land, that the interview itself would change my subsequent life for many years or that I was entering an embracing new world where technology and science intermingle into a sublime art.

It was true that Land, as a pioneer in understanding visual perception, as the inventor of polarizing plastic, stereographic movies, instant photography, and so many other wonders, had been my childhood hero, but I was nonetheless unprepared for the way in which his ideas and personality would set my mind in motion. Talking with Land, that day and on later occasions at Polaroid and at The Rowland Institute for Science, I began to understand the open-ended but far from obvious idea that images have a

special ability to trigger, in a controlled way, the exceedingly refined mechanisms of human visual perception. Indeed, as Land has shown, images, under certain special conditions, can be used to dramatically reveal the strategies the eye/brain uses to create our visual world.

In studying the mechanisms of visual perception, one soon acquires a rather different view of the visual world we experience, recognizing that, made as it is from ephemeral energies reaching the retina, it is quite a marvelous achievement. One comes to view the eye/brain as a *synthesizer* improbably creating a stable world of things from the inchoate world of light. It is just these generative powers of visual perception that are marvelously exploited by the technologies of visualization.

I was very fortunate to learn a great deal about the technology of imaging in a period of unparalleled technological advancement. As a consultant for the Polaroid Corporation in the early 1980s, I had the opportunity to learn about marvelous developments, mostly having to do with computers, in the imaging industry in the United States and abroad and to interview luminaries in computer science, visual perception, and all facets of imaging. It was under these ideal conditions that I began to realize that a new field, a discipline called "visualization," was emerging. Technologically speaking, the barriers separating the fields of diagnostic imaging, computer graphics, remote sensing, image processing, and many other disciplines that use images were dissolving because of the digital computer. All sorts of new hybrid techniques could be attempted because the data from one application, since it was in digital form, could be easily interpreted by machines ostensibly designed for a completely different application. Algorithms developed in one field could be borrowed for use in others. There seemed to be an extraordinary potential for developing a defined body of interrelated visualization techniques as well as entirely new kinds of visualization machines by combining methods from different disciplines—a potential that is now being fulfilled (see *Emergent Technologies*).

In 1982, it sometimes felt a bit odd traveling from hospitals to the motion picture special effects studios of Hollywood, to NASA, to architectural firms and pharmaceutical companies to talk about "visualization." Using the computer to make images was still, then, a relatively unknown activity. I was encouraged, however, to discover that I was becoming in my travels a kind of messenger. Experts in diagnostic imaging would ask me what I had learned about a new technique in computer graphics. A developer of biochemical modeling software would want to know what I had seen at a conference on three-dimensional display. On one occasion, I was asked by individuals working with a flight simulator if I could help them acquire a data base of the buildings of Manhattan developed by an architectural firm. It was in this unanticipated role of messenger, moving from field to field, that I began to think of one day writing a book called *Visualization,* which would set forth for the public what I began to recognize as the basic techniques, problems, and philosophical issues of an emerging field.

I felt then, and am even more convinced today, that the ultimate impact of visual computing will eventually match or exceed the tremendous societal changes already wrought by computers. This is the reason for thinking of visualization as a "second" computer revolution. Visually oriented computers, computers with a window, open up a whole new kind of communication between man and machine. There are many applications that simply cannot be contemplated without a visual interface, and the visual interface makes many complex applications accessible to non-specialists for the first time. The future seems filled with potential.

Preparation of this volume has been a privileged journey. I owe a great debt of gratitude to all of the distinguished people in the fields of imaging technology, computer science, visual perception, and art who have shown interest in it and who have given their time, ideas, images, and above all, moral support to it. I sincerely hope that I have been faithful to the promise of this project and that I have conveyed the living excitement of this field. Powerful computers capable of the intensive computations required for visual applications are becoming more and more commonplace every day. It does, indeed, seem an auspicious moment to explore the function of visualization, to try to define the boundaries of this new discipline, and to consider, through its revelatory and enchanting images, its enormous significance for the future.

Richard Mark Friedhoff
Los Angeles, California
January, 1989

introduction: visual thinking with computers

The most striking—and a unique—feature of mind is the acceptance and use of things as symbols standing for other things. Symbols may stand for, refer to, or mean other things which may or may not lie within the world of physics. . . . In this sense we find Mind in computing machines.
Richard L. Gregory in <u>Mind in Science</u>

The first images were found rather than made. People looking into the night sky, saw human figures, animals, and magic symbols in the stars. They did not realize that they were creating these images from scattered points of light, but felt that they were discovering what was already there. So real and so awesome were these celestial apparitions that they were sometimes taken to be gods.

Art historian E.H. Gombrich has suggested that the earliest painters did not consciously create. Prehistoric man, accustomed to searching for signs of his prey, discovered likenesses of buffalo and other animals in the irregular features of the walls of caves. At Lascaux and elsewhere pictures were rendered only to make vivid what was perceived to already exist in the stone. These too were found images.

The tendency to impose form, whether on the surface irregularities of a cave, or in inkblots, clouds, or shadows, is suggestive of an organizing function of vision—an organizing tendency so strong that random shapes can trigger the perception of vivid illusions. It is in this organizing function that we begin to see the power of visualization.

Jacob Bronowski, the twentieth-century scientist and philosopher, has suggested that the auditory sense connects us with other living things but that it is vision which we use to understand the physical world. The importance of the visual system is further affirmed by the fact that a surprisingly large proportion of the brain is devoted to vision and visual analysis and the fact that the information-carrying capacity (the "bandwidth") of the visual system is greater than for any other sense. These facts alone, however, do not fully convey the central theme of this volume: that *the visual system*—the eye and those parts of the brain that are dedicated to organizing visual information—*can be made to take the place of conscious thought.*

In order to understand how this occurs we first have to accept the distinction made by perceptual psychologists between conscious and preconscious processes. The term *preconscious* refers to lower-order information processing that is outside of voluntary control. This is distinct from the conscious or problem-solving self. (Preconscious, it should be noted, is different from unconscious, a term from psychoanalysis that refers to repressed thoughts.) Our preconscious brains are almost unknown to us, although they create the world that we consciously experience. Major portions of the visual system including the retina, the structures ascending to the visual cortex, and parts of the visual cortex itself fall into the preconscious category. More powerful, if a comparison can be made, than a supercomputer, they relentlessly and silently perform information-processing miracles, creating the three-dimensional, colored visual environment that our conscious self, free of these responsibilities, enjoys so effortlessly.

When we visualize through the use of external means such as computers, we restructure a problem so that more of it is processed by the preconscious part of our brain—the visual system that is our silent partner. In this way, consciousness can be devoted to the highest levels of analysis and synthesis.

To explore this premise, the following chapter, *We Create the World We See,* has been devoted entirely to vision, specifically to the preconscious processes underlying color, depth, and form perception. The connection between vision and visualization is becoming more obvious every day. For example, Margaret Livingstone of Harvard University Medical School has pointed out that by understanding the differences between the separate channels for color and form in the visual system, we can better select color schemes for visualizing complex scientific problems so as to maximally exploit the capabilities of the visual system. Until recently, we did not know that a poorly chosen color scheme would cause messages from the color channel to conflict with messages from the form channel thus obscuring important forms and producing visual artifacts. In this case, despite visualization, conscious attention is required to decipher target forms. Conversely, a better color scheme results in congruent messages via the color and form channels so that forms are readily identified without conscious effort (see page 43).

Understanding the differences between the color and form channels is also useful for understanding artistic images. Notice how the diffuse colors of Picasso's *Mother and Child* (following page) seem to gravitate to the sharply delineated forms. This is because the color channel of the visual system has lower visual acuity than the form channel.

Image processing with computers can be used to make all of the qualities of an image congruent with the way in which the human visual system processes visual information. The computer can be used to enhance, by various means, the informational value of an image pattern. The image-processing computer does not comprehend the content of the image but can do much to prepare it for human perception. The computer can be used, for instance, to remove blurring from images, to improve focus *post hoc,* and to identify important features, by comparing ensembles of images (see *Images from Energy*).

In the chapter on *Emergent Technologies* a number of cases are described in which the computer is used to imitate human stereopsis so that it can build a three-dimensional model in its memory from a pair of flat images. Here the computer is imitating human perception—building a three-dimensional world from a pair of images just as the brain builds our visual world from retinal images. This is but another example of the way in which computers can be used as an extension of preconscious visual processes.

visual thinking
is real
Although this volume does not deal with the subject directly, another implicit theme is that there is a legitimate and distinctive mode of thinking that is visual. This is important to consider because computer graphics profoundly enhances our ability to think visually *en rapport* with the computer (see *Computer Graphics* and *Visual Experiments*). Anecdotal evidence of inspirations resulting from visual thinking abound. A well-known instance concerns Friedrich Kekulé's insight, in 1865, regarding the molecular structure of the chemical benzene—an inspiration that came in the form of a dream involving a snake biting its own tail. This mental image led Kekulé to the idea that the benzene molecule has a ring structure. Other scientists, including Albert Einstein, have commented on the importance of visual thinking in model building and in grappling with complex problems.

Although there are many anecdotal reports of the importance of visual thinking in science, the phenomenon has often been treated skeptically by experimental psychologists. In the late nineteenth and

inkblot A simple inkblot reveals the visual system's organizing power. Although its shape is arbitrary, it triggers the perception of recognizable forms. Prehistoric people similarly found forms, which were the basis of the first paintings, in the surface irregularities of the walls of their cave dwellings.

Picasso
22

color channel/form channel Margaret Livingstone has suggested that the color channel of visual perception has lower visual acuity than the form channel. This helps to explain why the diffuse patches of color in Picasso's *Mother and Child* naturally relate to the sharply delineated forms.

Pablo Picasso. *Mother and Child*. 1922. Oil on canvas, 39⅜ x 31⅞". The Baltimore Museum of Art: The Cone Collection, formed by Dr. Claribel Cone and Miss Etta Cone of Baltimore, Maryland.

early twentieth centuries, psychologists became distrustful of all inner qualities of mind, since they could not be readily measured except by the self-reporting individual. Experimental psychology had been nearly crippled by too great a trust in introspection, and many experimental psychologists in the first decades of the present century rightly demanded more objective kinds of data. The behaviorists went so far as to banish all forms of self-reporting and introspection, even denying the reality of inner experience.

Fortunately, in recent years there has been a new focus on visual thinking among psychologists who have found more objective ways to measure it. Perhaps some of the most interesting information comes from neurophysiology, through Dr. Roger Sperry's work at the California Institute of Technology with epilepsy patients who have had to have the

connection between the cerebral hemispheres, the right and left halves of the brain, cut to prevent chronic seizures. The two hemispheres are normally connected by a brain structure called the corpus callosum. When this structure is cut in neurosurgery, it is possible to present information exclusively to one hemisphere by, for example, limiting it to one half of the visual field. Generally speaking, in this situation, one hemisphere does not know what the other is doing. In this way, the different capacities of the two hemispheres can be compared. It is almost as though one person now has two independent minds.

The dominant hemisphere has proven to be better at mediating speaking, writing, and calculation. The non-dominant hemisphere is superior for *visual* tasks. If a line drawing of a cube is presented to the dominant, usually the left, hemisphere, the subject will find it difficult to draw an accurate copy. If it is presented to the non-dominant, usually the right, hemisphere, the subject has little trouble copying despite the fact that the drawing is executed with the left hand, not normally used for such tasks. The non-dominant hemisphere is also superior at discriminating between items by touch and at matching tactile with visual stimuli.

Another kind of experiment, developed by psychologist Roger Shepard at Stanford University, also points to the reality of visual thinking and has helped to center attention on the subject in recent years. Individuals were shown the pairs of drawings seen at right and asked to determine whether they were identical. Shepard discovered that the length of time subjects required to reach a decision was proportional to the angle through which the figure had to be mentally rotated so that it had the same orientation as the target figure. If a figure had to be rotated by a large amount to match a target figure, it required longer for the decision than if the figure had only to be rotated a small amount. Shepard interprets this as support for the idea, confirmed in interviewing the subjects, that they answered the question by mentally rotating the forms.

Another experiment, conducted in 1960 by the Russian psychologist R. Natadze (reported in the United States by Stephen Kosslyn) should also be mentioned because it demonstrates how visual thinking can function as a substitute for real-world action.

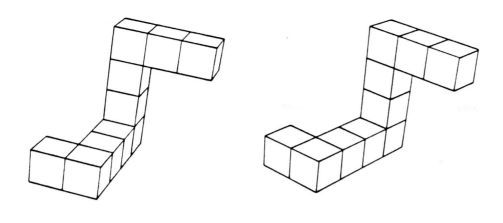

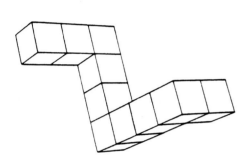

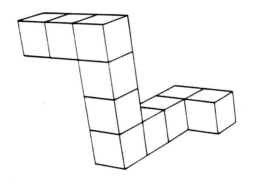

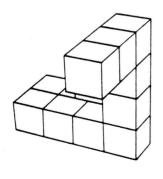

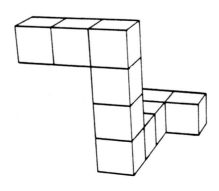

mental rotation These stimuli were devised by psychologists Lynn Cooper and Roger Shepard to evaluate an aspect of visual thinking—specifically the idea that we can rotate objects in our minds. The second member of each pair of drawings is either a rotation of the object shown in the first drawing or its mirror image. Subjects were asked to determine whether the two objects were identical and were timed as they thought about it. The results showed that the time elapsed was proportional to the angle through which the object in one view had to be rotated to be matched with the other. The greater the rotation between the two figures, the longer it required to match them. This seems to support the subjects' contention that they rotated the figures mentally.

This experiment simulates, using visual thinking, the conditions that produce the so-called weight contrast illusion. In the normal demonstration of weight contrast, subjects are asked to lift a very heavy weight with one hand and a light weight with the other. They are then given weights that are identical. In comparing the identical weights, they generally report that the hand that first held the heavier weight is now holding the lighter weight even though the second pair of weights are identical. Interestingly, Natadze's subjects found the same phenomenon when the entire experiment was *visualized in the mind of the subject;* that is, when no actual weights were manipulated.

Two findings are quite persistent in research on visual thinking. The first is that the way in which people think visually is different from individual to individual. The second important finding is that the degree to which individuals rely on visual thinking is, like almost every other measurable characteristic, distributed in the population. Some individuals think more visually than others.

An important aspect of visualization with the computer is that it tends to even out these differences among people. Why should it require a Kekulé with an unusual gift for visualization to discover the molecular structure of benzene? Using a computer simulation, such as described in the *Visual Experiments* chapter, even a beginning student of chemistry might be able to deduce benzene's structure. *Visual Experiments* also discusses the importance of the computer as a means for communicating visual ideas. Visualization need no longer be a solitary inner experience. The computer makes it possible for groups of individuals, even if they are separated by great distance, to collaborate in visual exploration whether in the artistic, design, or scientific spheres. The computer *democratizes* visual thinking.

the emergence of a new discipline

The central premise of this volume, the reason for writing it, is that much is to be gained by recognizing that visualization, because of the computer, is emerging as a distinctive new discipline. Consider the Miranda fly-over discussed in *Emergent Technologies*—a breathtaking flight over the surface of this moon of the distant planet Uranus.

To produce the fly-over movie, the programmers simulated, entirely within the computer, a camera moving over Miranda at a low altitude. Although the raw data that was the basis for this animation was transmitted back to Earth from a space probe and was two dimensional, the fly-over that we see was constructed with a computer-graphics system and is three dimensional and actually took place within the computer following the commands of the programmer who directed its movements.

The important point is that the fly-over technology, and others described in *Emergent Technologies,* go well beyond the disciplines from which they emerged. The fly-over technique properly belongs neither to image processing nor to computer graphics but to the nascent discipline of visualization. There are many other visualization technologies emerging from the combination of image processing, computer graphics, holography, and simulation, which transcend the particular applications for which they might have been developed—these are the new techniques of visualization.

If this new discipline of visualization is to realize its full potential, however, it will also have to borrow ideas from those areas traditionally concerned with imagery such as art history and perceptual and cognitive psychology. The field of visualization should not be so absorbed by the miracles that are its technical basis that it ignores a larger interest in the way in which images can be used to enhance the power of our thinking. It is, after all, the power of images to fuse the human mind with the computer that drives invention in this new discipline. In the following chapters, an attempt has been made to create a framework, borrowing from many fields, which will be useful to everyone who visualizes whether in art, science, medicine, entertainment, design, or any of the disciplines that every day are being irrevocably changed by the computer.

large-scale structures of the universe Problems of perception are always a factor in visualizing the unknown. These two visualizations, created with supercomputers, were made to help answer questions regarding the larger-scale structures of the Universe. The image at bottom was produced entirely within the computer by simulating early forces of creation as they are understood by astrophysicists. The image here is a frame from an animation showing the Universe forming after the Big Bang. The filament-like structures represent volumes that are dense with galaxies. © Joan Centrella, Drexel University, Philadelphia, Pennsylvania.

The top image, showing our Local Supercluster, was derived from astronomical data rather than from a simulation. The positions of known galaxies were compiled into a three-dimensional model within the supercomputer and the image was rendered with computer-graphics techniques. Our own galaxy, the Milky Way, is a point at the center of the image. The space between the two purple areas is empty because the dust and stars of the Milky Way make observations of this region impossible. The magenta cone encloses a volume of space that has not been completely mapped.

Both images create a dilemma for astrophysicists because it is difficult to know whether the large structures they contain are real or visual artifacts. By changing the basic assumptions of the simulation shown in the bottom image, galaxies will be distributed in different patterns and the filaments visible in the image may or may not appear. The structures in the top image also depend on the criteria used. The orange areas identify volumes of space with a relatively high density of galaxies. If the density criterion is made less stringent, however, larger entities, indicated in green, are visualized.

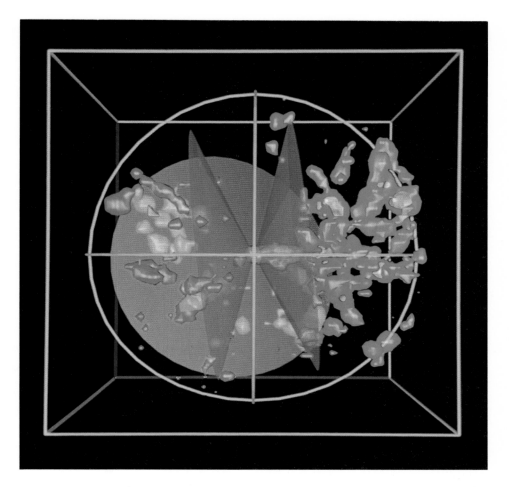

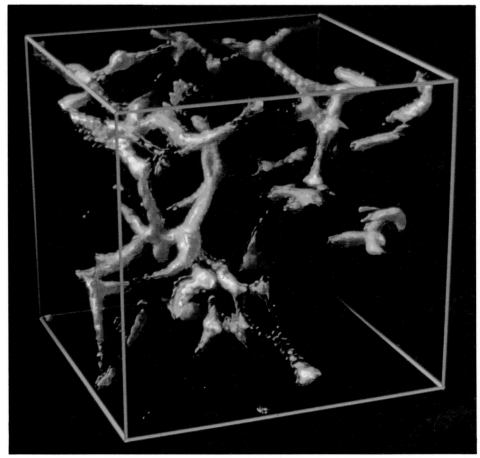

we create the world we see

The perception of solid form is entirely a matter of experience. We see nothing but flat colours; and it is only by a series of experiments that we find out that a stain of black or grey indicates the dark side of a solid substance, or that a faint hue indicates that the object in which it appears is far away. The whole technical power of painting depends on our recovery of what may be called the innocence of the eye; that is to say, a sort of childish perception of these flat stains of colour, merely as such, without consciousness of what they signify—as a blind man would see them if suddenly gifted with sight.

John Ruskin in The Elements of Drawing

Visual theorists of ancient times imagined that vision depends on particles flowing outward from the eyes. In the fifth century B.C., inspired by luminescent animal eyes, Empedocles proposed that the "eye is like a lantern." Plato, too, had an emanation theory but, reasoning that vision cannot occur in the dark, thought that rays flowing from the eyes mix with outer rays—an awkward theory but one that, because it is pivoted between inner and outer, between the person seeing and the things seen, can now be said to have a poetic truthfulness. Modern theories of vision tell us that the eye and visual brain are active creators of the visual world we experience.

As we look around, our eyes make thousands of movements, grabbing what they can from the fluctuating lights reaching them, building a visual world in an instant. In spite of its tenuous origin in light, it is a world characterized by stability—a world in which things simply seem to be there. The visual system is not a passive instrument "photographing" the environment but a synthesizer which sublimely makes "things" from light. Visual science also tells us that vision is not a single sense. There

are a variety of subsenses working simultaneously that contribute different components to vision. Here we look at some of the most successful attempts to differentiate and understand these subsenses, specifically the color sense, stereopsis (two-eyed depth perception), and form perception. It is becoming clearer that understanding the mechanisms of visual perception helps us to understand the nature of visualization.

color perception
The ubiquity of photography has given rise to the popular notion that the function of the eye is similar to a camera. In certain ways, of course, the structure of the eye does resemble a camera. Both have a lens and an iris and both project an image. The critical difference is that the camera is a passive instrument while the eye, considered (as it should be) as a part of the brain, is fundamentally an organizer. The eye and the camera part company at the moment light reaches the retina. The camera passively transforms the pattern of light into a pattern of chemical change. The eye/brain, starting even with the activity of the retina, is building a world of objects. It is mostly because of advances made in the last two decades that we can

begin to appreciate the nature of this achievement—and the strategies the eye/brain uses to synthesize a visual world.

Modern color theory begins with Isaac Newton who articulated the fundamental problems that still challenge theorists today. Newton's *Opticks,* published in 1704, describes a number of experiments begun some forty years earlier that revealed puzzling properties of color. Working in his room at Cambridge, Newton found that by using a prism, he could separate sunlight into the spectrum of colors. This is possible because light of different wavelengths is diverted by varying degrees when passing from one medium (air) to another (a glass or crystal prism). Newton saw seven colors in sunlight—violet, indigo, blue, green, yellow, orange, and red—although we now know that hundreds of distinguishable hues can be seen under more carefully controlled conditions.

Newton also found that by adding a second prism, the seven colors would recombine into a single spot of sunlight. The separation and recombination of sunlight raise the fundamental question of color theory: what are colors and how do they combine to create new colors that do not appear to contain their components? Red and green light produce yellow, a color that does not give any hint that it might be made of these ingredients. It is different with sound. When musical notes are combined, they can still be distinguished in the resulting chord. Combined colors, on the other hand, tend to take on an entirely new character. Is it a physical property of light itself, or does it result in some way from our perceptual processes?

Since ancient times, artists have known that a few colored pigments could be mixed to make many more. (Note that while lights combine additively paints combine subtractively, since pigments appear to be the color they do not absorb.) Newton's *Opticks* stimulated a great deal of interest in systematizing color mixing and it soon became evident that three colors could be mixed to make the other principal colors of the spectrum. A number of investigators felt that color mixing could be explained by thinking of the eye as having three separate sensitivities to "primary" colors. This idea, the concept of trivariance, is usually credited to its first forceful exponent, Thomas Young, working in the beginning of the nineteenth century, although others had stated related concepts earlier. Young thought it unlikely that the retina would be equally sensitive at every location to every part of the spectrum and proposed that it has three different types of light-sensitive "particles." Colors, Young proposed, are a combination of three responses: the independent responses of red-, green-, and blue-sensitive particles. It is an idea that is still fundamental to color theory, although Young was never satisfied that he had found three wavelengths that perfectly produce, when combined in different proportions, every color.

The physiologist and physicist Hermann von Helmholtz, working in the nineteenth century, refined Young's idea, although von Helmholtz, too, had difficulty settling on three wavelengths. In present-day color vision research, the Young-Helmholtz theory has come to mean that there are three kinds of receptors within the eye. Each of the three receptor types is optimally sensitive to a particular wavelength—the wavelengths of the three primaries: red, green, and blue. Since color perception is built on the combined responses of these three kinds of receptors, it is not possible to distinguish a pure wavelength from a color that is mixed from primaries. According to the Young-Helmholtz theory, both stimuli trigger identical responses among the three receptor types and so are perceptually indistinguishable. For example, red and green light appear yellow when mixed because they stimulate the same responses of the red and green receptors that a pure spectral yellow would.

The Young-Helmholtz theory, while fundamental to color science, has been shown in recent years to be inadequate for explaining certain aspects of real-world color perception. First of all, we now know that it is *not* true that there are three colors from which all other colors can be mixed even though this remains the technical basis for color photography, color television, and color printing. A remarkable range of colors can be made from three well-chosen primaries, but not every hue.

electromagnetic radiation From the physicist's perspective, visible light is a small segment of the continuum of electromagnetic radiation that includes radio waves, radar, microwaves, infrared and ultraviolet light, X-rays, and gamma rays. Although the properties of these types of radiation are different from one another, they are all electromagnetic oscillations—periodic waxing and waning of an electromagnetic field. Visible light, for example, has a frequency of approximately 10,000,000,000,000,000 oscillations per second. Those above visible light oscillate more slowly while those below oscillate more quickly.

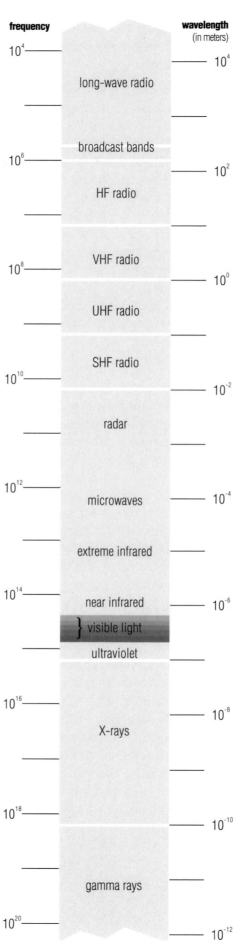

frequency

10^4

10^6

10^8

10^{10}

10^{12}

10^{14}

10^{16}

10^{18}

10^{20}

long-wave radio

broadcast bands

HF radio

VHF radio

UHF radio

SHF radio

radar

microwaves

extreme infrared

near infrared

} visible light

ultraviolet

X-rays

gamma rays

wavelength
(in meters)

10^4

10^2

10^0

10^{-2}

10^{-4}

10^{-6}

10^{-8}

10^{-10}

10^{-12}

The speed of light is 186,281 miles, or 300,000 kilometers, per second. The distance traveled by light during one oscillation is its wavelength. Wavelength and frequency can be interconverted since the length of a wave tells us how many oscillations will fit into the 186,281 miles light travels in a second—its frequency. The equation: wavelength = the speed of light/frequency is a mathematical statement of this relationship—a way of converting back and forth from wavelength to frequency.

A convenient unit of length used to describe the wavelength of visible light is the nanometer (NM) which is equivalent to one-millionth of a millimeter. The blue light of the spectrum has a wavelength of about 480 nanometers; spectral green falls between 480 and 560 NM; yellows are between 560 and 590 NM; orange between 590 and 630 NM; and reds are visible wavelengths longer than 630 NM.

The Young-Helmholtz theory also fails to explain why the appearance of a color is often affected by its context of surrounding colors, a fact well known to artists and painters and wonderfully articulated by John Ruskin who believed that "every hue throughout your work is altered by every touch that you add in other places." Another complication is color constancy—the idea that colors stay the same under varying kinds of illumination. Objects seen through green sunglasses, for example, retain their familiar colors in spite of the fact that the proportions of the three primary wavelengths are altered dramatically.

LAND'S RETINEX THEORY In the 1950s, Edwin Land, the scientist and inventor popularly known for creating the Polaroid instant camera, became interested in aspects of color not explained within the Young-Helmholtz framework. He began a series of experiments that eventually led him to propose a radical new theory of color perception.

The experiments are visually astonishing. While working on a color film for instant photography, Land was projecting three black-and-white slides of a colored scene through red, green, and blue filters. Accidentally, a technician dropped the green filter so that the three slides were illuminated by only red and blue filters and the white projection light. Surprisingly, the colors on the projection screen did not seem to change very much with the loss of the green filter. The greens remained vivid—indeed, all the colors remained much the same in spite of the loss of the green-light component, one of the presumptive primaries. This adventitious discovery led Land to re-examine the idea of three primaries by trying to create color images from many different combinations of wavelengths. He found that full-color images could be made from a large assortment of wavelength combinations—pairs or trios of wavelengths entirely different from the traditional primaries.

It soon became evident that colored lights mix differently when they illuminate *images* than when they are projected as simple spots. Red, blue, and white *spots* of light cannot be mixed to produce any shade of green. When black-and-white transparencies of a colorful scene are projected with these, or many other combinations of wavelengths, however, greens and other colors not possible with spots of light are quite vivid. Land began to realize that previous experiments in color vision had relied far too much on combining spots of light and had failed to examine an important aspect of the way in which the eye/brain builds the color world from information contained in the shadings of the scene that are recorded in the black-and-white images.

red and white make? In an experiment that has become a classic demonstration, two black-and-white transparencies are made of a colorful scene (see illustrations on the following pages). One photograph is exposed through a red filter and the other through a green filter. The resulting black-and-white transparencies are then projected with two slide projectors so they overlap on a projection screen. The observer, at first, sees a black-and-white projection. But when a red filter is placed over one projector opening, the result is not a pink image but a *full-color* image. Although the image is produced with only white light from one projector and the light passing through the red filter attached to the other projector, the image is resplendently colored. Remove the black-and-white transparencies, and the screen appears to be illuminated with pink light—an insipid blend of the red and white beams—just as the Young-Helmholtz theory, the idea of proportional stimulation, would predict.

As if this were not astonishing enough, experiments with photographs made through different pairs of filters showed that a large variety of wavelengths can be used to reproduce a colored scene—the critical requirement is only that the filters not be identical. In some areas of the spectrum, for example among the wavelengths normally considered to be green, wavelengths quite close together produce remarkably colorful images.

As Land and his colleagues explored these phenomena, they realized that one longer and one relatively shorter wavelength were all that were needed to create a full-color scene. Wavelengths from the middle region of the visible range could serve as either the longer or the shorter member of the pair. If long- and short-wavelength filters are reversed, an image composed of colors complementary to the true colors will be produced—for example, red in the place of green.

red and white make? Edwin Land was surprised to find that exposures made with various *pairs* of wavelengths could be used to create colored scenes. The top portion of the diagram shows how a pair of black-and-white images were exposed, respectively, through a red filter and a green filter. The bottom part of the diagram shows one way the resulting black-and-white transparencies can be projected to yield a resplendently colored projection. The image originally exposed through the red filter is projected through a red filter. The image exposed through the green filter is projected without a filter. Traditional color theory predicted that the double projection would result in a pinkish image. Instead, the image contains colors from all the color families including green.

Because of the limitations of the commercial printing process, the color image shown opposite top is given only as a normal photographic record of the original scene and does not attempt to show the recombined colors present in the red-and-white projection. Nevertheless, the reader could demonstrate the phenomenon by photographing the black-and-white images and projecting the resulting transparencies, one through a red filter, in a well darkened room. (The images at middle and bottom are records of the scene as photographed through a red or green filter, respectively.)

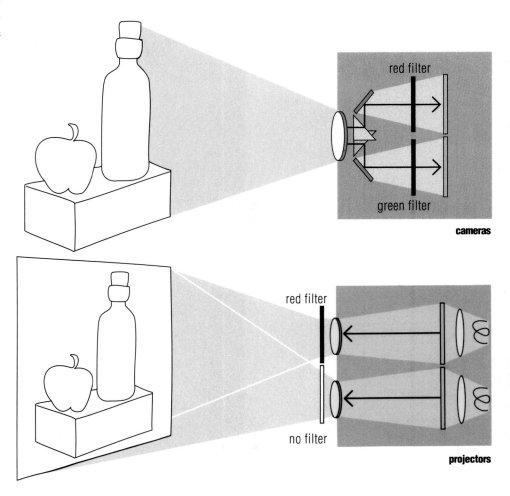

red filter

green filter

cameras

red filter

no filter

projectors

The variety of ways in which a full-color image can be produced suggested to Land one of the fundamental tenets of his theory of color vision: *the eye is able to see color independently of wavelength*. This is the most startling departure from the Young-Helmholtz theory, which postulates that colors originate in the eye's fixed response to three primary wavelengths.

The idea that color and wavelength are independent is studied in another series of experiments done in Land's laboratories. In the years following the first experiments with filters and transparencies, the light-absorbing properties of the pigment molecules of the visual cones (the cells of the retina that detect light for color vision) were measured. The light absorption of these substances is highly significant because the energy that is absorbed is the energy that initiates the response of the cone. If it is not absorbed by the visual pigments, it cannot be seen.

Experiments confirmed, however, that Young was correct in proposing that the retina is sensitive at three separate areas of the spectrum. There are, indeed, three overlapping bands of sensitivity with their peaks at the portions of the spectrum usually described as red, green, and blue.

Using this information, Land devised a series of experiments in which the relationship between wavelength and perceived color could be studied under carefully controlled conditions. The basic technique is to illuminate a collage of colored papers (usually called a "Mondrian" because of the similarity to certain paintings by the Dutch artist Piet Mondrian) with three independently controlled sources of light of the wavelengths of peak sensitivity. With this three-illuminator system, Land was able to separately control the amount of light each cone system received from the illuminated collage.

Using this apparatus, Land was able to create the situation in which a rectangle of one collage was reflecting the same wavelengths in exactly the same proportions as a rectangle on another collage and yet was differently colored. The rectangle on the first might be perceived as white while the rectangle on the second was green in spite of the fact that the light returning from them was exactly the same.

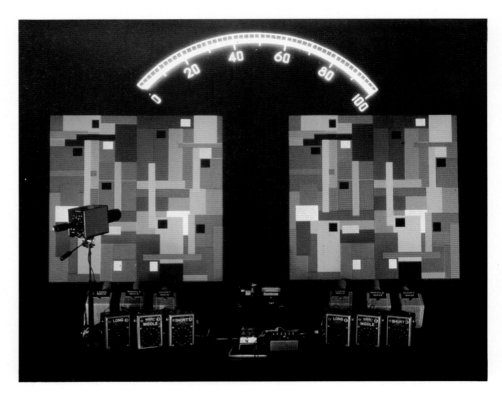

"mondrian" test stimuli Edwin Land developed these test stimuli, usually called "Mondrians" (because of their similarity to paintings by the Dutch artist Piet Mondrian), to test the interrelationship of wavelength and perceived color. In this experiment, two identical Mondrians are each illuminated by a set of three projectors. The three projectors are each fitted with a filter matching the peak sensitivity of retinal cones. Thus, in a darkened room, the amount of any of the three wavelengths involved in color vision returning from the Mondrian can be precisely controlled.

Light from each of the three projectors on the left can be turned up or down while light reflected from a test rectangle in the Mondrian is measured with a photometer (light meter). The light from the three projectors illuminating the right-hand Mondrian can be adjusted the same way. The illuminators can be adjusted so that, for example, a white rectangle in the left Mondrian will reflect exactly the same amounts of the three wavelengths as will a green rectangle in the right-hand Mondrian. The surprising result is that although the two test rectangles are reflecting the same wavelengths in the same quantity, they retain their familiar colors: white and green. The demonstration shows that the color perceived for an area within a scene is not a simple product of the three wavelengths returning from the area.

If the wavelengths coming from the test rectangle alone do not determine its color, what does? Perhaps the wavelengths coming from the test area are perceived, in some sense, in the context of the light reflected by the larger areas of the scene? Indeed, we are forced to this conclusion by these ingenious experiments since the test rectangle in isolation cannot be the carrier of the color message: the test rectangles themselves are reflecting exactly the same light yet retain their color differences. The eye must be making use of the larger field of view.

If the "Mondrian" is inspected under each of the three illuminators separately, three different patterns are observed. Areas that are light under one wavelength are dark when illuminated with a different wavelength. Similarly, areas that are dark under one illuminator will be light when illuminated with another. Note also that when the long- and short-wave photographic records in the experiments with natural images are compared, the whole pattern of light and dark is different in the two images.

Why is the pattern different for the different wavelengths? Each of the three wavelengths is reflected to a different degree by the colored papers in the collage. Under the light of a single illuminator, each rectangle will have a particular degree of lightness depending upon the degree to which it reflects that wavelength. Each wavelength that illuminates the collage will therefore produce its own overall pattern of lightness and darkness. Given three wavelengths, each color will have a unique reflectance profile— for example, light in one, dark in another, and somewhere in between in the third. This information could be used by the eye to determine the color, but the eye must first be able to determine the pattern of lightness independently of the brightness of the illumination in three wavelengths. These experiments demonstrate that the brightness of the wavelength components can be turned up and down without changing perceived color.

long- and short-wave records The long-, middle-, and short-wavelength records of a colored scene, in this case the Mondrian stimulus, contain different patterns of brightness. The pattern of brightness is processed by the visual system to determine reflectance values which are the basis of color perception.

Long wavelength

Middle wavelength

Short wavelength

147,375

College of St. Francis Library
Joliet, Illinois

brightness and reflectance How can a pattern of brightness be used to determine reflectance? This stimulus suggests that the edges between different areas are very important. Cover the area between the two squares with a pencil and note the change in apparent brightness of the the two squares.

brightness vs. reflectance

In order to determine color of a given rectangle reliably, it would be necessary to measure, not its brightness, but a value called reflectance. *Brightness* can be defined as the absolute amount of energy returning from a surface. *Reflectance* is defined as the degree to which a substance reflects light. A substance may have a very low reflectance, in the sense that it absorbs a high proportion of the light falling upon it, but may be illuminated so strongly as to have a high value for brightness. Conversely, a surface with a high reflectance but a low level of illumination will produce a low level of brightness. Once reflectance is known, color can be determined.

Land's theory proposes the revolutionary idea that the eye is able to determine reflectance at three sensitivities and that it does this as a prelude to assigning a color value to an object. According to Land, determination of reflectance is said to be a fundamental competency of the visual system. This competency exists at three different wavelength sensitivities so that the eye is able to compare reflectance at three different wavelengths. The resulting trio of reflectances determines color. This is in contrast to the Young-Helmholtz approach that measures the brightness of light reaching the eyes.

We should not underestimate the ingenuity of the eye in being able to make the leap from brightness to reflectance. Brightness is ephemeral, depending from moment to moment on the illumination of the scene. It is much better for an organism to sense, if possible, the actual reflective qualities of surfaces because these are constant, a property inherent in the objects themselves and therefore a valid basis for identifying them.

Land has suggested that this competency, the eye's ability to determine reflectance can be explored by moving to the simpler world of low-light rod vision which is uncomplicated by color. The visual rods are used primarily in night vision and are much more sensitive than the cones, which are involved in color perception. By lowering the illumination, or wearing goggles that block the light, we can study perception when only this system is operating.

In the low-illumination world, it becomes more obvious that the appearance of a stimulus is not dependent upon the quantity of light coming to the eye. A black piece of paper can be illuminated with a bright spotlight so that, according to a photometer, it is reflecting more light than a nearby white piece of paper. Nonetheless, the black paper appears black and the white paper appears white.

How does the eye/brain determine the reflectance of all the varied surfaces we see as we look around us? Land has developed a model of how this might be achieved. Consider for a moment a surface made of a white square contiguous with a black square. What would happen if we measured brightness at two points on this surface, one in the white area and one in the black area, with a photometer. The readings on the photometers would tell us nothing about the reflectance of the two squares because we would know nothing from these two readings alone about the illumination. A point on the black square might actually be returning more light than a point on the white square because it happens to be closer to the light source. If we were to move the photometers closer and closer together, however, until we reached the edge between white and black, the ratio of the two readings would be a more reliable indicator of the relative reflectances of the two surfaces.

Within that very narrow area—the edge—the illumination is unlikely to change very much so that the differences between the response of the first photometer and the second photometer would be mostly attributable to a change in the surface itself.

Land's theory proposes that the visual system is able to infer reflectance by analyzing such point-to-point brightness changes across large areas of the scene, and he has developed a simple mathematical model to show how this can be achieved. It is highly probable that the cellular interactions responsible for this occur in the retina and in the visual cortex. For this reason, Land has named his color theory *retinex* theory—making a contraction of retina and cortex to describe a process that involves mechanisms from the lowest to the highest areas of the visual system.

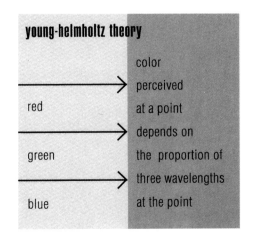

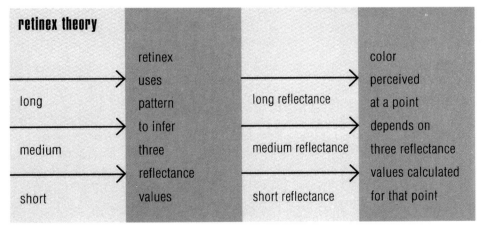

color vision theories The Young-Helmholtz theory of color vision posited that the perceived color of an area in a scene is determined by the relative amounts of light within three wavebands returning from that area. Retinex theory holds, instead, that the first step in color perception is the generation of three reflectance patterns from three brightness patterns. The perceived color is then determined by three reflectance values for each point in the scene.

color space The round tiles correspond to the rectangles of the Mondrian stimulus. The location of a tile on the three-coordinate system is determined by calculating three values of reflectance with Land's method. The co-ordinate system shows specific color areas corresponding to reflectance relationships. The color space summarizes why the two test rectangles in the Mondrian experiment retain their familiar colors despite the fact that they are returning identical ratios of light within the three wave-bands of cone sensitivity. The retinex system, after calcu-lating three reflectance values for the rectangles, places them in their appropriate area in the color space regard-less of the illumination.

Retinex theory states that color results from compar-ing reflectance determined by three retina-cortical systems sensitive at different wavebands. The theory suggests that the individual sensitive systems pro-cess the *whole image* into three reflectance patterns, which are then compared. A color, then, is a trio of reflectances. If we use a Cartesian coordinate sys-tem using x, y, and z axes to represent reflectance, we can create a color space, shown in the stereo-graph at left, in which colors reside in certain re-gions—as combinations of reflectance in the long, medium, and short wavelengths.

Once we calculate three reflectance values for a sur-face within a scene, we can find the corresponding region of the Cartesian map and correctly predict the color that will be perceived. Land has done this for the Mondrians, using his mathematical technique to estimate reflectance from brightness changes over a large area. However the collage might be illuminat-ed, each rectangle yields three reflectance values that place it in a region of the coordinate system. The resulting values are persistent and unique to the familiar color of the rectangle despite variations in the composition or brightness of the illumination and can be located at a specific region of the three-coordinate space associated with that color. This is why the two different colors of the test rectangles in the left and right Mondrian experiments are retained even when the projectors are set so that both reflect identical combinations of wavelengths. The eye/ brain correctly calculates their reflectances at three wavebands using information from the larger scene.

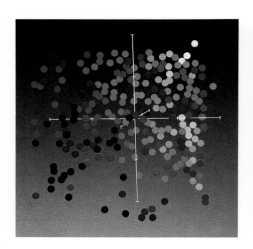 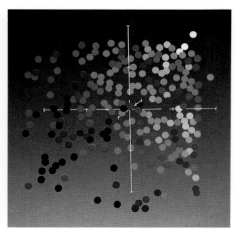

viewing stereographs When these pairs of images (and the other image pairs in the book) are placed in a stereo-scope, they will be seen in depth. It is also possible to see the depth by crossing your eyes so as to make the images overlap. If this is difficult, a playing-card–size cardboard placed between the images helps to fuse them.

The color space explains how we are able to build a color world from red and white projections and oth-er combinations of two and three wavelengths. Even when a scene is represented with only two wave-lengths, the visual system can derive at least two unique values for reflectance for each surface and, potentially, a third (although redundant) value be-cause the sensitivities of the cone systems overlap. These three reflectance values will locate colors within the color space.

The basic idea of the Young-Helmholtz approach, the notion that the eye has three separate sensitivities, fails to make the extremely significant distinction between brightness and reflectance. As a result, it does not explain the eye's marvelous ability, vividly demonstrated in Land's experiments, to perceive color independently of wavelength. Retinex theory avoids these problems by suggesting that vision begins with the jump from brightness to reflectance.

Retinex theory also explains why colors are affected by surrounding colors because shadings of various kinds can affect the accuracy with which reflectance is calculated from point-to-point brightness changes. The method used by the eye to determine reflectance is imperfect—a fact evident in the illustration on page 26. When a pencil is used to cover the edge between the two squares, their relative brightness appears to change even though we know that it does not. Color constancy is not a problem within retinex theory because changing the illumination does not affect the outcome of the determination of reflectance.

It seems that, in a way, we have three separate eyes within the eye, each translating the brightnesses reaching it into its own image of reflectance. It is only after these separate reflectance images have been created that a higher process begins. This superordinate process, an "eye" within the brain that looks down on images produced by lower processes, looks for differences among them. It is at this moment, when the three reflectance images are cross-compared, that a world of hues is created. The whole environment in all of its variety is marked with unique combinations of reflectance that is our familiar world of color.

constructing the third dimension

The visual system creates the three-dimensional world we experience from the two-dimensional patterns projected onto the retinas—a feat that, odd as it may seem, is a little bit like imagining a building from its blueprints. How is this achieved? The fact that we can see depth quite well with one eye closed, or in a photograph that provides only a monocular view, indicates that two eyes are not necessary for a satisfying sense of depth. The shape shown at right can be seen as a circle on its side or an ellipse printed flatly on the page. We see it as one shape or the other depending upon the assumption we make about what the pattern represents. In the familiar type of photo of a tourist "holding" the Leaning Tower of Pisa, the tower would be placed at the wrong distance by someone unfamiliar with the appearance of towers. The paradoxical quality of the image derives from conflicting cues: the attitude of the tourist places the image nearby while our familiarity with the scene, and the appearance of recognizable objects, place it at a distance.

These examples suggest an intimate relationship between what might be called "object recognition" and perception of three-dimensionality. When we look at a photograph, or see from a stationary monocular view, we need to know what we are seeing in order to know where it is located in space. Unfortunately, at this point we know little about how the brain identifies objects so a large part of "depth perception" is simply not understood. In spite of our lack of genuine insight into monocular or "pictorial" depth cues (as they are called by artists), it is possible to classify them into a number of categories (see page 32).

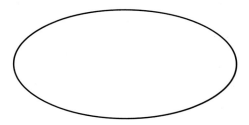

circle on its side or ellipse? The shape shown here can be seen as a circle on its side or as an ellipse printed flatly on the page.

STEREOPSIS: COOPERATION

BETWEEN THE EYES There is one mechanism for depth perception, however, that can be shown to function independently of the recognition of objects. Stereopsis (Greek meaning "solid sight") combines the views from the left and right eyes into a single three-dimensional view. Much of our understanding of this process comes from the work of Bela Julesz, a perceptual psychologist at Bell Laboratories, who developed an experimental technique for isolating the stereoptic sense. Before Julesz' technique, it was difficult to test the mechanism of stereopsis independently of processes that can act monocularly. Julesz devised a unique test stimulus that can *only* be perceived by stereopsis—the stimulus is unique because it simply cannot be seen with one eye.

Interestingly, Julesz' experiments indicate that 5 to 20 percent of people have trouble seeing stereoptically, although a large percent of these would have stereopsis if their vision were corrected for astigmatism. To our surprise, in researching this book, we have encountered a number of individuals working in visual arts fields who do not see well stereoptically. It is startling, at first glance, to discover graphic artists and painters who seemingly lack a visual capacity, but it is possible that diminished stereoptic perception may contribute to drawing and painting ability by facilitating the reduction of the visual environment to a flat pattern—what Ruskin has called "the innocence of the eye." A statistical study has not yet been attempted to determine if there is indeed a correlation between a deficit in stereopsis and drawing ability, but the idea could conceivably help to explain why some individuals naturally excel in drawing, painting, and other visual arts. Since not everyone has stereopsis, some of our readers, perhaps even some artists, will not see depth in the stereo test stimuli reproduced in this book. Many others will not see depth without a stereoviewer simply because they find it difficult to cross their eyes. In any case, a quantitative estimate of stereoptic competency requires administration of a graded series of tests under carefully controlled conditions.

There has been a great deal of misunderstanding about binocular depth perception. Many of us learned that the sense of depth is based on visual convergence—the way in which the eyes come together when we look at closer objects and diverge when we look at objects at a distance. Nearer objects require that the eyes converge to a greater degree than more distant objects in order to project the same image to corresponding regions of the retina.

It used to be thought that binocular depth perception might be achieved by a form of triangulation. Several different types of experiments suggest that such oculomotor feedback, to the extent that it is available, is relatively unimportant. For example, the eyes can be anesthetized and physically moved without the subject experiencing a changed perception of distance.

stereographs Stereographs such as these were popular in the late nineteenth and early twentieth centuries. They were viewed with the Wheatstone or Brewster stereoviewers, devices that facilitated fusion of the images by helping the viewer focus on them while they were held horizontal. The images are made from horizontally adjacent viewpoints. The visual system uses disparity between the images to determine the relative distance of objects.

The pair at left depicts Yosemite Valley at the turn of the century. The pair below was made by the Paris optical firm that first marketed the Brewster stereoviewer, shown at the lower right of the picture. Courtesy George Eastman House.

Experiments performed in the nineteenth century with a stereoscope also confirm that convergence is not necessary for the binocular perception of depth. Experimental subjects experienced the perception of depth in a stereopair even if the stereograph was illuminated with a flash of light too brief to permit movement of the eyes. The stereograph also eliminates another possible source of depth information—accommodation. The lens of the eye thickens when we focus on near objects and flattens when objects are at a distance—a potential source of distance information. In stereographic images, however, the eyes focus on the stereograph itself so that lens accommodation does not provide depth information, and depth is perceived nonetheless.

If neither convergence nor accommodation is important, what is the basis for depth perception involving two eyes? By holding a finger over this page, midway toward the eyes, you can readily see, by closing one eye and then the other, that the left and right eyes differ in their lines of sight: different parts of the page are obscured in each view. Examining the left and right images of a stereopair, such as the one on page 30, will also reveal small differences between them. Notice how portions obscured in one image are revealed in the other.

monocular and ''pictorial'' depth cues

The fact that two eyes are not necessary for a sense of depth is evident simply by closing one eye. Not very much is known about the mechanisms of monocular depth perception, but artists and perceptual psychologists like to speak of image qualities that are presumably used in some manner by the eye as "pictorial" depth cues. Pictorial depth cues are generally classed into these categories:

Linear Perspective: The concept of perspective drawing was formalized in the Renaissance. A *camera obscura* demonstrates a fundamental property of optical systems including the eye—objects of equal size at varying distances transect areas of the focusing plane inversely proportional to their distance. The farther away an object is, the smaller portion of the focusing plane (or retina) it will occupy. Thus the edges of a road, which are parallel, appear to converge in the distance because the gap between them decreases with increasing distance. Conversely, converging lines in an image give a sense of receding distance. Notice, too, that objects rise in the picture plane as they move into the distance, because we generally view the ground from above.

Interposition or oculation: When one object is in front of another it obscures it. This is a simple indication of the object's relative position.

Shadow: We generally assume that light comes from above. Shadows can give a sense of the way in which an object or a figure stands in relation to the ground or in relation to a background.

Detail perspective: Fine detail is lost in objects at a distance due to limitations of visual acuity. Textures become smoother and details disappear.

Aerial perspective: Airborne dust particles and the greater transparency of the atmosphere for shorter (blue) wavelengths make parts of a scene appear blue—a depth effect often utilized in landscape painting.

pictorial distance cues Canaletto's *View in Venice* is an example of classic linear perspective. Note, however, that shadow and obscuration also play an important role in revealing depth relations. E. H. Gombrich suggests, in *Art and Illusion*, that even perfect linear perspective does not automatically resolve the ambiguity of the third dimension in an image. In order to understand the spatial relations, the viewer tacitly assumes that the buildings and walls are constructed at right angles. The same appearance could be given by skewed buildings differently arranged in space—an aspect of visual perception often exploited by the designers of stage settings.

Canaletto, *View in Venice*, c. 1740. Oil on canvas, 28 x 44″. National Gallery of Art, Washington, D.C.; Widener Collection.

A simple experiment with surprisingly far-reaching implications will help to explicate the way in which the brain exploits these small differences between the left and the right line of sight to form a single three-dimensional view.

Julesz' random dot stereogram (RDS) reveals a great deal about the strategy used by the visual system to determine depth relations with two eyes. We have already seen how the left- and right-eye view, for example, of a finger held above this book, differ in line of sight. Objects in front of a background are shifted to the right in the left-eye view and shifted left in the right-eye view. Shifting a small portion of the RDS pattern to the left in the right-eye view and to the right in the left-eye view (a nasal shift) creates a stimulus that is equivalent to a real patch hovering in space above the page. A real floating patch would be shifted to the right in the left eye and to the left in the right eye because of the difference in line of sight. Thus, the RDS, because it duplicates this circumstance, appears three dimensional.

The difference in horizontal position of objects in the left and right eyes is called disparity, or binocular parallax. The RDS proves that differences in disparity and not convergence or accommodation are the basis of stereoptic depth perception. The only way the floating or receding patches of the RDS can be seen at all is by sensing the disparity between the two images. Look at the left member of the pair and then the right member separately. There is no hint of the floating plane, no linear perspective, obscuration, shadow—none of the so-called pictorial or monocular depth cues. Indeed, the monocular stimulus is a deliberately randomized pattern that, by definition, does not contain information about the depth planes visible when the two views are compared. The RDS shows us that we can perceive depth stereoptically, independently of recognizing objects.

As has already been mentioned, many of us were taught, incorrectly, that convergence is the basis of binocular depth perception, so it is important to distinguish convergence from disparity. A convergence theory necessitates that the visual system first recognize objects in the scene—recognize them within the visual pattern and converge on a distinct object so that distance can be estimated by the angle between the eyes. In a flow diagram of depth perception based on convergence, object recognition would occur *before* perception of depth. The RDS, however, shows that this is not the case. Perception of depth is possible even when there is no possibility of converging on the object first. Indeed, it is the other way around. The object, the floating patch, is perceived only as a result of sensing depth. In the flow chart of stereopsis, depth perception can occur before a distinct figure is recognized. (The two theories are contrasted in the diagram on page 36.)

making a random dot stereogram A coin toss is used to determine if boxes should be black or white. Then an exact copy of the preparation is made in order to produce a pair.

A different smaller random dot pattern is inset on the first.

The two insets have been shifted inwardly three boxes. When viewed stereoptically, this creates the impression that the inset floats above the page.

The two insets have been shifted outwardly three boxes. When viewed stereoptically, this creates the impression that the inset lies behind the plane of the page.

These figures were created simply to illustrate the way in which the random dot stereogram is made. In actual practice, it is easier to see depth in the smaller finely textured examples shown on the following page.

Stereopsis probably evolved because it discloses aspects of the environment that are unrecognizable by other means. It is extremely difficult to conceal an object from stereopsis by camouflage. The three-dimensional structure becomes evident by comparing monocular views even when the shape is obscured perfectly in *two* dimensions. Indeed, in the RDS, the object is perfectly camouflaged in the left and right view until it is "revealed" by disparity. An animal blended into a natural background by "protective coloration" becomes visible with stereopsis (if we are close enough to detect disparity). Based on this phenomenon, stereophotography was used during World War II to reveal camouflaged tanks and artillery that would not have been visible in single-image aerial photography.

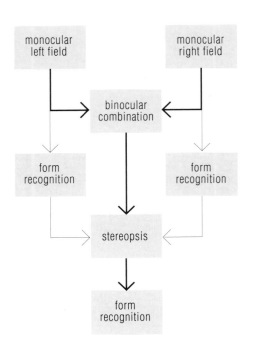

stereopsis The random dot stereogram demonstrates that binocular depth perception is based on disparity between retinal images and can occur without the complex processing involved in form recognition. Convergence theories required that objects be identified first, so that the eyes could converge permitting depth estimation from the angle of convergence. The diagram indicates that some form recognition may occur prior to stereopsis but does not have to. In the case of the random dot stereogram, there is no indication of the form until it is revealed stereoptically.

random dot stereogram A random dot stereogram formed with 100 x 100 squares. Nasal (inward) shifting of a T-shaped area causes it to float above the background when viewed stereoptically. Approximately one in five individuals will be unable to see this or other stereographic images due to limited stereopsis. However, some of these people may tend to do better at drawing and painting, since they are better able to translate the world into flat patterns. Many others will not see depth in the image without a proper stereograph simply because they find it difficult to fuse the images.

complex random dot stereogram A complex random dot stereogram made with specks instead of squares. After fusing the left and right images stereographically, a spiral form will appear as the brain gradually discovers the similarity between the two images. The appearance of the spiral can take as long as five minutes.

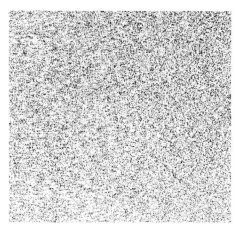

the mechanism of stereopsis How is the visual system able to determine depth on the basis of disparity alone? It is useful to imitate the process mechanically with a pair of images in order to consider methods of simplifying what seems, at first glance, like an inordinately complex task.

One way to do the pattern matching by hand would be to make large photographic transparencies of the left and right views and overlay them. Shifting the images horizontally left and right, we can look for instances in which areas of the two images are in superimposition.

A distant part of the scene will be in superimposition as soon as the images are overlaid, because distant objects do not appear differently to the left and right eyes at a distance. Superimposition of nearer objects requires horizontal movement—the nearer the object, the greater the shift. Shifting the images left and right, we could establish which objects are relatively near and which are relatively far—precisely the achievement of stereopsis.

This method for ranking distance can be further simplified so that a simple mechanical device could do it without having to measure superimposition as such. If we made one transparency a positive, and the other a negative, a simple light meter could be used to determine when the left and right patterns are matching. When portions of the pattern are perfectly superimposed, light will not pass through patches that are light in one image and dark in the other. Thus, by looking for areas of perfect opacity as one transparency is moved horizontally over the other, a simple device could rank areas of the image for distance. Superimposition, in this mechanical example, is an efficient way of comparing patterns for similarity without analyzing them for specific visual content. Indeed, using a light-measuring device and this technique, one can imagine a simple machine which could isolate and rank the distance of every area of the scene without, of course, ever recognizing any objects within it.

To be sure, the visual system determines disparity with more subtlety than this mechanical method of superimposition. We know, for example, that stereopsis is possible with image pairs even when one member of the pair has been considerably reduced in size. Such an image pair would fool this simple "positive/negative" machine but does not fool the brain. Specially designed random dot stereograms have shown that the eye can measure disparity with even more complex distortions that would defeat a mechanical method. Nonetheless, some sophisticated form of superimposition must occur since stereopsis is based on small differences between the left and right views.

The dependence of stereopsis on superimposition is sometimes revealed by patterns which repeat, such as wallpapers or fences. It is possible to misconstrue these types of stimuli, misplace them in distance, by mismatching the views from the two eyes. A portion of one eye is matched with a non-corresponding portion of the other. Such surfaces occasionally appear to hover in mid-air momentarily or seem too distant. Usually an irregularity or a shadow gives the misalignment away and the correct fusion is quickly achieved.

DISPARITY AND
VISUALIZATION

The technique used to create depth in the RDS, nasal or temporal shifting, can be utilized in visualization. For example, Richard Gregory, a perceptual psychologist at the University of Bristol, England, has devised a very simple device for creating a stereopair by drawing. His device uses two pens. Movement of a stylus controls the two pens and simultaneously creates the left and right images of a stereopair.

One pen is red and the other green, and the drawing is observed with glasses in which one lens is a red filter and one lens is a green filter. The red-filtered eye sees only the green drawing as black because red and white are indistinguishable through the red filter. The green-filtered eye similarly sees only the red drawing as black. These types of stereo image, in which the left and right views are kept separate with red and green filters, are called anaglyphs and may be familiar from three-dimensional comic books. Setting the distance between the two pens determines the degree of disparity and thus determines the depth plane of the drawn object. Increasing the distance between the two pens will increase the disparity and place the object relatively nearer. Decreasing the distance will cause the object to appear more distant.

Computer-graphics systems can be quite easily adapted for the production of stereopairs. The computer, using geometric principles described in *Computer Graphics*, generates a pair of images that correspond to the left- and right-eye view. The stereopair can be viewed with an ordinary stereo viewer, a special stereographic monitor, or projected for viewing with polarized glasses. A number of computer-graphic stereo movies have been made, for both scientific and entertainment purposes, by creating a sequence of stereopairs.

stereopaintings Stereopaintings can be created by depicting left and right perspectives, as Dali has done in his *Christ of Gala* (above). Magritte's *Man With a Newspaper* (right) contains two stereopairs, which are, however, difficult to fuse since the seated figure appears in only one image.

Salvador Dali. *Christ of Gala*. 1978. Oil on canvas, each canvas 39⅜ × 39⅜″. Museum Ludwig, Cologne.

René Magritte. *Man With a Newspaper*. 1928. Oil on canvas, 45½ × 32″. The Tate Gallery, London.

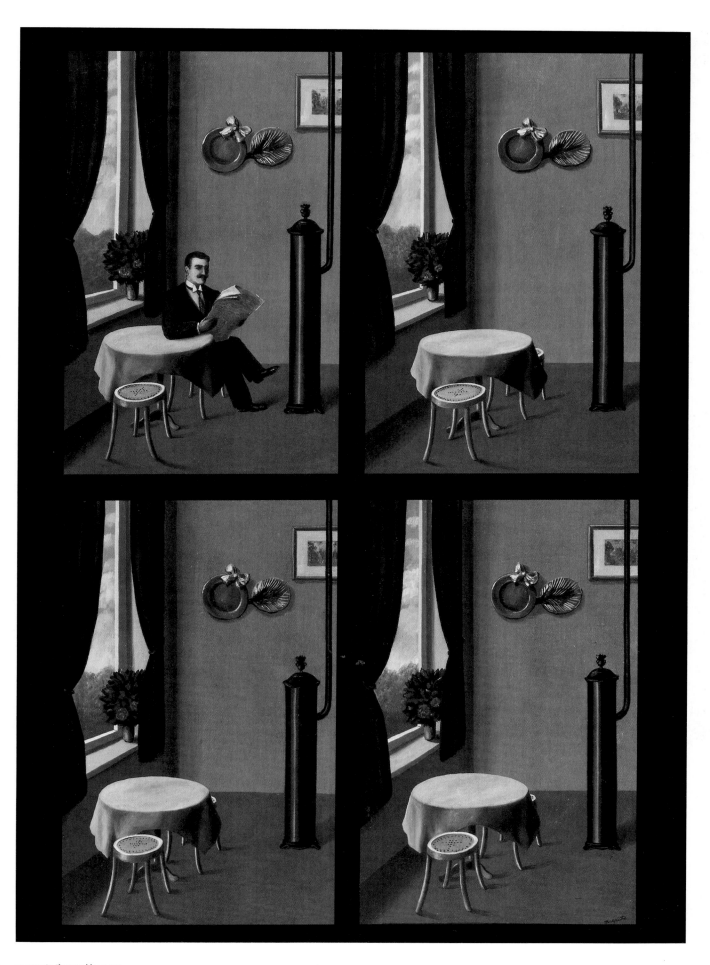

physiological mechanisms

So far, perceptual theories have been discussed—theories that attempt to quantify the relation between physically defined stimuli and the perceptions we experience. The visual system can also be studied physiologically, an approach that examines the cells or cellular structures of the visual system directly. There is no guarantee that these kinds of measurements will be easily related to perception. Nonetheless, some important advancements have recently been made.

The visual system is the general name for those portions of the brain, including the retina, that are known to be occupied with the sensing, transmission, or interpretation of visual information. The cells of the brain, including the visual system, are called neurons and they carry signals in the form of small, chemically mediated electric currents. The current originates in the cell body of the neuron and travels along its axon, a long extension of the cell that leads to other neurons. The point at which a neuron forms its connection with another neuron is called a synapse. Neurons carrying information from many different sources will synapse on a given neuron. That neuron will combine and relay the electrical signals from these different sources. The central mystery of neuroscience is how conscious thought, vision, motor behavior, and other functions of the nervous system arise from many billions of neurons interacting in this way.

THE RETINA

The design of the retina is quite intricate and has, perhaps, fifty distinguishable kinds of cells. The retina is derived in embryological development from the forebrain and consists of a layer of special neurons called receptors, which are specifically adapted to detect light, and others that process the signals from the receptors. Curiously, in humans the photosensitive neurons are not the outermost layer, closest to the incoming light, but lie behind these other transparent layers of processing neurons.

The picture at right shows the two kinds of receptor cells found in the retina: the rods and the cones. The long cylindrical rods are more sensitive than the cone-shaped receptors and are used in "scotopic" or low-light vision. There is only one type of rod, and rod vision is colorless. The cones, which are necessary for color vision, are densely concentrated in the center of the retina: an area called the fovea. Unlike the rods, the cones exist in three varieties with visual pigments sensitive to three separate areas of the spectrum.

The signal from the photoreceptors has already been processed in the retina itself before it is relayed along the million and a half axons of the optic nerve. At the "optic chiasma" the fibers of the optic nerve divide so that all of the pathways concerned with the left portions of the retinas, the left side of the visual field, travel together to the right half (hemisphere) of the brain while those concerned with the right side of the retinas (the right field of view) ascend in the left hemisphere.

The signal from the optic nerve is carried to two structures, the superior colliculus, a structure thought to be concerned with directing visual attention, and the lateral geniculate nucleus (LGN). After processing in the LGN, information is carried to an area of the cerebral cortex (the outermost surface of the brain) called the "striate" area because of its striped appearance.

The fibers going to the lateral geniculate and ascending from the lateral geniculate nucleus to the cortex run in parallel and retain the overall pattern impinging on the retina. Visual information from the retina is therefore said to be "topographically" mapped onto the lateral geniculate nucleus which is, in turn, topographicaly mapped on the striate cortex.

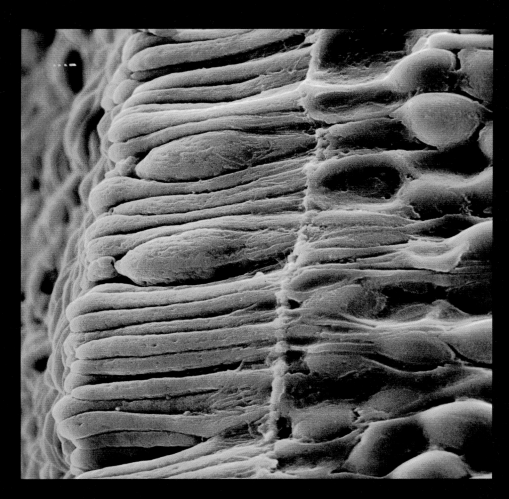

rods and cones The rods and cones are the visual receptor cells of the retina. The cones are slightly bulbous and the many slender rods are packed between them. The human retina has about 120 million rods and 7 million cones. The cones are concentrated in the center of the retina—an area called the fovea. This scanning electron micrograph has a magnification factor of about 45,000.

single-cell recording A fundamental technique of the physiological study of vision is single-cell recording. Recording micro-electrodes, tiny needles that pick up electrical activity, are inserted into individual cells while different stimuli are presented to the eye. By inserting micro-electrodes in the various structures of the visual brain, it is possible to determine the way in which information is handled as it ascends from the retina to the LGN and cortex.

David Hubel and Torsten Wiesel, who shared the 1981 Nobel Prize in medicine, are among those who have pioneered in this area. Hubel and Wiesel's experiments have shown how cells at various points in the visual system respond to an assortment of lines and spots of light used as stimuli. By placing an electrode in a cell they can study its "visual field"—the field of view that triggers the cell's response.

Hubel and Wiesel have found remarkable differences in the "receptive fields" of cells in various areas of the visual system. For example, the ganglion cells of the retina and the lateral geniculate nucleus have circular receptive fields. Sometimes they have an "inhibitory center"—a spot of light within the central area will cause them to decrease their rate of firing, while a spot in an outer region of the receptive fields will cause an increase. Some cells have an "excitatory center"—a spot of light in this area will cause an increase in their rate of firing; a spot outside this area will cause a decrease.

It is in the striate cortex that we first see cells that are triggered by something more complex than spot stimuli. The receptive field of a cortical cell might be a long and thin excitatory area surrounded by a much larger inhibitory area making the cell particularly responsive to a line segment. Such cells fire strongly when a short lighted bar is presented to the retina in a specific orientation. Other types of cells in the visual cortex require that a line segment be physically moved in a certain direction across the visual field to produce a response. Still other cells require that the moving line segment be of a particular length.

What causes the various cells of the visual system to respond with such specificity? It is tempting to think that it is a result of the way in which the cells are wired together—the "cytoarchitecture" of small cell groups. Hubel and Wiesel's work suggests that the visual system consists of small cellular information processors. Synaptic interconnections are organized so small groups of cells analyze the local pattern for specific qualities. The interconnections of the neurons made by the dendrites and synapses are thought to be analogous to the wiring of electrical circuits. Clusters of cells function like small computers by virtue of their interconnections.

It remains to be seen whether visual perception in its totality can be explained in terms of the responses of these small analyzers or whether a larger principle encompassing much larger patterns of neuronal activity is needed. The striate cortex, the highest center that has been intensively analyzed, is not the end of the road in visual perception. Information flows outwardly from this area of the cortex to surrounding areas as well as to other structures deeper in the brain. These other structures will need to be understood if we are ever to completely understand visual perception.

Hubel and Wiesel's research is important even if we cannot, at present, relate the behavior of single cells in the visual cortex to the experience of seeing. Their discoveries tell us that visual processing begins with small and precisely defined tasks. Visual processing is *parallel* processing: the scene is divided into many small segments that travel upward through the visual system in parallel and are processed simultaneously.

INTERACTION OF THE VISUAL SUBSENSES

In studying the responsiveness of cells in the visual system, it has become evident that separate pathways carry different qualities of the visual scene to the visual cortex and from one cortical area to the other. There appear to be at least three major distinguishable channels. One channel carries color information but does not "see" objects in great detail. Another channel appears to be principally concerned with movement and stereoscopic depth information. A third channel carries high-resolution information about shapes.

conflict between visual channels These two topographical maps of a foot made by Margaret Livingstone show how the different qualities of visual channels sometimes need to be considered in visualization. The topographical map on top uses the traditional color order derived from the spectrum (violet through red) to indicate altitude, while the map on bottom uses a color order consistent with the apparent brightness of colors as perceived by the shape channel (dark purple to light yellow).

When the spectral color order is used, the different perceived brightnesses of colors can make it difficult to properly interpret changes in altitude since, for example, a gradual change could be marked by sharp, and therefore misleading, transitions in brightness. The shape channel would tend to identify shapes—artifacts—that do not correspond to real altitude changes and would conflict with the color channel. When colors are chosen for their perceived brightness to the shape channel, however, the transition from color to color is accompanied by a comparable transition in brightness. Thus, altitude would be interpreted the same way by both color and shape channels, making a topographical map conceived in this way easy to interpret.

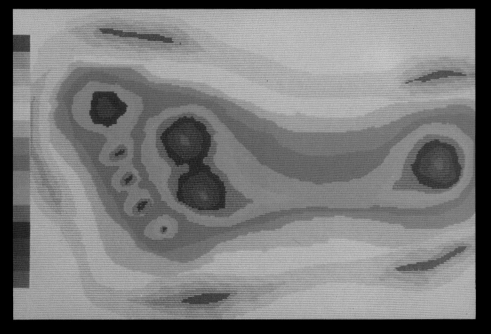

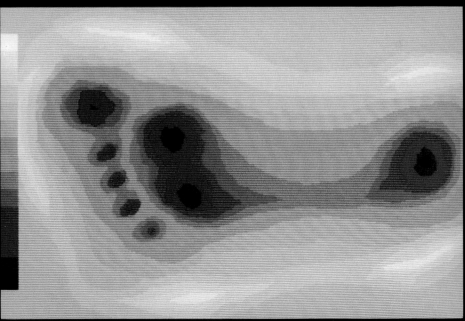

Margaret Livingstone of Harvard University Medical School has expressed the idea that information about these separate channels should be utilized in understanding art and visualization. Notice, for instance, that a contour map in which color indicates elevation is more easily understood when the relative *brightness* of colors is considered, so that, for example, the higher elevations are all light colors and the lower elevations are dark colors. This use of color is more effective than using a traditional color scale derived from the color order of the spectrum. Since color and shape are carried in separate channels, and since the shape channel is most sensitive to brightness changes, irrespective of color, the separate analytical pathways will conflict with one another if the color scale is not graded by brightness. If the color scale is simply derived from the order of the spectrum, then a high and a low elevation, although differently colored, may have the same brightness, making it difficult to perceive features. A map designed in this way requires conscious analysis to identify its features and to ignore shapes that are artifacts.

Physiological studies of the visual subsenses can help us understand artistic images too. In Matisse's *Self-Portrait,* shown here, notice that the shadows are primarily green. The green color is unusual but it does not interfere with sensing depth because the shape system is insensitive to color. In the accompanying black-and-white photograph, it is apparent that the brightness value of the green is normal for a shadow.

visual channels Although the shadowing in this painting is primarily green, it does not interfere with the sense of depth because depth, processed by the high acuity shape channel, depends primarily on brightness values, according to Margaret Livingstone. The black-and-white image shows that the brightness of the green area is appropriate for a shadow.

Henri Matisse. *Self-Portrait*. 1906. Oil on canvas, 21⅝ x 18⅛". Statens Museum for Kunst, Copenhagen, J. Rump Collection.

CONSCIOUS VS. PRECONSCIOUS VISUAL PROCESSING

In a tentative way, for the purposes of understanding visualization, we might divide visual processing into conscious and preconscious domains. Clearly consciousness plays a role in visual perception because we can consciously direct visual attention—we can think about and analyze what we see. The mechanisms studied by Land, Julesz, and Hubel and Wiesel are, however, *preconscious,* which means that the cellular mechanisms are beyond voluntary control and unrelated to conscious experience. The conscious mind receives information *after* it has been processed by the preconscious visual system.

It is in the distinction between the preconscious and conscious functioning of the brain that we find the most important reason for visualization. Images utilize the processing power of the retina, the LGN, and the visual cortex, among other structures which, in a sense, prepare information for consciousness. A successful visualization reveals the important feature of a problem to consciousness by allocating as much of the information processing as possible to the preconscious visual system (see *Visual Experiments*).

In visualization, as in all instances in which we see, the eye functions not as a camera, as is so often said, but, to go back to our earlier example, more like Empedocles' lantern. The eye and brain functioning together do not passively record but *actively create* the visual world. To be sure, modern physics disabuses us of any notion of emitted rays of energy, but the eye/brain is the source of the organizing power that creates and gives meaning to our visual environment. Visualization makes use of this illuminating power. This is its great appeal since, as will be seen in subsequent chapters, it is difficult to conceive of a means other than visualization by which we could so exquisitely prepare a problem for consciousness and, thus, higher orders of thought.

images from energy

My original decision to devote myself to science was a direct result of the discovery which has never ceased to fill me with enthusiasm since my early youth—the comprehension of the far from obvious fact that the laws of human reasoning coincide with the laws governing the sequences of the impressions we receive from the world about us; that, therefore, pure reasoning can enable man to gain an insight into the mechanism of the latter. In this connection, it is of paramount importance that the outside world is something independent from man, something absolute, and the quest for the laws which apply to this absolute appeared to me as the most sublime scientific pursuit in life.

Max Planck in Scientific Autobiography

Given the tremendous power of the visual system as an information processor, it is not surprising that many of the important inventions of the twentieth century are instruments designed to extend its reach, instruments that bring to the eyes things too small to be seen, the interior of the human body, unknown aspects of the Earth's surface, the planets, stars, and galaxies.

These instruments have enabled us to produce what are often "impossible" images—images from non-existent perspectives of non-visual phenomena. In the past two decades, great advances have been made by linking instruments for sensing patterns of energy to powerful digital computers. Much like our own visual systems, these instruments are ingenious not only in the way they gather image information but in the way they *make sense* of it. They grind through vast numbers of computations to interpret data that is often, by their very nature, scattered and difficult to decipher.

In considering these technologies, we soon realize that there is a reciprocal relationship between the technique by which an image is made and the way it must be interpreted. When an instrument takes the place of our eyes in the initial steps of seeing it plays an important role in determining the qualities we see. The necessity of understanding one's instruments is recognized in all fields of scientific measurement, but has a special importance in visualization. When a non-visual or visually inaccessible phenomenon is made into a visual form, the techniques must be designed so that the transformation is not misleading.

As technologies become more sophisticated, there are more and more subjective considerations, traditionally better understood by artists than by scientists, which must be appreciated. As we have already seen, the eye/brain has its strengths and its limitations, its peculiar way of making sense of patterns of light. Interpreting the images of visualization means not only understanding the technological strategy by which they are made, but also the subjective choices, the artistic technique, with which visualization is achieved.

The first step in these processes, is capturing or transducing a pattern of energy. Transduction is the transformation of energy from one form to another—in this case to make an image pattern. Photography is the oldest transduction technique. Here, light energy is changed into chemical energy and thereby into a pattern of very small silver grains. Black-and-white photographic film consists of light-sensitive silver salts that are dispersed in a thin layer of gelatin coated onto transparent plastic. When the film is exposed to light, individual crystals absorb light photons (the basic unit of light energy). This is the energy transduction step: light energy is transduced into chemical energy. The absorption of photons results in the liberation of silver atoms from the salt molecules. Regions of film that are exposed to bright areas of the image will be bombarded by many photons and will thus be dense with released silver particles. Regions that are exposed to dark areas will not be so heavily bombarded and will contain fewer silver particles. In this way, an image encoded as a pattern of light energy is transformed into a pattern of silver particles.

In general, whenever energy and matter interact there is an opportunity for visualization by transduction. Many methods have been developed. Just before the turn of the century, for example, Wilhelm Roentgen discovered the existence of X-ray radiation, which, like light, is a form of electromagnetic radiation that can be recorded on film. X-rays, having a shorter wavelength, can penetrate substances that are opaque to visible wavelengths, thereby providing a means for visualizing the interiors of objects. The image is made photographically because, conveniently, X-rays have the same effect on photographic materials as light does.

The electron microscope uses another form of energy: electrons. Developed in the late 1920s by Ernst Ruska, a German physicist, the electron microscope uses magnetic fields to focus a beam of electrons on an object. The portion of the beam that is transmitted through the object is then focused in a vacuum tube. The tube transduces the image pattern into a pattern of electrical current that, after amplification, is used to form an image on a cathode-ray tube (CRT). Because electrons are so much smaller than a wavelength of visible light, they can be used to resolve images much smaller than those accessible to light microscopes.

false color A false-colored scanning electron micrograph of an iron crystal. The colors indicate different magnetic polarities.

In 1931, while investigating the causes of static in telephone transmission lines, Karl Jansky, an electrical engineer at Bell Laboratories, discovered radio emissions coming from stellar objects and inadvertently discovered a transduction technique for visualizing the cosmos. Using this discovery, Grote Reber, in Wheaton, Illinois, constructed the first crude radio telescope, which is simply a radio antenna that detects very faint radio signals from space. Reber scanned the sky with his telescope and manually plotted the detected signals on a map. Thus began radio astronomy, which is important because the information it provides about the sky often reveals features not evident through light measurements.

the digital revolution and image processing
With the development of the digital computer, additional kinds of energy patterns could be made into images. The new computational techniques came to be called image processing and they opened up entirely new visual worlds.

Image processing uses computational techniques, many of which were first developed for the space program, to manipulate visual information. Space probes such as Ranger, Surveyor, and Mariner transmitted images back to Earth as strings of numbers representing the brightness values of the many points that make up an image. Since the data transmission was often interrupted by static and solar flares, methods were developed to repair the damage and to restore lost portions of images. It was inevitable that these methods would attract a great deal of interest because they permitted the refining and altering of images in ways that had never before been possible. Now these techniques are used in many fields, including medical diagnostics, electron microscopy, seismography, aerial reconnaissance, video, and the graphic arts.

The first step in image processing is to digitize the image, to turn it into numbers. The image is broken into discrete picture elements, called pixels, which are arranged in a rectangular grid, much like the stitches in needlepoint. For a black-and-white (monochromatic) image, each pixel is assigned a number that indicates its brightness. For a color image, each pixel is assigned three numbers, one for the brightness value of each of three primary colors (generally red, green, and blue). Thus the digitization represents an image as a two-dimensional array of numbers.

There are several ways of digitizing a photograph. A device called a scanning microdensitometer moves a print photograph or transparency past a small spot of light and measures the reflected or transmitted light at each point. The light is then assigned a number to indicate the brightness at that point. With another device, a flying spot scanner, the image is stationary while a small spot of light, created either by a laser or by a cathode-ray tube, is scanned across it. In both of these scanners the scan path follows a form called a raster, which is horizontal from left to right, line after line, from top to bottom.

More recently, digitizers have been based on arrays of light-sensitive semiconductor devices, called charge-coupled devices (CCD). These devices can read more than one point of the photograph at the same moment. A one-dimensional array of CCDs (a row of light-sensitive units) can digitize an entire row of points in an image at once. Thus, a scanner using such an array must be moved from one edge of the image to the other, to digitize successive rows. With a two-dimensional CCD digitizer (a rectangular array of light-sensitive units) scanning is unnecessary: all the points in the image can be digitized simultaneously. The most sophisticated CCDs can digitize millions of pixels in an instant, approaching resolution close to that of a photograph. CCDs are used in lightweight video cameras and prototypes of electronic still cameras.

The numbers that encode the image can be stored in the memory of a computer and the computer can display the image on a monitor, typically a cathode-ray tube (CRT). In order to keep the image flicker-free, the CRT repaints the image 30 times a second. This places such a great demand on the computer's processing power that the screen display is generally managed by a separate portion of the computer's memory called a frame buffer, which is devoted exclusively to the display.

There are several ways of producing hard copy. One method is simply to use a camera to photograph the CRT screen. It is also possible to record an image directly onto photographic film by, in effect, running a flying spot scanner or a microdensitometer in reverse. Image data is used to modulate a focused light beam that is scanned over the film in the raster pattern. These images are generally of higher quality than those photographed from the CRT screen. Hard copy can also be produced by a variety of printing devices that essentially print the rows of pixels, usually by scanning in a raster pattern.

0	1	2	3	4	5	6	7	8	9	10	11

digitizing a photograph Before an image can be processed by a digital computer, it must be translated into numbers or *digitized*. The image is first divided into a grid of small rectangular picture elements, or *pixels*. The area within the pixel is then electronically matched to a grey scale and a number that corresponds to its average brightness is selected.

Grey scales can have any number of levels from black to white. Sixty-four levels of grey are sufficient to create a realistic black-and-white image. In the case of a color image, the color of a pixel is represented as a combination of three brightness values, one for each of the primaries.

The number of pixels (the number of rows and columns in the grid) depends upon the resolution required. Low resolution is, conventionally, 512 rows by 512 columns or 262,144 pixels. Higher resolution is often multiples of this, for example, 2048 x 2048 (4,194,304 pixels). High resolution is required for special applications such as motion picture special effects where large-screen projections will be made. High resolution is required so that the individual pixels will remain small enough to be unnoticeable.

In the early days of image processing, images were sometimes digitized manually. Now, the process is usually accomplished with special digitizing machines or with a computer that uses the output of a video or other electronic camera.

1	1	1	1	10	11	1	1	1	1	1	1	1	1	1	1	1	9	8
1	1	1	1	10	11	1	1	1	1	1	1	1	1	1	1	2	8	9
1	1	1	1	10	11	1	1	1	1	1	1	1	1	1	1	4	8	10
1	1	1	1	10	11	1	1	1	1	1	1	1	1	1	1	4	8	10
1	1	1	1	10	11	1	1	1	1	1	1	1	1	1	1	5	8	10
1	1	1	1	10	11	1	1	1	1	1	1	1	1	1	1	5	8	8
1	0	0	0	10	11	0	0	0	0	0	1	1	0	0	0	5	8	8
0	2	2	2	10	11	2	3	3	4	4	5	5	7	7	7	6	8	8
3	5	9	8	10	11	7	7	7	7	8	8	8	7	6	6	6	8	8
11	9	9	6	10	11	7	8	8	8	8	8	6	5	5	5	6	8	8
10	9	9	6	10	11	7	8	8	8	8	8	3	5	6	4	6	8	8
10	7	6	6	10	11	6	7	7	6	6	6	4	3	2	2	5	8	8
4	3	8	7	10	11	5	4	3	2	2	2	2	2	2	4	8	8	8
6	4	2	2	10	11	2	2	2	2	3	2	2	2	7	9	8	8	8
2	2	2	2	10	11	2	2	2	2	2	2	5	7	9	9	7	8	8
2	2	2	2	10	11	2	2	2	4	2	8	9	9	10	9	8	7	8
2	2	2	2	10	11	2	2	2	2	5	7	9	10	11	9	10	9	7
2	2	2	2	10	11	2	2	2	2	7	9	9	9	10	11	10	9	7
2	2	5	7	9	8	2	2	2	2	7	9	9	9	10	11	11	11	10	7
7	9	7	5	2	2	2	2	2	2	8	9	9	10	11	11	11	11	11	10

IMAGE-PROCESSING TECHNIQUES Although the underlying principles of image processing are often conceptually complex, the techniques themselves are more and more being used in art, publishing (including desktop publishing), science, design, advertising, and in other areas by individuals who are not computer scientists and who simply employ commercially available software packages. The computer provides a completely new way of enhancing, altering, and combining images.

There are four broad categories of image-processing operations: (1) In geometric processing, the shape of an image or areas within an image are modified. (2) In point-by-point processing, the image is modified by making simple changes in pixel values. (3) In ensemble processing, information from multiple images is compared on a pixel-by-pixel basis to derive a new image. (4) Finally, in Fourier-domain processing, the values for pixels are altered in complex ways based upon brightnesses of surrounding pixels or properties of larger areas of the image.

geometric processing
In geometric processing an image, or part of an image, is magnified, reduced, rotated, repositioned, or intentionally distorted, much as if the image were on a rubber sheet: the shape of the image is changed by mathematically stretching or twisting the rubber sheet. Geometric processing is often used to bring pairs of images into precise registration and alignment prior to more sophisticated processing operations. A pair of medical images produced at different times may not match exactly. Satellite images made from the same point of view, but at different times, may be different because of different atmospheric conditions.

point-by-point processing
The simplest point-by-point process would be the addition of a constant to each pixel. In digitization, the brightness of each image point is translated into a number. By adding a number to the value for each pixel, the brightness can be increased for the image—an operation similar at least in certain respects to increasing the exposure time of a photograph.

CONTRAST STRETCHING Contrast stretching is a more sophisticated point-by-point process, which would be used when visual inspection shows that an image lacks contrast. In a low-contrast image, the difference in brightness between the brightest and the darkest regions is small, which indicates that the full range of values in the grey scale has not been used. Contrast stretching "spreads" the pixel values out on a graduated scale from white to black so that the full range of greys is utilized.

For example, if an image consists entirely of pixels with brightness values between 32 and 63, it is possible to stretch that contrast over the full range of available values, 0 (white) to 63 (black), with a simple arithmetic procedure. The lowest value is simply subtracted from each pixel and the result is multiplied by a constant. In this case 32 is subtracted from each pixel and the result is multiplied by two. The newly calculated image is more intelligible because it has greater contrast. Contrast stretching epitomizes the kind of numerical manipulations that are used in image processing—the idea that you can alter a *quality* of an image with mathematics.

Contrast stretching can reveal hidden details in an image. The human visual system responds to a limited range of brightnesses and, within that range, has a certain capacity to recognize differences. In a low-contrast image, all of the brightness information is concentrated into a relatively narrow region of the visual system's responsiveness. Since contrast stretching makes the difference between brightnesses greater, a much broader range of the visual system's responsiveness is utilized.

The procedure for contrast stretching—subtract the lowest value in the image from each pixel and multiply the result by a constant—is an example of an algorithm. It is important to discuss the idea of an algorithm here because algorithms are fundamental to computing and to using the computer in visualization. Algorithms are simply computational procedures, equivalent to a recipe, for achieving a particular result. The name is derived from that of Al-khowarizmi, the ninth-century Muslim mathematician who systematized the calculating techniques we think of as arithmetic. Addition, subtraction, multiplication, and division are simple procedures that, when formally described, are themselves algorithms. For a procedure to be an algorithm each step must be explicitly stated and the procedure must be complete (no steps left out) and finite (it cannot have an endless number of steps)

Algorithms have been developed to accomplish many kinds of tasks with the computer, both basic and esoteric. Some of the important algorithms in visualization are even simpler than contrast stretching, but many are much more complex. Fortunately, it is not necessary to understand the intricacies of algorithms in order to use many visualization technologies—any more than it is necessary to understand automotive mechanics to drive an automobile.

contrast enhancement This photograph of San Francisco has been contrast enhanced by a technique called histogram equalization, which is similar to contrast stretching but slightly more sophisticated. In contrast stretching, the range between the darkest and the lightest pixel is increased and intermediate pixels are redistributed. In histogram equalization, the computer, in essence, produces a histogram (bar chart) showing the number of pixels at each brightness. The computer then alters the brightness levels of selected pixels so that there are an equal number for each brightness level. Either method of contrast enhancement can improve the legibility of an image by converting it into a form where it better matches the eye's remarkable ability to see brightnesses across a wide range. The image at right is an equalized version of the top right area of the lower image.

FALSE COLORING False coloring (or pseudocoloring) is another point-by-point process that serves a purpose similar to that of contrast stretching. Assume that an image already uses the full range of available brightness values. The goal is to process the image in a way that increases our capacity to detect patterns in regions of the image where the grey scale differences are all very small. Since the image already uses the full range of grey-scale values there is no way of stretching it. In false coloring, different portions of the grey scale are given different hues. Each hue then has a full range of brightnesses. In this way, some of the grey-scale differences become translated into hue differences while formerly small differences become larger brightness differences within a hue. Here, as in contrast stretching, a visualization process is used to adapt images to the eye's information-processing capacity.

ANTI-LOGARITHMIC PROCESSING A final type of point-by-point processing, anti-logarithmic processing, is used to prepare images for other kinds of image processing. For example, photographic film does not darken in direct proportion to the actual brightness of the light it receives. Since many image-processing techniques work best if applied to actual brightness values, it is necessary to recover these values. This is done by applying a mathematical function called the anti-logarithm to the brightness value of each pixel. The resulting image data reflect the actual brightness values in the light that made the image and not the grey level of the photograph.

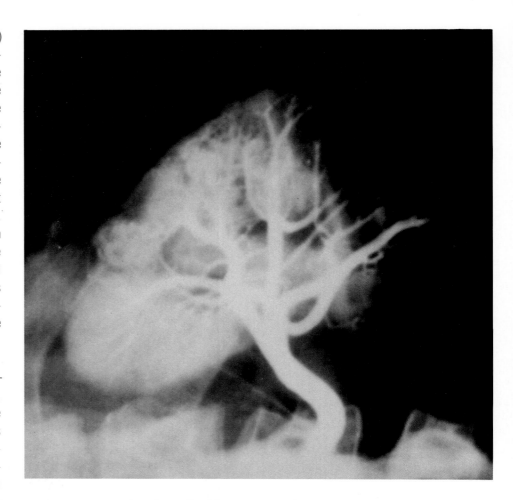

information processing demands of image processing Image processing and graphics require a great deal of computing power. Even to display the image requires a great deal of computing power. A 512 × 512 image—a medium-resolution display—has 262,144 pixels. To display a color image, the intensity for each of the primary colors, red, green, and blue, at each pixel must be specified. If each of the primaries can display over 256 levels of brightness, a single image will require 6,291,456 bits of information. Each bit is held in the computer's working memory and read to the display electronics. To maintain the image on the CRT, the information in the computer's memory must be read 30 times a second which, for a 6,291,456-bit image, is 188,743,680 bits a second. Reading these bits to the CRT is not complicated, but it consumes a great deal of processor time which could be more fruitfully devoted to transformation of image data. Of course, the numbers become more formidable when greater resolution is required, as it often is. Systems with greater resolution use a 1024 × 1024 or 2048 × 2048 pixel format. In this case, even more processor time would be required just to sustain the image on the screen.

Computer designers have dealt with this problem by using frame buffers—a part of the computer's memory that is strictly dedicated to holding image data for display. Once an image has been calculated, it is moved to the frame buffer where it is then read to the CRT. The rest of the computer's memory is kept available for further image calculations, or for any other kind of information processing.

The computational demands of image processing are so extreme that visually oriented computers are likely to include special graphics processors as well. These special microchips handle large numbers of relatively simple graphics calculations, such as those required to reduce or enlarge an image or a portion of the image, thereby freeing the main processor for more complex operations.

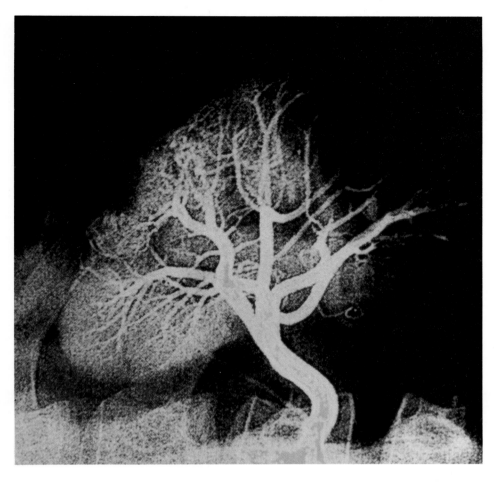

edge enhancement and false coloring In edge enhancement, the brightness value of pixels is changed in a way that depends on the brightness of adjacent pixels. Pixels that are similar to adjacent pixels in brightness will be unchanged whereas pixels that are different from their neighbors (suggesting an edge) will have the difference increased. The figure at near left shows how edge enhancement can clarify detail.

In false coloring, the computer colors a black-and-white image by substituting colors for grey-scale values. The darkest region of greys, for example, could be assigned to blue, the next brightest region to green, and the brightest levels to red. Thus, each portion of the grey scale is spread out over a full range of brightnesses within a color therefore exploiting the eye's ability to discriminate small differences in color.

After false coloring, colored areas do not necessarily correspond to features within the image. Visual artifacts can be produced when changes in brightness not corresponding to important features are made salient in the colored image. False coloring is thus something of an art; it is not always easy to assign colors to an image so that the coloring reveals the features of interest. It is best to utilize a color scale in which colors are ordered according to their perceived brightness by the shape channel in order to ensure that the color and shape channels of visual perception work harmoniously (see *We Create the World We See*).

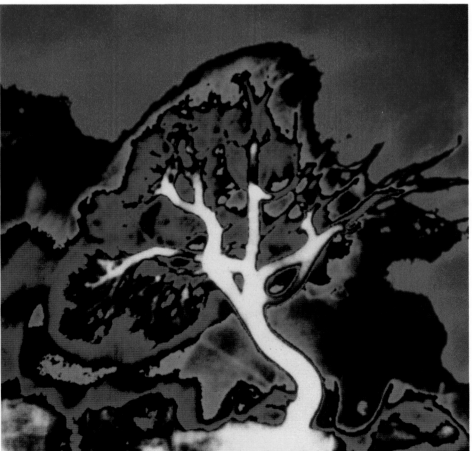

side-imaging radar Side-imaging radar (SIR) is an imaging technique in which the motion of an airplane or, in this case the space shuttle, is used to simulate the effect of an impossibly large radar instrument. With radar, a beam is sent from the radar instrument and is reflected back by objects in its path. The time it takes for the beam to return indicates the objects' distances. By moving the radar instrument, SIR produces an image of a broad portion of terrain by integrating radar reflections as they return. The process is akin to the way in which the geometry of an unseen object could be sensed by running a finger over it. SIR images have high resolution and provide very good depth information. The top image depicts a high plateau in northern Peru. The bottom illustration shows the mouth of the Ganges River in Bangladesh during flooding. SIR is a monochromatic technique—both images here are false colored.

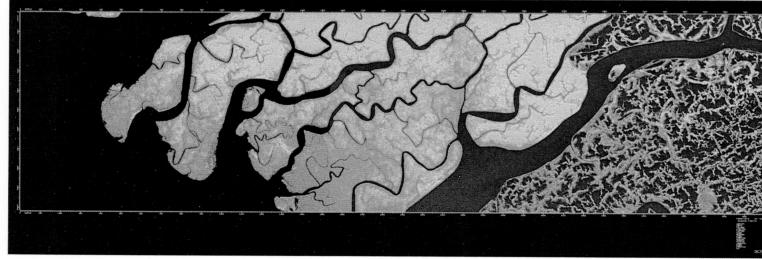

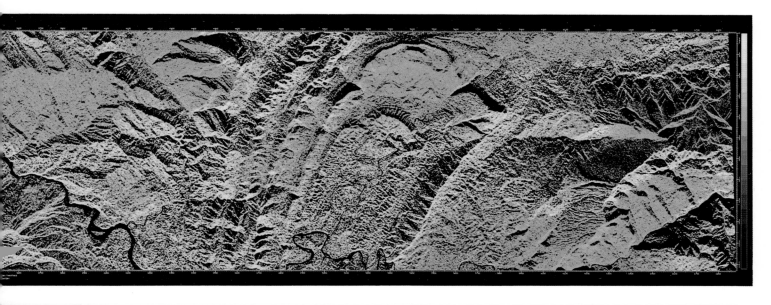

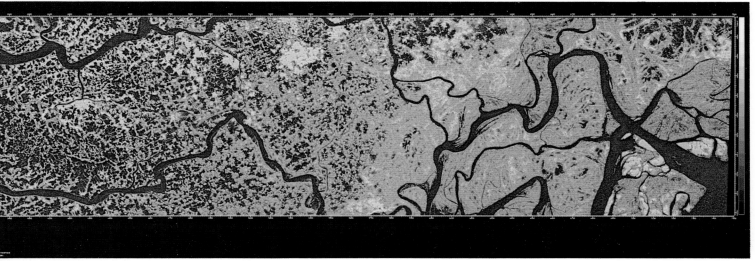

ensemble processing One of the most exciting applications of image processing is being able to use the computer to compare images made at different times or under different conditions in order to search for significant differences. After all, this is precisely the way in which both the color sense and stereopsis operate in the human vision system. The computer can be made to take the role of a preconscious visual process—isolating features on the basis of comparisons among different images to prepare a higher-order image in which significant structures are identified. Image processing in which multiple images are used to produce a higher-order image is called ensemble processing.

The medical diagnostic technique of digital subtraction angiography, which is used to visualize the circulatory system, is an example of ensemble processing. With this technique, which is based on X-ray, the image data is obtained as follows: first a background or mask image is obtained. A contrast dye is then introduced into the patient's circulatory system through a vein. When the dye has had a chance to distribute itself through the circulatory system, another image is made with the same point of view as the mask image. The value for a given pixel in the mask image is then subtracted from the corresponding pixel in the second image. This proceeds pixel-by-pixel for all later images. Since the only difference between the mask image and later images is the presence of contrast dye in the veins and arteries, the result of the subtraction process is an image in which only the dye in the circulatory system is visible. It should be noted that, since the patient generally moves involuntarily when the dye is injected, it is also necessary to use geometric processing in order to register the mask image with successive dye-filled images.

Dual-energy radiography is another diagnostic technique that uses ensemble processing. X-ray images are made using two different wavelengths of X-ray energy. These images are then combined to emphasize subtle distinctions in tissues that can be noted because of the differences with which they absorb X-rays at the two wavelengths.

Still another application of ensemble processing is in the analysis of multispectral remote-sensing images, taken from aircraft or satellites. The Landsat multispectral scanner, for example, is sensitive to four spectral bands (each band containing a limited range of adjacent wavelengths), while the thematic mapper, a more sophisticated multispectral instrument, is sensitive to seven bands. More recent airborne instruments use between 100 and 200 bands. An image of the terrain is made in each of the bands. The computer is then used to search for specific relationships among the resulting images. New images are then calculated in which the value of a pixel indicates its spectral signature, that is, its response to several wavelengths rather than to just one. This new image can then be pseudocolored with distinct colors denoting specific relationships between corresponding pixels in an ensemble of images. The resulting image helps in the search for terrain characteristics such as mineral deposits or specific kinds of vegetation. Distinctive colors mark areas in the resulting images that have particular spectral signatures.

multispectral scanning Multispectral scanning—recording satellite images at two or more wavelengths—can be used to analyze the surface of the Earth, in this case Eleuthera Island, Bahamas. Copyright © 1988 CNES.

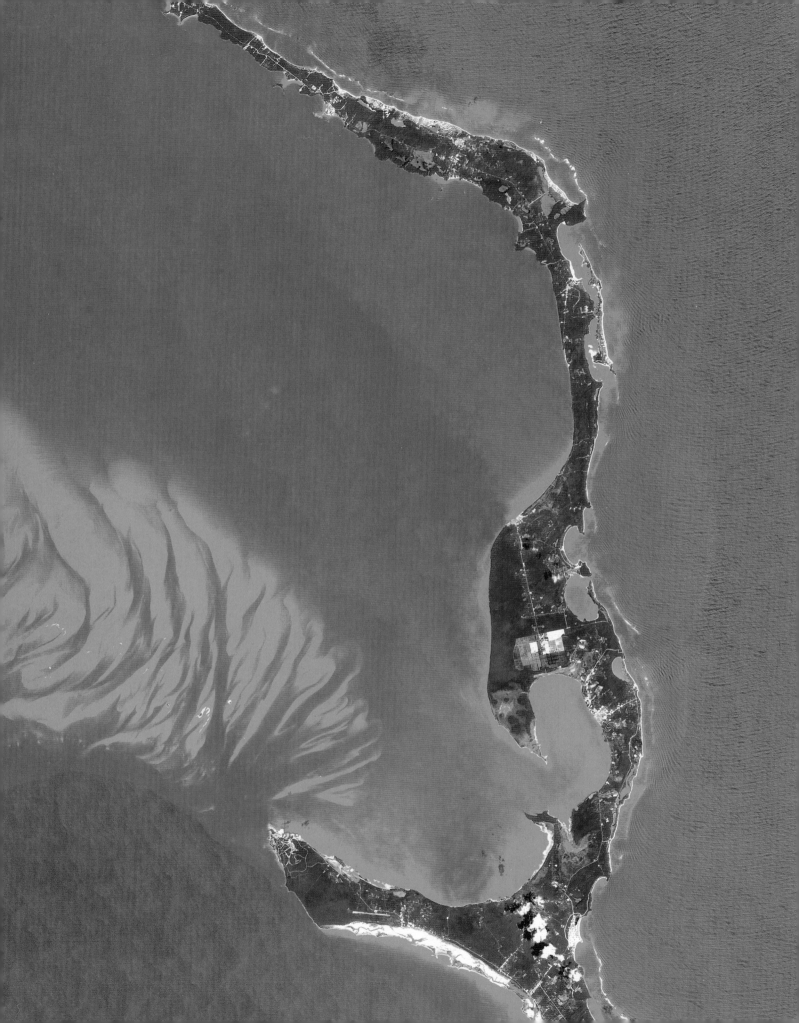

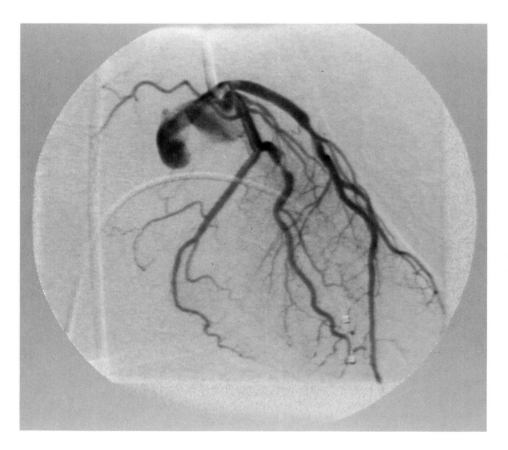

digital subtraction angiography Digital subtraction angiography, an example of ensemble processing, is used to visualize the circulatory system, which is problematical for diagnosticians because it has almost the same X-ray absorption properties as the tissues surrounding it.

To visualize the circulatory system, an X-ray is made by directing a pulsed X-ray beam through the patient to a high-resolution video camera. This produces a mask image. A contrast dye is then injected into the patient's circulatory system and another X-ray image is made. The two images are then aligned in the computer and the second image is digitally subtracted from the first. The result is an image of the circulatory system without surrounding tissues.

These pseudocolored images are produced by a method that is, in certain ways, analogous to the Young-Helmholtz color theory, which postulates that color is calculated in the eye and brain by comparing separate images made at long, medium, and short wavelengths. According to one theory, color is a percept that depends on differences in brightness among three images. The images resulting from multispectral scanning similarly reveal features by cross-comparison of separate images made at different wavelengths. The same thing can be said of dual energy radiography, which also compares images made with energy at different wavelengths.

It remains to be seen whether, in the case of multispectral scanning, there would be an advantage to switching to reflectance rather than the brightnesses. In cross-comparing narrow band images with the computer, it is conceivable that it might be easier to recognize features if reflectance, as defined in Land's color theory, calculated from brightness changes from point to point, were calculated prior to ensemble processing. If so, it would be an interesting application of perceptual theory to image processing.

edge detection In general, portions of an image in which there is a sharp change in brightness over a small area are likely to be edges. The computer searches for these areas by comparing the grey-scale values of closely spaced pixels. Sharp changes are replaced with white and all other areas are made black. The resulting image shows "edges" quite clearly.

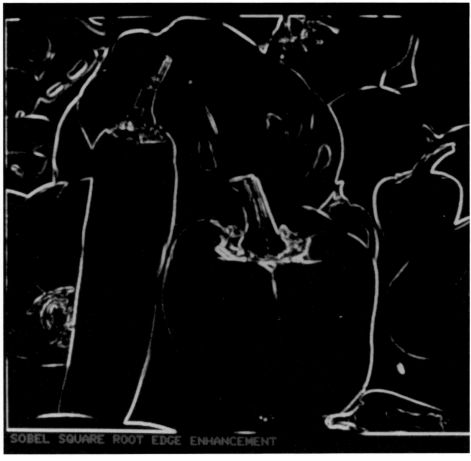

SOBEL SQUARE ROOT EDGE ENHANCEMENT

fourier-domain processing In point-by-point techniques the values of individual pixels are considered in isolation. In calculating a new value for a given pixel, the values of adjacent pixels or pixels in other parts of the image are not considered. Another category of image-processing techniques, Fourier-domain operations (so-called because they rely on a form of mathematical analysis invented by the nineteenth-century French mathematician J.B.J. Fourier) consider the individual pixel, not as an element in isolation, but as one indicator of the whole image pattern. Fourier techniques sometimes seem to achieve the impossible. They can be used to remove blurring, to sharpen edges, to improve contrast, to restore detail, to improve the focus in an image after it has been made, and to combine elements from separate images seamlessly. Fourier techniques are also the basis of several fundamentally new visualization techniques: tomography, synthetic aperture astronomy, and side-imaging radar, among others.

Fourier technique was developed to analyze wave forms. Fourier discovered that a complex wave form can be represented as the sum of simple waves of various frequencies and amplitudes. This idea is easiest to understand with sound waves. When the treble control on a stereo is adjusted, the high-frequency portion of the signal is affected independently of the low-frequency portion. Similarly, the bass control affects only the low-frequency components of the signal. The music itself is a highly complex sound wave, but electronics can be used selectively to operate on its different component frequencies. This is the essence of Fourier analysis: the isolation of different frequency components in a complex signal.

It is intuitively difficult to imagine an image, which is a pattern of light and dark, as being constituted of *spatial* frequencies. The pattern, however, can be thought of as a signal that changes from point to point much as a sound wave changes from moment to moment. While sound waves are temporal changes in air pressure, images can be thought of as spatial changes in brightness. Those changes can be characterized as a wave form with high- and low-frequency components just like the treble and bass of a musical signal.

With digital computers it is possible to use Fourier analysis to separate an image into its different spatial frequency components. A Fourier analysis calculates the power (the amount of activity) at every frequency. The high-frequency components of an image are strongest in those regions where brightness varies greatly over a small distance; for example, the pattern of a hound's-tooth check has powerful high-frequency components. The low-frequency components of the image are strongest in those regions where brightness varies gradually over a relatively large area (such as a clear sky). An out-of-focus image is strong in the low-frequency components but weak in the high-frequency components. By using Fourier analysis, it is possible to turn up the visual "treble" or to turn down the visual "bass." When the high frequencies are turned up, the sharp changes in the image become more pronounced. When the low frequencies are turned up, the image becomes softer.

Edge enhancement is one of the simplest Fourier techniques. The high spatial frequencies, which are strongest at edges, are increased. Fourier techniques can also be used to correct an image that has been blurred because the camera was not properly focused. By closely examining the Fourier transformation of the image, clues can be obtained about the nature of the blur—its "signature"—and the imperfection can be mathematically corrected.

deblurring The blur in the image top left was caused by camera movement while the blur in the bottom left image is attributable to poor focus. In both cases, Fourier analysis was used to determine the "signatures" of the blur and then to correct the images. The "halo" in the deblurred images results from two factors: 1) the absence of information in the original images and 2) the deblurring process itself. Deblurring process restored some information to the image but some was unrecoverable.

DEBLURRING Detecting the cause of a blur in a photograph is not as difficult as it might seem. The simplest case is an image of a dot. If a camera is moved while photographing a dot, the dot becomes a short line. If the camera is out of focus, a dot will become aureoled. If the dot is moving during the exposure, it will photograph as a line or a curve.

In general, natural images are more complex than a single dot. Nonetheless, once the nature of the blur has been determined, the blur component can be corrected. In the case of camera movement, the trace that turned a dot into a line can be mathematically corrected, leaving a sharp image of the dot. In a more complex image, every point can be corrected for that same component, restoring clarity to the image. Similarly, images that have been blurred because of poor focus can be restored by deblurring the component that spreads the points into an aureole. In the case of a moving subject in the image, only one portion of the image needs correction.

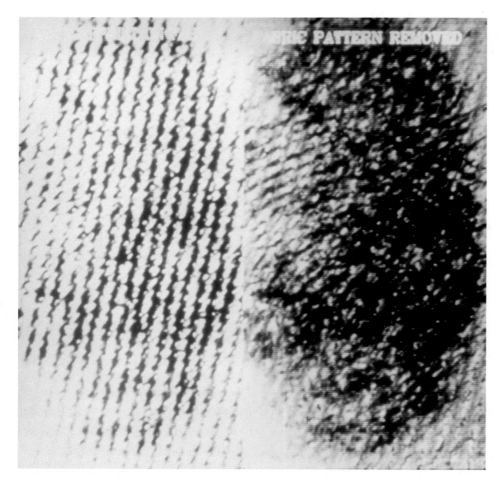

revealing a fingerprint Pattern removal techniques have been used to reveal a fingerprint on a patterned fabric. The left image shows a barely discernible fingerprint. In the right image, the fabric pattern has been removed with a Fourier technique and the fingerprint has been made distinct.

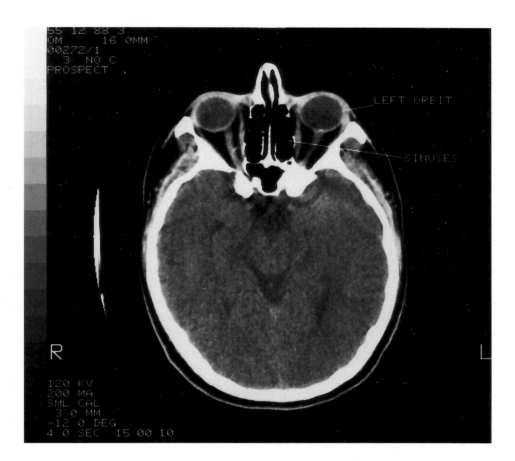

55 12 88 3
OM   16 0MM
00272/1
3 NO C
PROSPECT

120 KV
200 MA
SML CAL
3 0 MM
-12 0 DEG
4 0 SEC 15 00 10

R

L

LEFT ORBIT

SINUSES

computer tomography (CT) A conventional X-ray image collapses the three-dimensional structure of the body into two dimensions, making it difficult to understand spatial relationships. Furthermore, features of interest can be obscured by other X-ray absorbing structures anywhere in the path between the X-ray source and the X-ray plate. Computer tomography fulfilled a long standing hope of diagnosticians by visualizing planes within the body as if portions of the body had been cut away. In the image shown, for example, the horizontal plane formed by the two eyes has been visualized. The only way to produce a comparable image with traditional X-ray would be to physically remove a slab of tissue from the head.

Tomography is an example of the marvelous results that can be achieved with digital image processing. The image of tissue density is inferred from data collected by passing an X-ray emitter around a plane of tissue. As the X-ray beam is rotated, a detector on the other side of the plane monitors the absorption of X-rays. The raw data is a set of numbers indicating the X-ray density of each straight line through the tissue plane. The computer compares these values to calculate the X-ray density of discrete volumes within the plane. Typically, the process is repeated so that the diagnostician is provided with a series of images of adjacent planes through the body.

X-ray tomography In CT scanning, narrow beams of parallel X-rays are transmitted through a slice of the body by an X-ray emitter which circumscribes a cross-section. Opposite the emitter, on the other side of the cross-section, an X-ray detector measures the transmitted rays at these different angles. If the body were perfectly transparent to X-rays, the beams would pass through the body unchanged. In actuality, many of the rays in the beam are deflected and others are absorbed depending upon the density of the tissue in a given line through the cross-section. The output of the detector is then used by the computer to calculate the distribution of tissue densities in a slice which would yield the measured pattern of X-ray deletion. These densities are then represented as an image. The process yields a result that would be identical to physically removing and making a conventional X-ray of a slab of tissue.

COMPUTED TOMOGRAPHY (CT) Fourier analysis is useful in visualization way beyond image enhancement and restoration. These techniques are used in the very creation of images in computed tomography, aperture synthesis radio astronomy, side-imaging radar, and X-ray diffraction crystallography. Here, the basic transduction process alone, without the computer, does not yield an image. The information obtained must first be subjected to Fourier processing.

The best-known application of tomography uses X-ray. Tomography solves many of the problems inherent in standard X-ray. For example, traditional X-ray does not produce a good image of the brain because it can visualize only extreme differences in tissue density, such as that between bone and soft tissue. The brain is essentially a mass of soft tissue surrounded by bone—the skull. Consequently, standard X-ray images of the head are basically images of the skull. The subtle differences in tissue density that indicate a small tumor, for example, are usually indiscernible. Another liability of X-ray is that it is a "shadow" technique; it collapses the three-dimensional structure of the body onto a two-dimensional plane. CT solves these two problems; it isolates individual planes of interest and visualizes them without the obscuration of bone or other dense structures.

The basic CT scan visualizes a single slice through the body, a two-dimensional image. Adjacent slices can also be calculated and "stacked up" into a three-dimensional image of the body's interior. Through the techniques of computer graphics, this data can be used to create a three-dimensional computer-graphic model of body structure.

Such three-dimensional visualizations are extremely useful in medical diagnostics. For example, injuries are often difficult to assess fully without a three-dimensional model, and surgeons increasingly want to visualize the three-dimensional structure of an organ in anticipation of surgery.

The principle of computed tomography is also used in other diagnostic technologies such as positron emission tomography (PET) and magnetic resonance imaging (MRI). In PET, various naturally occurring compounds in the body, called biological substrates, are synthesized in a mildly radioactive form. The radioactive particles emitted from these substrates (called isotopes when radioactive) are detected and tomographically analyzed in order to visualize the metabolic activity of tissues, thus providing a portrait of the functioning of internal organs.

While the X-ray CT image shows tissue density, the PET image visualizes metabolic activity. It is, therefore, an image of biological *function* rather than of structure. On page 66, we see PET scans of the brain. In this case, glucose-like molecules were made radioactive and, thus, these images visualize glucose metabolism.

The illustration shows brain activity during different kinds of mental tasks of a manic-depressive patient. Differences in brain activity correspond to different kinds of perceptual and cognitive activity indicating how well PET scanning visualizes subtle changes in metabolism.

Computed tomography is not limited to diagnostic images, or to the transduction of electromagnetic energy. It can also be used, for example, by geologists to create images of the Earth's interior from seismic data. Instead of using X-rays, positron emissions, or magnetic resonance, geologists work from the mechanical waves generated by earthquakes. These waves travel with relatively little attenuation and are detected by seismometers all over the world. Tomographic analysis of wave velocity yields an image of the distribution of "slow" and "fast" regions in the Earth's interior. Since seismic waves speed up or slow down according to both the density and the temperature of the material through which they travel, this technique allows scientists to visualize the Earth's inner structure.

Although developed for diagnostic purposes, computer tomography is occasionally used outside of medicine. In this case, it was used to create the computer model of a sculpture by Joan Miró which was to be installed in an office building plaza. A series of CT scans were made of a 36-inch maquette (a size small enough to fit into a CT scanner). A computer-graphics system was then used to compile the slices into a three-dimensional model within the computer, which was then incorporated into the three-dimensional computer model of the building and plaza. The same computer model was also used to design the supporting structure of the actual 30-foot-high sculpture.

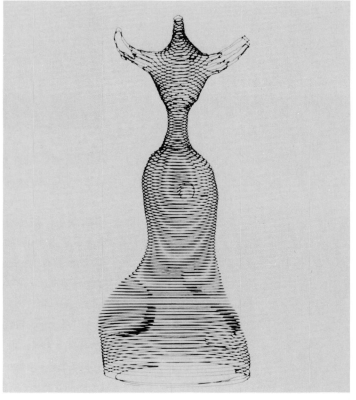

positron emission tomography (PET) The tomographic technique can be used with energies other than X-ray. Positron emission tomography, for example, measures the emission of positrons from mildly radioactive substances—isotopes—injected into the body. By creating an isotope of biologically significant compounds, aspects of metabolism can be visualized. In the images here, an isotope of a glucose-like substance is used. Thus, positrons are emitted in greater numbers from areas of the body where a great deal of glucose is being utilized. False color can be used to help identify active areas.

The PET scans seen here depict glucose metabolism in the brain during different types of mental activity. In this case, the cool colors indicate low utilization of glucose while warm colors indicate rapid glucose metabolism. In the experiments shown, subjects were asked to perform visual, auditory, cognitive, memory, and motor tasks, which caused different regions of the brain to become active as indicated in the images.

While CT scanning visualizes structure, PET is used to visualize metabolic function of the brain and other organs of the body. PET is particularly useful for studying the brain since there are no other comparable techniques for visualizing brain activity.

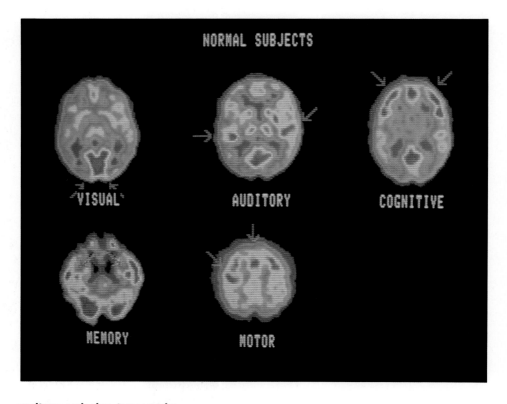

positron emission tomography In PET, biological substrates such as water, oxygen, glucose, fats, amino acids, and neurotransmitters are labeled with radioisotopes which decay very quickly (thus minimizing the patient's exposure to radioactivity). The isotopes emit positrons (positively charged electrons) that travel for very short distances in the body (less than a few millimeters) until they collide with electrons by chance. Each proton-electron collision generates two gamma-ray photons traveling in almost exactly opposite directions. When two detectors exactly opposite one another simultaneously detect gamma-ray photons, an emission is recorded. The computer assigns the emission to the narrow cylinder of tissue between the two detectors. The cylinder of tissue is analogous to the row of voxels penetrated by the X-ray beam in X-ray CT. The total score of emissions for any cylinder is thus analogous to the strength of the transmitted beam, for a particular path, in X-ray CT. After collecting data from many pairs of gamma-ray detectors, defining many cylinders of tissue in the image plane, Fourier techniques can be used to calculate the distribution of metabolic activity in the image plane. This distribution is then displayed as an image.

magnetic resonance imaging Magnetic resonance imaging (MRI), like X-ray CT, is used to visualize internal structure. One advantage MRI has over CT is that it has a higher resolution and it is more sensitive to soft tissue detail. MRI uses magnetic fields and pulses of radio waves to detect the distribution of hydrogen atoms in the body—which are abundantly present since most soft tissue mass is water (consisting of hydrogen and oxygen).

In MRI, the subject is placed in a very strong magnetic field, which causes positively-charged particles, or protons (for example, the nuclei of the hydrogen atoms), to line up their magnetic spins. The effect is analogous to the way in which a compass needle lines up with a magnetic field. A relatively weak radio wave pulse is then introduced, which causes some of the protons to pick up energy and become aligned against the magnetic field. When the radio pulses stop, the protons become realigned with the magnetic field, giving up energy in the process. It is that energy which is detected and subjected to Fourier analysis to produce an image.

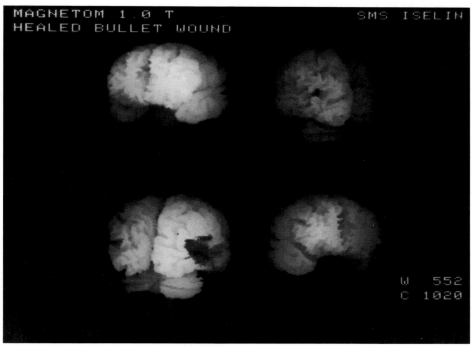

magnetic resonance Another application of the tomographic method is in magnetic resonance imaging. The sequence of images above depict a healing bullet wound in the brain. Magnetic resonance visualizes differences in tissue composition and so is ideal for rendering images of soft tissues that are not distinguishable in X-ray images. In the images here, the new tissue forming around the wound, which is only slightly different in composition from uninjured tissue, would be invisible to CT but can be visualized with MR. Tomographic slices have been compiled into a three-dimensional image by a technique called volume visualization (see *Emergent Technologies*), which permits the physician to explore the wound in three dimensions.

holography

Holography has excited the imaginations of scientists and the public since its principles were first proposed in the 1940s. As imperfect as the first holograms were, they attracted attention with good reason. Holography is the realization of an aspiration latent in all the visual arts and in all forms of imaging—the possibility of controlling light in order to to be able to produce truly perfect three-dimensional illusions. Ideally, holographic images would be visually indistinguishable from the objects and scenes they portray. This degree of perfection has yet to be attained but many very beautiful kinds of holograms have been created.

Before going further, it is important to clarify the distinction between holography and other imaging techniques that capture or display three-dimensional information. Stereo photography, for example, although often referred to as three-dimensional photography, is not a true three-dimensional imaging technique. A stereograph is simply two pictures, typically seen through a viewer or polarized glasses, so that one picture reaches the right eye and the other reaches the left eye. The images are themselves flat and provide only one perspective determined at the moment the photographs are made.

The only true three-dimensional photography is holography. Holography re-creates the three-dimensional environment of light reflecting from the original scene. No special viewer is required to see a hologram and a hologram can be inspected from different perspectives just as is possible with the real objects. For instance, if a hologram contains a magnifying glass held over a page of postage stamps, the stamps seen through the magnifier will change as we shift our viewing angle exactly as they would if we were viewing the real scene. The magnifying glass *in the hologram* magnifies different objects as we change our point of view.

In holography, and only in holography, the *wave* properties of light (or other forms of energy) are used to create an image. The idea of using wave properties to make images was first proposed as a technique for increasing the resolution of electron microscopy by Dennis Gabor in 1948 in his paper "Image Formation by Reconstructed Wave Fronts."

Gabor proposed recording an image with very short waves, and reconstructing it with long waves to achieve greater magnification than had been possible. Gabor, who received the Nobel Prize in 1971 for his idea, recognized that the technique could be used to make light images but, in the era before the laser, was only able to produce small, crude holographic images of flat objects. Because holography exploits the wave properties of light, larger-scale holograms must be made with laser light. The light from lasers, called *coherent* light, is purer than ordinary light in the sense that its waves oscillate in unison.

As has been noted earlier, light behaves at times like a particle and at other times like a wave. The dualistic quality of light confuses many non-scientists and, indeed, has challenged the greatest minds in physics. As mysterious as light ultimately is, its wave properties can be demonstrated in a simple experiment. If two adjacent pinholes are made in opaque paper and light is permitted to pass through them, a pattern such as is shown in the diagram at right bottom will be formed. The best way of explaining the appearance of the pattern is to assume that the pinpoint sources of light are sending out concentric waves that are *interfering* with each other. The pattern produced by the two pinpoint sources of light is similar to the pattern formed when concentric water waves interact in a water tank. When corks are bobbed in a regular tempo at two points at the edge of the tank, concentric waves radiate outward and form a standing pattern because they interfere with each other.

As depicted in the diagram at right top, waves interact as they pass through each other. When two troughs meet, the downward displacement of the water is increased. When a crest and a trough meet in the water tank they cancel each other. When two crests meet, the upward displacement of water is increased. In the water tank, the bobbing corks cause the wave to repeat and the result is a standing interference pattern. In the pinhole experiment with light, we cannot see the waves themselves but the absence of light in some areas and the brightness in other areas indicate that repeated wave forms are interfering, causing a standing pattern of brightness and darkness.

constructive interference

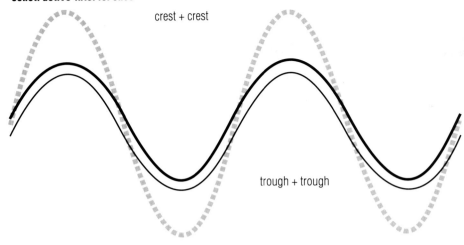

crest + crest

trough + trough

wave interference When waves, for example water waves, pass through one another they "interfere." If the crests (high points) of two waves meet, their combined amplitude momentarily produces a crest much higher than either crest alone—a phenomenon called constructive interference. When a crest meets a trough, however, the waves momentarily cancel each other in "destructive" interference. Light waves also constructively and destructively interfere when they pass through each other—a property of light exploited in holography.

destructive interference

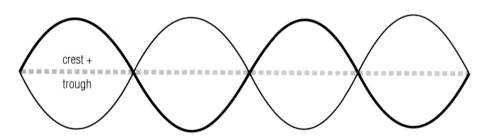

crest + trough

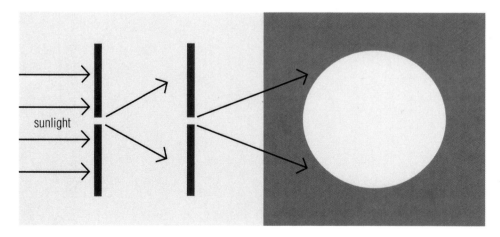

wave theory of light The wave theory of light was advanced by this experiment devised by Thomas Young at the beginning of the nineteenth century. Top: Sunlight passing through the first pinhole and then through another pinhole forms a spot. Bottom: When two holes are made in the second barrier, however, a bar pattern is produced. The bar pattern is evidence that light behaves like a wave, since overlapping spots would be expected if light behaves like particles traveling in straight lines.

Young recognized that the bar pattern is a cross-section of a field of wave interactions and that the bright bars indicate additive interference and the dark bars destructive interference. If either hole in the second barrier is covered, the bar pattern disappears.

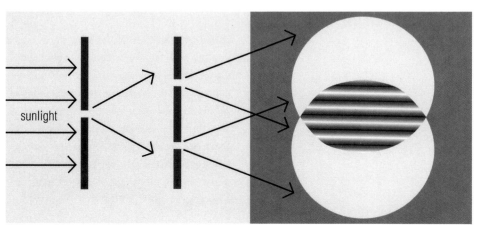

A method for producing areas of darkness and lightness has, of course, potential for imaging. There are, however, many difficulties in trying to exploit the wave property of light. If we were to try the above light experiment on a larger scale, with two flashlights instead of pinholes, it would not produce a persistent interference pattern. Unlike pinhole sources of light, which produce fairly regular concentric waveforms, ordinary light, such as light from the sun, light bulbs, or fluorescent tubes is a jumble of wave fronts traveling in different directions so that no single interference pattern is formed. It is technically possible to use pinhole sources of light to make holograms but they are limited in size and in the kinds of images that can be made.

It is better to use laser light because the waves making up the entire beam oscillate in unison. If ordinary light is similar to a rushing throng, laser light can be thought of as rows of soldiers marching in formation. When two laser lights pass through each other, vivid interference patterns are formed. The coherence of laser light makes it useful for making the interference patterns needed for holography. The invention of the laser in 1960 stimulated Emmett Leith and J. Upatnieks to attempt light holography, and they very soon succeeded in improving the technique to produce true three-dimensional images.

Stated most simply, holography depends upon the following phenomenon: if light A interacts with light B to form an interference pattern that is captured on photographic film, it is sometimes possible to project light A into the developed film, the frozen interference pattern, to recreate light B. If light B was reflected from an object, then the reconstructed light is a holographic image of that object.

In holography, light A is called the "reference" beam while the light coming from the object is called the "object" beam. The reference beam interacts with the object beam to produce an interference pattern recorded on film. This photographically captured pattern is the hologram. To see the image, the reference beam is projected into the photographically processed hologram, and the object beam is re-created. The technical term for the effect of the hologram on the reference beam is *demodulation*. (Happily, the viewing light does not *always* need to be the same laser and, in some cases, need not be a laser at all.)

setup for making a transmission hologram The laser is at the top right. The beam is divided by a beam splitter. One beam travels to the mirror at the bottom of the frame, then through a filter to the object. The other beam reflecting from the beam splitter goes to a mirror, through another filter to a collimator lens, and directly to the plateholder (bottom left). An interference pattern is formed at the photographic plate because of interaction of light reflecting from the object and light from the collimator lens.

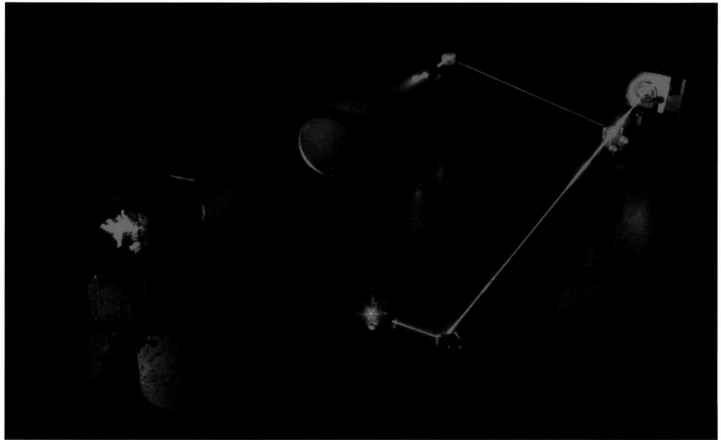

reflection hologram A reflection hologram can be made dichromatic or trichromatic by using chemicals to swell the photographic emulsion prior to exposure to different color components of the scene. During development of the hologram, the emulsion shrinks back to its normal size. The holographic fringes shrink with the emulsion so that the different recorded images reflect different wavelengths of light. In *Peppers* the preswelling technique was used to add green to a hologram that would otherwise have played back entirely in red. Hologram by Julie Walker. Courtesy, The Spatial Imaging Group, The Massachusetts Institute of Technology.

transmission hologram

The transmission hologram was invented by Leith and Upatnieks in 1964 and marks the beginning of true holographic imaging. It is called a transmission hologram because it is viewed by transmitting laser light through it. When light is projected through the hologram, an image appears on the opposite side of the holographic plate.

Since the transmission hologram is the grandparent of them all, it is worth taking a moment to describe how it is made. A laser is set up on a sand table (to minimize vibration) as shown in the illustration. Vibration must be minimized to avoid forming multiple interference patterns on the film during exposure. If we follow the beam of light in the diagram, we see that it first passes through a beam splitter, which separates into reference and object beams. The object beam travels to the object, which reflects it onto the photographic plate. Simultaneously, the reference beam travels to a mirror and is reflected to the plate. The two beams thus meet at the plate and form an interference pattern that the plate records as a hologram. After exposure, the plate is developed and the interference pattern, the "holographic fringes," can be seen under the microscope.

For viewing, the hologram can be replaced in the plate holder so that it will be in the same position with respect to the laser as when exposed. The interaction between the reference beam and the hologram will re-create the pattern of light that reflected from the object during exposure. The image is seen by looking through the hologram to where the object originally was. The hologram, in a sense, functions as a window in which the object is seen.

The transmission hologram, of which there are several varieties, provides spectacular depth effects and can be made in very large formats. Ideally, transmission holograms are illuminated with laser light but they can be made for spot sources of non-laser light or with sunlight. When inferior (non-coherent) light sources are used, however, color fringing and blurring limit the depth of the image.

Although holography stands apart from the other new transduction technologies because it does not require digital image processing, it is a fundamental and profoundly important method for visualization. There are many research efforts under way to improve the technique—to make it easier both to create holograms and to display them. Furthermore, there are already a number of techniques that have been developed combining the computer with holography (discussed in the last chapter).

laser-transmission hologram In *One Bad Banana* by Julie Walker, the bananas are presented holographically; the hand is real.

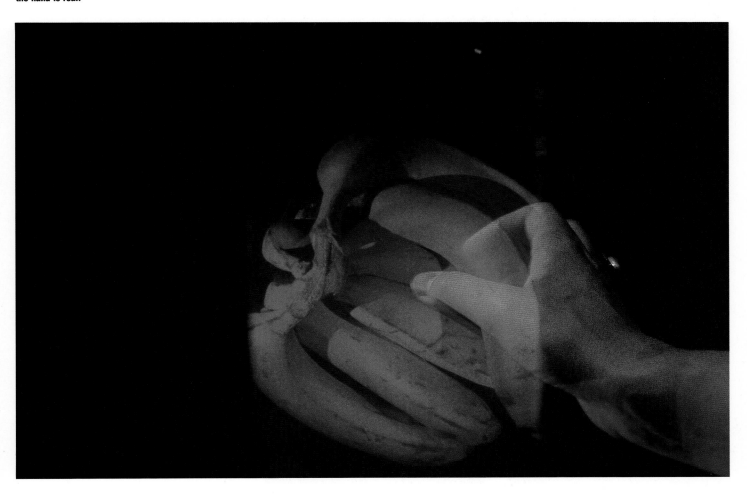

other holographic techniques

WHITE-LIGHT TRANSMISSION HOLOGRAM The white-light transmission hologram was invented by Stephen Benton in 1968 at the Polaroid Corporation. The significant advantage of this type of hologram is that it yields a bright image with good depth when illuminated with an ordinary light source such as an incandescent bulb. Benton developed a way of eliminating the need for a laser when displaying the hologram by eliminating the vertical parallax of the image. Vertical parallax is the change in viewpoint as the perspective is raised or lowered. Horizontal parallax is retained so that, moving horizontally, there is a change in viewpoint and the left and right eyes receive disparate viewpoints so that stereopsis is possible. If we raise or lower our perspective, the viewpoint does not change. Interestingly, few spectators notice the absence of vertical parallax since we generally view an image moving horizontally and since only horizontal parallax is necessary for stereopsis.

A form of this type of hologram, where the hologram is embossed on mirrorized plastic, is used on credit cards to prevent counterfeiting. A quick glance at one of these will verify the absence of vertical parallax.

REFLECTION HOLOGRAMS A reflection hologram is a hologram that is viewed by reflecting light off it, rather than by transmitting light through it. It is based on the work of Y.N. Denisyuk of the Soviet Union who first developed it in the early 1960s, at about the same time as Leith and Upatnieks were working on the transmission hologram. A reflection hologram can be made by passing the laser light through a photosensitive emulsion, to the object, and then back to the emulsion where it interacts with the oncoming light to produce the interference pattern: the hologram. To view a reflecting hologram, light is projected from the same side as the original reference beam and an object is seen on the other side, or behind, the hologram. The holographic fringes in this kind of hologram act as reflectors, and special photosensitive materials have been developed with high reflectivity. Although laser light is ideal for viewing, a number of techniques have been developed which use ordinary sources of light. Holographic novelty items such as pendants and buttons are often of this form.

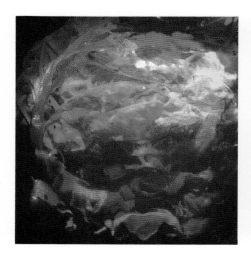 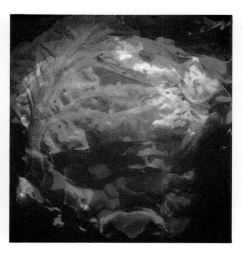

white light transmission hologram *Cabbage* by Julie Walker incorporates organic shapes and multiple colors in an abstract composition. The three-dimensionality of the hologram is evident only by fusing the stereograph pair. Hologram by Julie Walker. Courtesy, The Spatial Imaging Group, The Massachusetts Institute of Technology.

HOLOGRAPHIC STEREOGRAM Unlike true holograms, the holographic stereogram is actually a series of holograms of conventional, two-dimensional photographs. Holography is used as a medium for displaying left and right members of the stereopair separately to the two eyes, obviating the need for a special viewer. The depth effects can be quite good and, although it is really a hybrid between holography and stereo photography, the technique has an important advantage over both. Unlike the holographic techniques described above, it begins with ordinary photography, sometimes a motion-picture sequence. Thus, the hologram begins under ordinary studio conditions, without the problems of vibration, laser light, and so on which complicate holographic imaging. Unlike conventional stereo photography, the image is seen without the need of polarized glasses or a special viewer.

The most common form of the holographic stereogram is the cylindrical rainbow type invented in 1973 by Lloyd Cross. Also known as multiplex, integral, or Cross hologram, the image is seen in the center of a plexiglass drum that is illuminated with an ordinary light bulb at its base. As we walk around the holographic stereogram, the image in the center can move.

If we look at the hologram closely, we can see narrow vertical lines that are themselves individual holograms. Each vertical strip is a single hologram of one photograph that can be seen only within a narrow viewing arc because the hologram itself was made of the photograph in a slit. As we move left and right, these strip holograms are viewable in sequence. The viewing arc is narrow enough so that separate views reach the left and right eyes.

To produce a sequence of photographic frames suitable for the holographic stereogram, a motion-picture camera is generally used to photograph a subject rotating on a turntable. Thus, each frame captures a view from a different point of the circle surrounding the subject. When the cylindrical hologram, a composite of perhaps one or two thousand holograms, is viewed, each hologram of a photograph is visible within a narrow arc and the subject is seen in depth in the center of the drum. If the subject moves while the turntable is turning, the movement will be captured in the sequence of frames and will be visible to the viewer as the drum is circumscribed. In a well-known example, a girl appearing inside the cylinder winks and blows a kiss to the circling spectator. A number of techniques have been developed for making flat holographic stereographs using the same general idea: strip holograms that come into view within a narrow viewing arc.

PULSED HOLOGRAM Holography is a difficult imaging technique although it is possible even for hobbyists working on a limited budget to make sophisticated holograms. One of the principal difficulties, apart from the requirement that laser light be employed, is that the holographic record must be made in a vibration-free environment. The wavelengths of light, and the interference fringes they produce, are so small that even the tiniest movements will produce overlapping exposures on the photographic plate. For the most part, this rules out holographic imaging of living subjects. It is much more usual to make holograms of relatively small objects carefully placed on a specially constructed vibration-free table. Very fine-grained photographic emulsions must be used.

One way to make a holographic portrait of a living person is to pulse the laser so that only a very brief exposure is made, limiting the effect of vibration. It is technically difficult to produce a laser that pulses sufficiently brightly for a very brief duration while maintaining its coherence and purity of frequency. Techniques for pulsed lasers have been developed, however, and, although they are very expensive devices and are difficult to use, many holographic portraits have been made.

calibration and problems of interpretation

Engineers and scientists are faced with the problem of instrument calibration. The instrument's response has to be periodically measured against recognized standards in order to ascertain its accuracy. This is certainly true with all the technologies we have been discussing—with an additional complication. These technologies produce images rather than numbers, which are processed by the visual system. In perception of unfamiliar visual worlds, it becomes necessary to guard against what are called perceptual artifacts.

A famous example of perceptual artifacts was the "canals" seen on Mars by early astronomers. Early in this century, J.E. Evans and E.W. Maunder investigated the question of canals on Mars by making maps that included all of the observed features except for the canals. They then asked a group of schoolboys to make copies of the maps. When the maps were placed far enough away so that the smallest features were just discernible, the students "saw" linear structures and drew them. The drawings showed the "canals" even though there were no canals in the maps they were copying. This experiment is an indication of the human tendency to pattern visual information.

Although we now know that there are no canals on Mars, the question of perceptual artifacts is still a complicating factor in astronomy. A major controversy concerns the large-scale structure of the Universe. Astronomers are now "seeing" filaments in large-scale maps of the Universe, and hypothesize that these filaments indicate that galaxies may be distributed in large bubble-like patterns. Are these filaments real or are they merely perceptual artifacts produced by the fact that the astronomers are working at the limits of their present capacity for visualization?

Color also presents complex issues of calibration and interpretation. Consider the problem of coloring images made by the Mars Viking Lander. The Lander recorded color images by making exposures through three different color filters. The composition of the Martian atmosphere is different from the composition of the Earth's atmosphere, which means that the distribution of wavelengths reaching the surface of Mars is different from the distribution of wavelengths reaching the Earth's surface and that the light reflected from the Martian surface features is thus different from the light reflected from similar features on Earth. Calibration can be used to adjust the image so that objects appear 1) as they would if the observer were standing on Mars, 2) as they would if the object were on the Earth, or 3) as they would without any atmosphere at all. Now, in fact, most Mars images have been colored to appear as they would to an observer on Mars, although some of the initial published photos were colored to resemble conditions on Earth. In either case, interpretation of the image requires knowledge of how the image was calibrated.

False color of course raises additional questions of interpretation. Color has conventional associations. Red is hot and blue and green are cool. In a false-color image, color simply indicates a certain intensity value specific only to a particular application. Further, there is always the possibility that, by exaggerating small differences, false coloring will produce the appearance of well-defined features where, in fact, they do not exist. Thus coloring an image is often more of an art than a science, since the goal is to enhance actual structures without misleading.

Visualizing a three-dimensional object with a two-dimensional image has its own calibration problems. The familiar image of the tourist seeming to hold the Tower of Pisa highlights the influence of object recognition and context analysis on the determination of size and distance. In many kinds of visualization, such as in images returned by space probes, the scenes are completely unfamiliar and it is impossible to use familiar forms as a way of estimating distance. The temptation, of course, is to relate these alien scenes to scenes that are familiar. The Martian landscape begins to look more and more like the deserts of New Mexico. The boulders and prominences in the scene take on definite proportions and we have to remind ourselves that the image itself, without additional contextual information, gives us no information about the scale or spatial relationship of the objects.

Discerning spatial relationships is particularly important in diagnostic imaging. The heartbeat, the expansion and contraction of the lungs, and the movement of the skeletal muscles are three-dimensional phenomena. Images from microscopy, astronomy, and many other fields of visualization can present very significant problems of interpretation specifically because the phenomenon of interest is spatial and the image is ambiguous in the third dimension. When familiar depth clues are absent, the image becomes more like an abstract pattern. Unfortunately, many of the images of electron microscopy have such an "abstract" quality only because we cannot sense the third dimension.

MANIPULATING VISUAL REALITY Image processing is used in more and more areas outside of scientific and medical imaging. The same hardware and software used to modify images for medical and scientific purposes are easily adapted for applications in printing, reprography, advertising, and art. Simple image processing is used in preparing photographs for printing. After digitization, images can be cropped, flaws can be repaired, and colors can be corrected—procedures that have traditionally been done manually. The computer can also be used to produce cyan, magenta, yellow, and black color separations for four-color printing.

Geometric techniques are frequently used to alter images to make them more suitable for the needs of magazine publishing. In 1982, the publishers of *National Geographic* created a minor controversy by image processing the cover photograph of the pyramids of Egypt. Two pyramids were moved closer together in order to make the image more suitable for the vertical format of the magazine's cover. Some readers felt that *National Geographic,* as a respected photographic journal, should not, as a policy, alter images. The issue is complicated because a similar (although not identical) result could have been achieved by photographing the pyramids from a different angle. This instance is undoubtedly innocuous, but does serve the purpose of raising important questions about the presumed veracity of photographs in the age of image processing.

The determination of the veracity of photographs is further complicated by the use of image processing to combine images, to make seamless photographic collages. Image-processing techniques can go way beyond what is possible with manual cut-and-paste. With traditional collage techniques it is very difficult to combine images completely imperceptibly. In order to conceal edges, airbrush techniques are often employed but are still imperfect. With image processing, low- and high-frequency components of the image, or areas within the image, can be adjusted independently to eliminate the sudden changes in brightness that reveal foreign elements.

Although the image-manipulating possibilities of computerized visualization technologies demand ethical vigilance they do open up new aesthetic possibilities. The artists using these techniques are encouraged, by the very nature of the image-processing medium, to create a new kind of photo-realistic collage utilizing images from large numbers of sources. Of course, artists from all periods of history have been influenced by existing imagery, but image processing puts a new twist on this practice because of the ease with which full-blown image worlds can be assembled and modified.

cherry boulevard The combination of image-processing technology and video has engendered a new style of television commercial that combines diverse elements to create a visual world. This sequence of images is from a commercial for Cherry Coke made by Charlex, Inc., a pioneer in video "cut-and-paste" techniques.

Above: The Cherry Coke man was shot live and his arms and legs were removed in a digital paintbox (see *Computer Graphics*) so that they could be manipulated and foreshortened.

Right: The close-up hands were shot live and their motion was created with a digital device that allows the user to move video images in complex three-dimensional paths. The diner and buildings (immediately below the can of Cherry Coke) were created as images in the paintbox. The waitress was shot live.

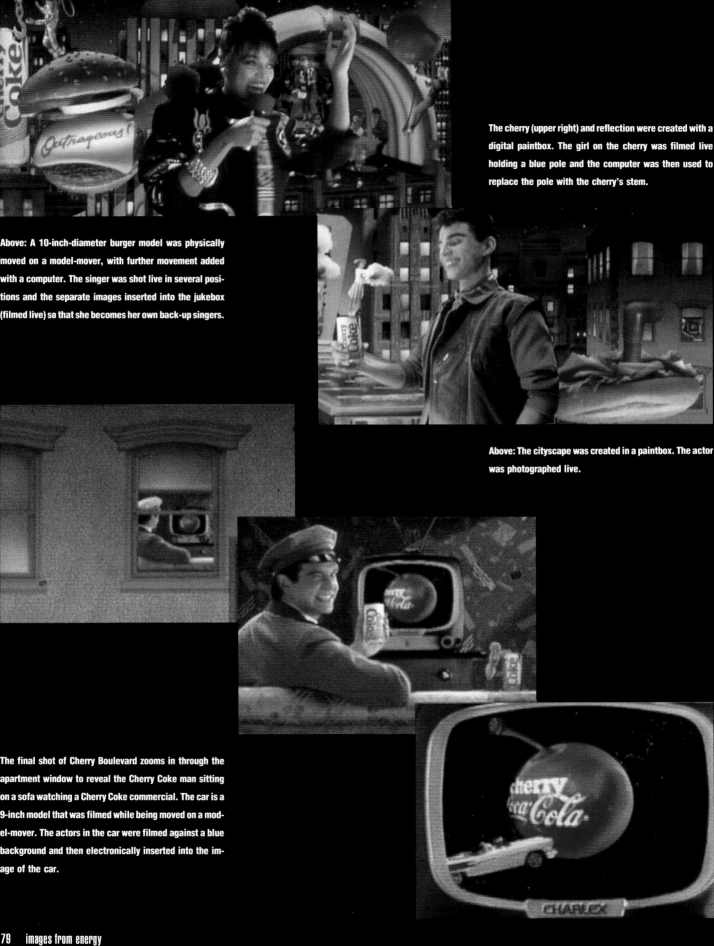

The cherry (upper right) and reflection were created with a digital paintbox. The girl on the cherry was filmed live holding a blue pole and the computer was then used to replace the pole with the cherry's stem.

Above: A 10-inch-diameter burger model was physically moved on a model-mover, with further movement added with a computer. The singer was shot live in several positions and the separate images inserted into the jukebox (filmed live) so that she becomes her own back-up singers.

Above: The cityscape was created in a paintbox. The actor was photographed live.

The final shot of Cherry Boulevard zooms in through the apartment window to reveal the Cherry Coke man sitting on a sofa watching a Cherry Coke commercial. The car is a 9-inch model that was filmed while being moved on a model-mover. The actors in the car were filmed against a blue background and then electronically inserted into the image of the car.

digital image processing *Crowd__Three* by Alyce
Xaprow was created by combining and modifying photographs with digital image processing.

technique and interpretation

It is not only in the artistic uses of these computer technologies that we see a relationship between the inherent properties of the technology and the character of the resulting images. In all of visualization there is an intimate connection between the technique by which images are made and the way they must be interpreted.

PET scanning is, perhaps, the clearest example of the way in which the visualization technique determines the images we see. PET scanning became possible through the development of three new techniques: 1) methods for preparing very short-lived radioactive isotopes that decay so rapidly that large doses can be given to patients without fear of radiation danger, 2) the development of sensors to detect the decay of these isotopes, and 3) tomographic image processing. The PET scan image is a function, not only of the data analysis performed by the computer, but also of the selection of the radioactive label. When fluorodeoxyglucose is used, for example, the resulting image depicts glucose metabolism, the energy consumption of tissues. If a different label is used, then an entirely different aspect of tissue functioning is visualized.

The image resulting from this elaborate process is a construction of great complexity. Interpretation requires knowledge not only of metabolism, but of the behavior of the isotope, of tomography, and of the conventions used in false coloring the image. There is the ever-present danger of visualizing artifacts, or of missing important clinical indicators. To be sure, PET scanning is an unusually complex process, but it contains an important lesson for visualization of all kinds. PET reveals the interdependence between technique and interpretation and reminds us that the images of science increasingly have kinship with art. The scientist shares the serious artist's goal of depicting a hidden truth and, like the artist, the scientist must master technique both to create and to interpret an illusion.

computer graphics

To know the world, one must construct it.
Giovanni Battista Vico

The visualizations in the last chapter begin in the physical world. Although the computer is essential for constructing images, the data originates in energy emitted or reflected from a real object or phenomenon. It is completely different in computer graphics. Here, the computer becomes a kind of laboratory in which three-dimensional objects, light, and other phenomena are imitated with mathematics. Images, often with photographic realism, can be made of entirely imaginary scenes.

Instead of a pattern of energy, computer-graphics visualization begins with a visual idea. Although popularly associated with computer games and motion-picture special effects, the real importance of computer graphics, its revolutionary significance, is as a tool for visual experimentation. Computer graphics provides a seamless fusion between the massive processing power of the visual system and the power of the digital computer. In this and in the next chapter, *Visual Experiments,* we shall see that computer graphics, because it bonds mind and machine in a unique partnership, creates an entirely new way of thinking.

a new visual vocabulary

Computer graphics is an enterprise built on artistic as well as technological discovery. As computer graphicists create this entirely new method of representing reality, it is interesting to see the impact of new discoveries and techniques as they spread through the discipline. E.H. Gombrich has called the epochal inventions of artists—their conventions for representation—"schemata," and the concept has some relevance to understanding what is going on in computer graphics. Once "invented," schemata are passed from teacher to student becoming not only standards for the way we make images but also conventions in the way we think and perceive. In creating images, artists continuously develop a visual vocabulary from which progressively more complex representations can be constructed.

object-based computer graphics Object-based computer graphics are increasingly used in animation. This image is a frame from a short film entitled *Red's Dream*, which utilized many computer techniques such as procedural texturing, motion blur, particle techniques, and sophisticated lighting models that allow objects to cast shadows on themselves. In the film, Red, a unicycle relegated to the discount section of a big city bicycle shop, dreams of running off to the circus. The images in the animation are renderings of a three-dimensional world that exists solely within the computer. © 1987 Pixar.

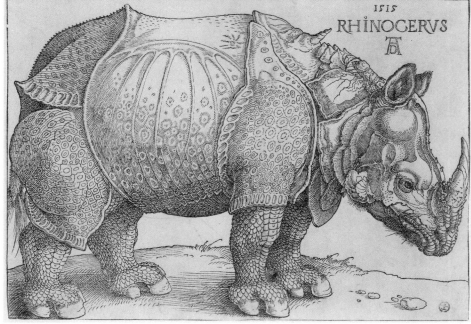

1Tach Chriſtus gepurt.1513. Jar. Adi.(.May. Hat man dem großmechtigen Rünig von Portugall Emanuell gen Lyſabona pꝛacht auß India/ein ſollich lebendig Thier. Das nennen ſie Rhinocerus.Das iſt hye mit aller ſeiner geſtalt Abconderfet.Es hat ein farb wie ein geſpꝛeckelte Schildtkrot. Vnd iſt vō dicken Schalen vberlegt faſt feſt.Vnd iſt in der größ als der Helffandt Aber nydertrechtiger von paynen/ vnd faſt weh afftig. Es hat ein ſcharff ſtarck Hoꝛn voꝛn auff der naſen/Das begyndt es allweg zu werzen wo es bey ſtaynen iſt.Das doſig Thier iſt des Helffanns todt feynde. Der Helffandt fürcht es faſt vbel/dann wo es Jn ankumbt/ſo laufft Jm das Thier mit dem kopff zwiſchen dye foꝛdern payn/vnd reyſſt den Helffandt vnden am pauch auff vñ erwürgt Jn/des mag er ſich nit erwern.Dann das Thier iſt alſo gewapent/das Jm der Helffandt nichts kan thūn.Sie ſagen auch das der Rhynocerus Schnell/Frayoig vnd Liſtig ſey.

1515
RHINOCERVS

visual schema Although a misrepresentation, Dürer's image of a rhinoceros nevertheless served as a model for other artists—showing the staying power of a visual convention.

Albrecht Dürer. *The Rhinoceros*. 1515. Woodcut, 9¼ x 11¾" (image and text). The National Gallery of Art, Washington, D.C. Rosenwald Collection.

An illuminating example of the influence of a visual schema is an engraving of a rhinoceros by Albrecht Dürer, published in 1515. In making his engraving, Dürer, who had never actually seen a rhinoceros, worked from the descriptions of others. Perhaps because the rhinoceros has such a thick hide, Dürer was given the impression that a rhinoceros is covered with armor-like plating and he depicted it this way.

It is interesting that Dürer's representation served as the model of a rhinoceros for other artists until the end of the eighteenth century. In 1790, James Bruce published an engraving of the animal with much fanfare about its being drawn "from the life" and with the assertion that his engraving corrected Dürer's inaccuracies. The astonishing thing, however, is that Bruce's "from the life" engraving also depicts the rhinoceros with a kind of armor plating— confirming the staying power of a visual convention.

To create three-dimensional objects within the computer requires the invention of entirely *new* kinds of visual schemata. Visual and structural qualities of objects have to be defined mathematically. In computer graphics these mathematical techniques are usually called algorithms but they correspond, in many ways, to the art historian's schemata. As with schemata, a successful algorithm becomes part of an ever expanding vocabulary among computer graphicists and profoundly influences both the conception and appearance of their images.

geometric affinities Present-day computer graphicists might find inspiration in the work of artists such as Léger, who utilized such geometric shapes as cylinders, cones, and spheres.

Fernand Léger. *Nudes in the Forest*. 1909–10. Oil on canvas, 47¼ x 66⅞". Rijksmuseum Kröller-Müller, Otterlo, The Netherlands.

With the emergence of fractal techniques a few years ago, for example, it suddenly became feasible to produce images of complex objects when their large-scale geometry is similar to the small scale (see "fractals"). Suddenly, mountains and clouds, which have this attribute, appeared everywhere in computer graphics. As might be expected, all these mountains and clouds had a characteristic appearance.

The central issue in computer graphics today is naturalism. The goal is to dispatch forever the angular, harshly colored images of the past and to move toward images that are so realistic as to be indistinguishable from photographs. Computer graphicists want the ability to synthesize any three-dimensional form in the computer and are currently working on models of trees, human figures, landscapes, and other complex objects. These are extraordinarily challenging problems but, as we shall see, the computer *can* be used to synthesize these and other natural forms.

simple pixel-based graphics

(paint systems)

There are two general kinds of computer-graphics technologies—pixel-based and object-based systems. With object-based systems, the computer is used to represent the three-dimensional geometry of objects and to simulate light and other phenomena. Pixel-based graphics systems are simply systems for creating two-dimensional images with the computer, often a personal computer, by methods that are analogous to the artist's use of brush and paint. To make an image, a stylus is moved across a sensitized pad to produce strokes that are viewed on a monitor. Generally speaking, a pixel-based or a "paint" program provides a series of lists or menus from which different brushstrokes, colors, and textures can be chosen, either with the stylus or with a separate control called a "mouse," which moves an arrow pointer on the monitor. With these tools, different "brush" shapes are chosen to produce different kinds of lines.

Paint systems usually have features that do not have a direct equivalent in conventional painting. For example, they provide ways of drawing simple geometric shapes—circles, ellipses, rectangles, squares—with a single stroke. The computer also makes it possible to "cut-and-paste" portions of images as is done with word processing. By recopying small elements, a complex pattern can be produced without the need to draw every detail. Portions of images can also be borrowed for use (perhaps with modification) in other images.

Many existing pixel-based software packages also offer simple image-processing algorithms. Images, or portions within the image, can be stretched; a color scheme can be modified automatically (for example, changing green for blue); colors can be automatically blended so that shading is smoothed. A "zoom" feature enlarges a small part of the image so that it fills the entire screen. The artist can see, and modify, individual pixels and so has a high degree of control over fine detail.

Increasingly, these paint systems are being used in the fine arts. Painters who turn to pixel-based computer graphics find both advantages and disadvantages. Of course, no system based on three primary colors, as all computer-graphics systems are, can provide the subtle colors of the painter's palette. Artists do tend to enjoy, however, the great freedom of experimentation provided by computer graphics because images can be made quickly and modified endlessly.

The speed with which images can be created and modified on pixel-based systems makes them particularly useful in commercial art. In advertising agencies, where concepts often need to be developed and revised very rapidly, paint systems can be used to produce variations of a print advertisement or a video storyboard much more quickly than can be done with conventional paste-ups. In television network news rooms, where time is an important factor, paint systems are useful because images already on file can be incorporated into an illustration for a breaking news story.

computer variations. The series of images on the following pages demonstrates some of the capabilities of a pixel-based paint system. Images created for *Visualization* by Charlex, Inc.

Right: Grant Wood. *American Gothic*. 1930. Oil on beaver board, 29⅞ x 24⅞". Art Institute of Chicago. Friends of American Art Collection, 1930.934. © 1988 The Art Institute of Chicago, All rights reserved.

Below: Sandro Botticelli. *The Birth of Venus* (detail). c.1480. Tempera on canvas, 5'8⅞" x 9'1⅞". Uffizi Gallery, Florence, Italy.

Below right: A ram.

American Gothic does not have the same aspect ratio as the screen on the graphics system. The paintbox program was therefore used to create left and right additions to the image.

One figure is painted out. The paintbox allows the artist to "pick up" color in one area and use it in another. The artist was thus able to paint over, or subtract, Wood's figure with transitions that are scarcely noticeable.

This image blends the original painting with a version in which both figures have been painted out.

The man's jacket was repainted with the paintbox.

en recolored with i

The computer replaced the colors with shades of grey in the areas containing the figures.

The pixels making up the figures have been averaged to form larger pixels.

The ram's head was electronically "cut" from a stock image and then pasted over the man's head. Paintbox techniques were used to blend the new head with the original image.

Portions of *Venus* were cut and overlaid on Wood's figure. The Botticelli elements had to be right-left reversed to fit—a simple operation with the computer. Notice the paintbox program has been used to repaint the man's expression.

Wood's figures have been "cut" from the painting, and electronically "pasted" onto "boards." The computer is then used to rotate the boards in "space." This is done with a warping algorithm—an example of geometric image processing. Notice the shadows the cut-outs cast on the ground. These were added with the paintbox.

object-based

systems

A completely different way of creating images with the computer is to define the geometry of objects within the computer's memory. Although we normally think of an object as being three dimensional, the term "object-based" refers to computer-graphics systems that produce images starting with geometrically defined forms whether of two, three, or more dimensions. The important point is that the computer does not store an image, but a geometric description from which images can be rendered.

Although the user need never be aware of it, object-based systems usually utilize methods of analytic geometry. The computer stores the "object" as lists of points or as equations that define shapes on Cartesian coordinates. For example, the equation $x^2 + y^2 = r^2$ defines a circle with its center at the intersection of the x and y coordinates and a radius equal to r. Plotting points whose x and y values satisfy the equation produces a circle. When objects are very complex, the geometric description is, of course, much longer, but this is the idea behind these kinds of systems—they work from geometric descriptions.

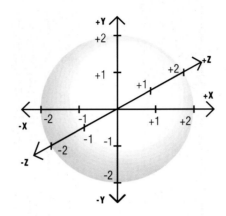

cartesian coordinates A sphere is described by the equation $x^2 + y^2 + z^2 = r^2$. The equations of analytical geometry are used by object-based graphics systems to encode the form of an object but the designer need never be aware of the encoding process and has the experience of directly creating and combining geometrical forms.

THREE-DIMENSIONAL

GRAPHICS

In three-dimensional graphics, a z axis is added to the x and y axes. Just as a circle (a two-dimensional form) can be defined with a two-variable equation, a sphere (a three-dimensional form) can be described by the three-variable equation $x^2 \times y^2 \times z^2 = r^2$, where the sphere has its center at the intersection of the axes and a radius equal to r. Points whose x,y,z values satisfy the equation form the surface of a sphere. Other three-dimensional forms, such as cylinders, ellipsoids, and cones, are defined by other equations familiar from geometry. Three-dimensional models are constructed in computer graphics by combining these elemental shapes.

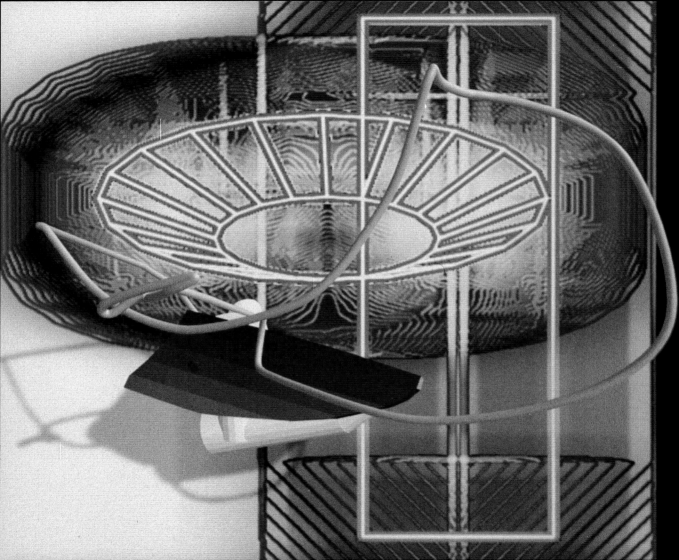

perspective This famous woodcut by Dürer illustrates the principle of perspective drawing.

Albrecht Dürer. *Demonstration of Perspective* from the artist's treatise on geometry. 1525. Woodcut. The Metropolitan Museum of Art, New York. Harris Brisbane Dick Fund, 1941. (41.48.3)

CREATING OBJECTS IN THE COMPUTER

To create a three-dimensional computer-graphics scene, each object must be described in precise detail. To create the egg, shown on page 96, the computer was instructed to create an icosahedron—a three-dimensional object with twenty equilateral triangular faces. Since the computer demands that forms be specified geometrically, a common strategy is to create a simple approximation of the form and then to modify it. In this case, the icosahedron, which the computer was able to produce automatically, served as a rough model of the egg form. In order to reduce the angularity of the icosahedron, two separate techniques were employed. In the first step, each face of the icosahedron was divided, as with a ruler, into many smaller triangles. In a second step, the vertices of the triangles were pushed away from the center as if the icosahedron were being gently inflated with air. The net result of these two steps was to create a form approximating a sphere. In order to produce the egg shape, this spherical form was automatically tapered with a function that narrows a form at one end. (As noted above, object-based systems generally have functions that produce spheres automatically. Such a function was not used in this case for technical reasons. The texture mapping that was eventually applied to the forms would have been more difficult had the form not been generated with triangles.)

To create the spiral, a program that produces a helix was used. To define the helix, the programmer specified its length, the number of revolutions, and its diameter. The resulting line had no thickness so a separate tubing feature was used to make the figure into a thick tube. Again, a tapering program was used to narrow the spiral tube to a point at one end.

simple wire-frame rendering In order to see the progress of the design, it is necessary to create a two-dimensional image on the computer monitor of the three-dimensional object in the computer's memory. The computer must calculate values for pixels so that the monitor functions as a window through which we can look at the evolving forms. This process, calculating an image of the object stored in the computer's memory, is called "rendering." Renderings can be both simple and complex. The wire-frame-type rendering is the simplest and shows just the outline of forms. More sophisticated rendering techniques produce realistic images that resemble photographs.

To render an image, the computer calculates a "projection." This graphic technique, first developed by artists and geometers during the Renaissance, is illustrated in a woodcut by Albrecht Dürer (shown at left). The artist in Dürer's woodcut looks through the frame at a lute. The panel at the rear edge of the frame shows how the lute would appear when projected onto a plane (such as a piece of glass). As an exercise in making projections, we may imagine that there is glass in the frame but that the string can pass through it. Wherever the string passes through the glass, the glass is turned black. By fixing one end of the string to the viewpoint, and tracing the outline of the lute with the other end, an image, an outline of the lute, is made. The string represents lines, called projectors, which pass from points on the lute, through the image plane, to the fixed point-of-view. In three-dimensional computer graphics, the user specifies a point-of-view with relation to the objects and the computer does the equivalent of calculating projectors passing through the image plane. In this way the computer determines values for each pixel in the image.

The illustration on page 96 shows a simple wire frame rendering of the egg and spiral. So far, in this first stage of design, the computer has been told nothing about the possible opacity of the objects, in other words, what can be seen from a particular viewpoint and what is obscured. The computer, therefore, assumes the objects are transparent and depicts all of their surfaces.

more realistic renderings The first step in making a more realistic rendering is to remove, or at least not to render, surfaces that would not be seen if the objects were opaque as most real objects tend to be (see page 97). This is often done with a "z buffer," a separate allotment of computer memory in which a depth image of the scene is created. (The name derives from the fact that distance into the image is conventionally represented along the z axis of Cartesian coordinates where the x and y axes represent, respectively, the horizontal and vertical directions.) A depth image is not an image in the conventional sense. In a depth image each pixel is a number representing the distance of the nearest surface to the viewpoint. Before a point on the surface of an object is displayed, its distance from the viewpoint is compared to the depth in the z buffer. When the point in question is farther away than the z buffer value, it means that another surface obscures it. It is therefore ignored by the rendering program. Thus, the computer renders only the visible faces of the object.

The next step in the rendering process is usually to choose colors for the objects. This can be done in two ways. The most direct way is to choose a color from a palette that appears on the screen. It is, however, sometimes desirable to specify color quantitatively as percentages of the red, green, and blue primaries. Entered from the keyboard, these numerical values will determine the intensity of red, green, and blue components for each surface. The illustration shows the egg after it has been colored blue and the spiral colored red.

shading

shading The next step is shading the image, creating the illusion that light falls on the objects and is reflected and absorbed as it would be on real objects. It is in this phase of creating a computer-graphics scene that we are reminded that the computer gives us an artificial universe where the behavior of light need not always correspond to reality. There are a variety of ways of imitating light and each method has advantages, disadvantages, and a characteristic appearance. Sometimes, such a high degree of photographic realism is required that computationally intensive methods, directly derived from physics and optics, are employed. At other times, a rough approximation of the behavior of light is all that is needed so that quicker and more economical methods of shading can be used.

The first step is to choose a light source. Is it local, for example a lamp, or is it effectively "infinite," set at a great distance from the scene as sunlight would be? Rays coming from local light sources travel in diverging directions while rays coming from a distant source are nearly parallel. This distinction is important when it comes to modeling light with the computer. For the examples on page 98, an infinite light source is assumed for simplicity.

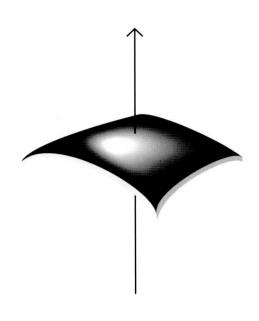

surface normal A surface normal is simply a line perpendicular to the plane of a polygon. In Lambert shading, this line is compared to the direction of the illumination—the so-called "vector of illumination." The polygon is brightened in proportion to the degree of parallelism between the surface normal and vector of illumination since this is a measure of the degree to which the polygon faces the light source.

LAMBERT SHADING One of the simplest methods, called Lambert shading, is to draw a line, called the "surface normal," perpendicular to the plane of every polygon on the surface of the objects. Prior to shading, surfaces are defined as inter-connecting polygons. Using a principle from optics discovered by Johann Heinrich Lambert in the eighteenth century, the computer estimates brightness by calculating the angle between the surface normal and the angle of illumination. If the polygon is directly facing the light source, the surface normal and a line representing the direction of the illumination, the "vector of illumination," will be parallel. The computer will brighten that polygon because it is directly facing the light. A polygon that is not facing the light, according to this test, is darkened. Lambert shading adjusts the brightness of each polygon upward or downward. Since polygons are adjusted separately, and adjacent polygons may have significantly different values, Lambert shading is quick and simple, but sometimes gives the appearance of facets and is therefore not always satisfactory for curved surfaces (see page 98).

GOURAUD SHADING To produce a subtler effect, modifications of the Lambert method have been developed. For example, in Gouraud shading, instead of comparing a surface normal to the angle of illumination, the computer calculates an average normal for each vertex (intersection of edges) of the polygon. This normal is calculated by averaging the normals for the polygons sharing the vertex. This produces a brightness value for each vertex instead of for each surface. The computer then interpolates values from one vertex of the polygon to the other so that a brightness value is determined for each point along the edges. A brightness value for every point in the polygon is then interpolated from the values along the edges. The result of the technique is that the polygon has gradations of brightness within its borders, producing a smoother appearance than Lambert shading (see page 98).

PHONG SHADING Neither Lambert nor Gouraud shading can create highlights. Highlights are produced on very smooth surfaces because an image of the light source, typically distorted, is reflected to the observer as it would be with a mirror. To produce highlights it is necessary to take into account not only the position of the light source, as is done in Lambert and Gouraud shading, but the location of the observer. With this information, the computer can determine which areas of the surface should have that intensely bright reflection of the light source.

In Phong shading, the brightness of every point on the object's surface is increased in proportion to how closely the ray reflected from that point comes to the viewpoint. In order to make this determination it is necessary to calculate a surface normal for *every point* on the object's surface. Because each point is calculated separately, the technique, unlike Lambert and Gouraud shading, will produce peak brightnesses within the borders of a polygon. As might be imagined, Phong shading is more computationally expensive but useful for creating the appearance of slick, metallic, or polished surfaces (see page 98).

The various shading processes take into account the designated color of the object. The computer will change the brightness of the polygons within the colors chosen by the designer. There are also occasions when the light source itself is colored. In this instance, the color of the surface will be determined not only by its designated color but by the color of the light. The shading procedures are, effectively, implemented for each primary separately.

Many other kinds of light effects are possible with computer graphics. A simple way to create the effect of transparency, for example, is to instruct the computer to ignore the depth information—to skip the removal of hidden surfaces. A more realistic image will be produced if, additionally, highlights are calculated for the front surfaces of the objects. Other algorithms produce glowing, iridescence, sparkling, and other light effects. Some of these algorithms are directly derived from optical laws, while others are improvised through experience.

It is exciting to remember that in the synthetic universe created in the computer, one can make light and objects interact in ways that are visually interesting but that are impossible in the real world. For example, it is a relatively easy matter to have "negative transparency." Objects are brighter (rather than darker) if they lie behind other transparent objects. This technique has been used, for instance, in an animated commercial for window cleaner so that a scene through a window appears brighter.

TEXTURE MAPPING The digital nature of computer graphics makes it possible to incorporate real-world or synthesized textures and patterns onto the geometric forms in the computer's memory. "Texture mapping" is the equivalent of "wrapping" a digitized pattern around an object.

A variety of textures, for example the grid texture that was created by a pixel-based paint program, has been wrapped around the egg and spiral (see page 99). Other textures, for example wood grain, can also be obtained by digitizing photographs which can then be wrapped around a computer-graphics object.

wire frame The egg and spiral are rendered with the wire-frame technique. While the equations in the computer describe these shapes with smooth surfaces, it is more convenient in rendering an image to depict the surfaces as small connecting polygons—usually triangles or rectangles. Image sequence created for *Visualization*.

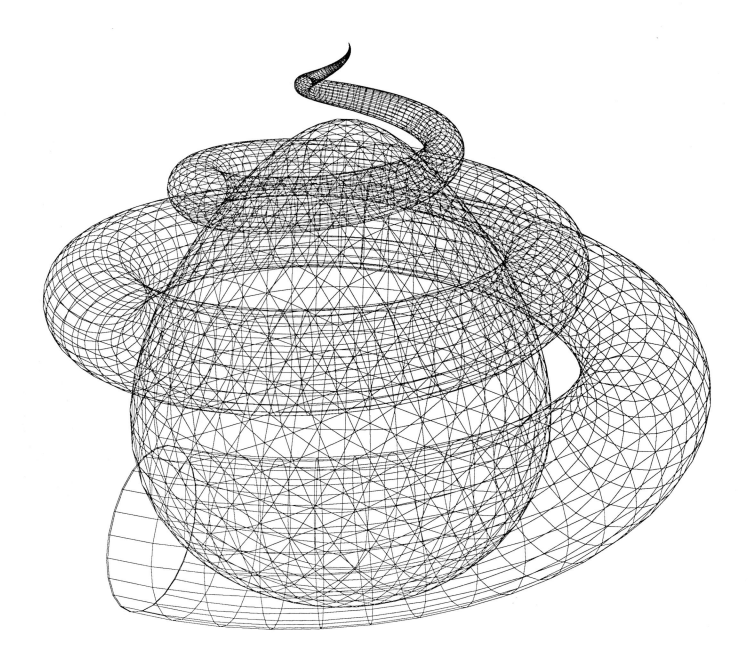

hidden surfaces removed In order to delete rear surfaces, the computer is instructed not to render a surface when one or more surfaces lie between it and the viewpoint. This gives objects the appearance of solidity.

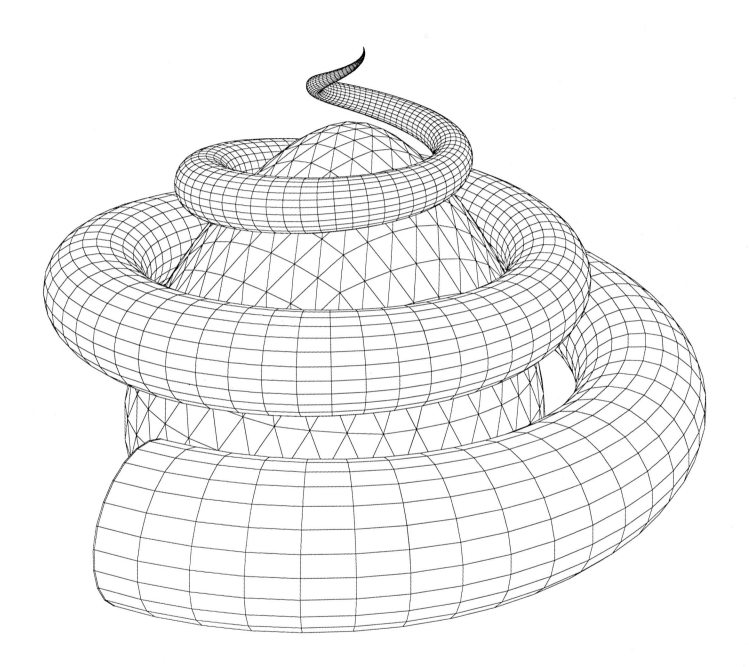

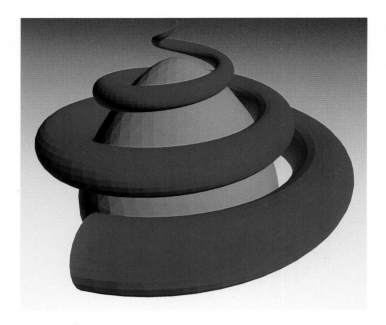

lambert shading Lambert shading (left) is the simplest shading technique. The faceted quality is present because the surfaces, for the purposes of shading, are defined as connecting flat polygons.

gouraud shading Gouraud shading (right) is a technique for varying brightness across each polygon to produce a "smoother" shading effect.

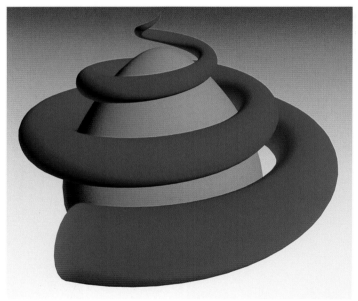

phong shading Phong shading (left) yields the specular highlights characteristic of shiny surfaces.

texture mapping In texture mapping (left), a two-dimensional pattern, either derived from a digitized photograph or produced with a paintbox program, is "wrapped" around a three-dimensional computer-graphics object. The checked pattern was created with a paintbox program and then texture-mapped onto the spiral. The sky and clouds are from a black-and-white photograph that was colored with a paintbox program.

bump-mapping The etched appearance of the spiral was produced with a technique called "bump-mapping" (right). In bump-mapping, the angles of the surface normals used in shading are varied so as to produce the effect of light reflecting from an irregular surface.

transparent rendering The background of this image (left) is an underwater photograph looking toward the sun. The egg and spiral were rendered to appear transparent. The stripes on the egg were created with a paint program and texture-mapped onto the egg. The spiral was bump-mapped.

RAY-TRACING One of the most interesting techniques for realistic rendering is called ray-tracing. Ray-tracing simulation originated in research on the effects of nuclear weapons: the idea was to use the computer to simulate the way in which radioactive particles would be emitted from nuclear explosions. Nuclear emissions travel in straight lines and will penetrate some materials but are absorbed or reflected by others. The computer algorithms developed for this kind of modeling were thus readily adapted to simulating the way in which light travels in straight lines, penetrating substances transparent to light while being absorbed or reflected by translucent or opaque objects.

In ray-tracing, in addition to the geometry, the optical properties of every surface must be specified. If an object is reflective, the surface must be described in terms of how it scatters light. When materials are transparent, for example water or glass, it is necessary to specify a "refractive index," the degree to which the object will "bend" the light passing through it. The refractive index is the same value used by lens makers to calculate the way in which a particular lens will focus light. Indeed, if the geometry of a lens-shaped figure is described to the computer, a ray-traced image will represent objects on the other side of the lens, magnified or diminished, just as they would look as seen from the same viewpoint through a real lens.

An enormous amount of computation is required for ray-tracing. The calculations become very extensive when light rays from several sources interact with the objects of a complex environment, which might have many kinds of surfaces. To reduce the amount of computation required, the computer models only those rays of light that would reach the viewer. To determine which rays do reach the viewer, the computer actually works in reverse—drawing lines from the viewpoint (which would be on our side of the computer monitor) through each pixel "into" the scene. If the line, after reflecting off the surfaces within the scene, fails to finally encounter a light source, the pixel will be dark. If the line eventually does encounter a light source, the pixel's value will be determined by the intensity of the light source as well as the reflective and refractive characteristics of all of the intervening surfaces. Using this strategy, the computer vastly reduces the amount of calculation since it does not have to simulate all the rays in the scene.

Ray-tracing, in spite of this simplification, is still quite computationally expensive. In a case where the image will be made with a million pixels (1000 x 1000 resolution), the computer must calculate the paths of reflection and refraction for a million rays. Each surface presents its particular complications. Does, for example, a surface have a matte finish (light scattering), or is it shiny (reflecting light at an angle equal to the angle of its approach)? If the object is transparent, the way in which light will be refracted depends upon its shape. If some of the surfaces are mirrored, the ray-tracing program must follow each ray of light from mirror to mirror so that, in the final rendering, mirrors will reflect other objects in the scene as they would in reality. Although the economics of computing are changing rapidly, at present, the expense of ray-tracing generally limits its use to those applications where its almost photographic realism is essential.

realistic images can be artificially synthesized. To produce an image, three-dimensional objects are defined
geometrically. The artist can then manipulate the way in
which the objects reflect and transmit light. For instance,
an object that is first defined as opaque and metallic can
be changed into transparent glass with a few simple commands. Much of the complexity of Search's images comes
from the fact that the spheres reflect and refract light
from colored objects and planes that are not directly visible in the rendered image.

ray-traced image This ray-traced image, *1984* by Thomas Porter, based on research by Robert Cook, simulates a short photographic time exposure. The computer, using the laws of motion, calculated the trajectory of the balls during an imaginary shutter opening. Ray-tracing was used to render an image of the pool balls sampled over the time of the exposure. In effect, rays of light were modeled in the scene at different times throughout the imaginary exposure.

Notice, too, the surrounding room reflected in the balls. To create this effect, a paint program was used to create an image of the poolroom walls, which the ray-tracing procedure rendered as a reflection. Image © 1984 Pixar. All Rights Reserved.

reflection mapping Both the teapot and the surrounding room were created with three-dimensional graphics in the computer. To create the reflective appearance of the teapot, the "camera" in the computer was placed in the position of the teapot and renderings were made of the walls, ceiling, and floor. These renderings were then mapped onto the teapot surfaces. This "reflection mapping" technique is sometimes called "half-a-ray tracing" because it, in effect, follows the light rays from the surface of the object (the teapot) to the limits of the surrounding space (the room), but no farther.

PROCEDURAL GRAPHICS If there is a barrier to the even wider application of computer graphics it is that the effort required to define complex objects geometrically is often forbidding. Even after great effort, forms frequently have an undesirable angular quality as a result of having been built with a limited number of regular geometric shapes. The problem is especially troubling when modeling natural forms such as plants, landscapes, and human figures.

To solve this problem, in the last few years, there has been considerable interest in eliminating the requirement that every geometrical detail of an object be explicitly defined. The idea is to let the computer create much of the detail in response to a general instruction in which the basic parameters of an object are described. Such techniques are called "procedural" because the computer produces the detailed geometry of the object by following programmed procedures. A few simple commands can substitute for the laborious, perhaps insurmountable, task of defining a complex object in exact geometrical detail.

In certain cases of procedural modeling, the computer generates a tremendous amount of data from a few descriptions, a process sometimes called "data base amplification" (a term coined by Alvy Ray Smith of the Pixar Corporation of San Rafael, California). Consider, for example, the difficulty in modeling an explosion such as that depicted in a landmark computer-graphics sequence of the motion picture *Star Trek II*. In the so-called "Genesis" sequence (see next pages), an explosion that creates a living planet is constituted of thousands of particles of fiery light. Since modeling an explosion with a normal object-based system would have been impractical (because the designer would be required to specify the position of every particle for every frame in the animated sequence) procedural techniques were essential. The behavior and visual qualities of a few particles were defined and then duplicated. The computer then "automatically" propelled them along their trajectories from frame to frame.

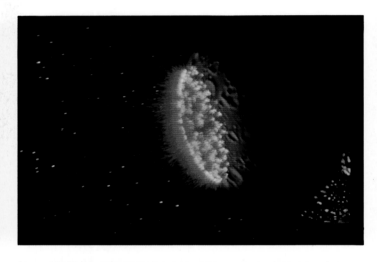
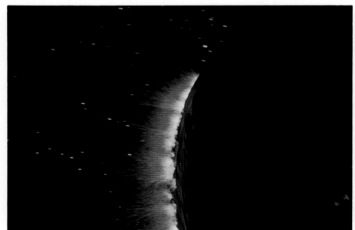
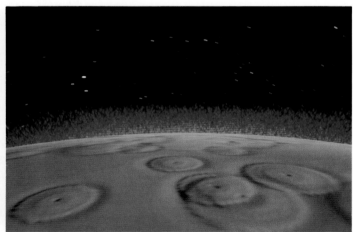

procedural graphics This sequence of frames from the motion picture *Star Trek II: The Wrath of Khan* is an example of procedural modeling. The "Genesis" sequence portrays the emergence of life on a dead planet as a fiery explosion. The technique involves defining a particle of light. The computer then reproduces hundreds of thousands of the particles and propels them, frame by frame, in three dimensions. Defining such a three-dimensional scene with conventional computer-graphics techniques, which would require specifying the location of each particle for each frame in the animation, would be unfeasible. Images © 1982 Paramount Pictures Corporation. All Rights Reserved.

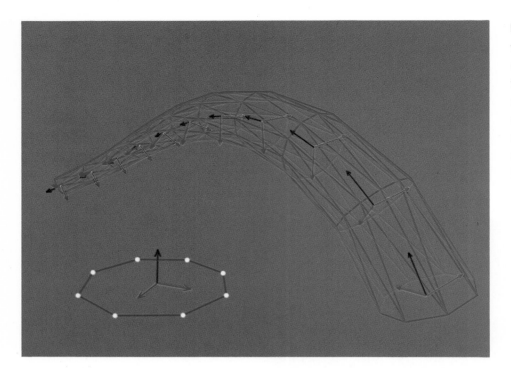

modeling a maple tree Computer graphicists have developed numerous techniques to facilitate the modeling of complex objects. This sequence of images showing a three-dimensional computer model of a maple tree was created using a combination of strategies including procedural and transduction techniques. Image sequence courtesy Jules Bloomenthal © New York Institute of Technology, Computer Graphics Laboratory, Old Westbury, New York.

growing a tree form The first step in modeling the tree was to procedurally create an outline in which the trunk and branches are defined as lines. The image above demonstrates how thickness is given to a line representing a branch. The black vectors (arrows) point along the shape-defining line that becomes the center of a cylinder. The blue circles define the changing diameter of the cylinder from point to point along the branch. The triangular shapes joining the circles define the surface of the branch.

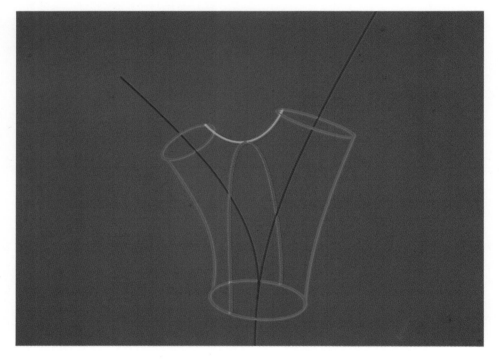

curvature at branch point The blue line shows the basic skeleton of the tree form at a branch point. The green, red, and yellow lines highlight the construction of a continuous surface around the branch point.

the base of the tree Since the shape at the base of a tree reflects the spreading of root structures below the soil, it is not easily modeled using the technique at left top based on tapering cylinders. Instead, a blob shape, the bottom of the trunk, was modified to the nearly cylindrical shape at the top of the figure.

modeling the
geometry of nature
To reproduce complex forms in the computer requires that, in some sense, we discover the essence of their geometry. To "grow" realistic looking trees procedurally, or make authentic looking mountains, we have to develop algorithms that imitate their characteristic geometry. This requires insight into the overall geometric quality of an object, and occasionally the introduction of real-world data into the modeling process.

Jules Bloomenthal at Xerox PARC has been using a combination of strategies for modeling realistic looking maple trees. First, he had the computer create a wire-frame model of the trunk and the branches of the tree procedurally. The overall shape of the tree was not geometrically specified as it would be with a simpler object-based system. The branching pattern was generated *recursively,* that is the same procedures that produce the trunk and first branching structure were employed again to produce successive branches. The branching angle, the length, radius, and taper of a branch and number of branches were randomly determined from within certain parameters. The outermost branches will be smaller and will differ in other respects from the base branches although they are produced by the same process. Significantly, the range of values the computer uses to decide branching angle, number, length, and so on have been extrapolated from measurements of real trees.

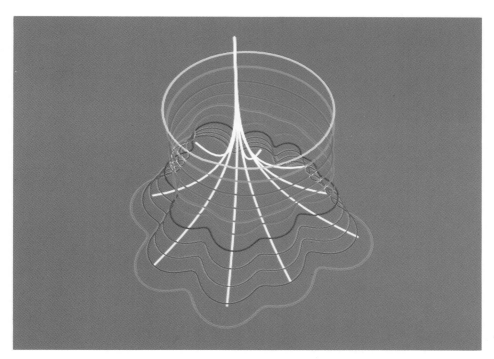

growing the tree The "growth" of the tree in the computer is here represented with colors. Red represents the trunk and successive branches are represented by orange, yellow, green, blue, and white, respectively. Although the tree was grown as lines, the branches have been given volume in this illustration.

bark The bark texture was derived from real bark and bump-mapped onto the tree form.

Once the overall form of the tree was generated, Bloomenthal abandoned the procedural strategy. In order to produce realistic bark, he found it necessary to borrow bark patterns from real trees. To digitize the surface of bark, a plaster cast was made and then X-rayed. The two-dimensional X-ray image is a portrait of the three-dimensional structure of the bark because thicker areas in the plaster produce lighter regions in the X-ray. The X-ray pattern is converted by the computer into a "bump-map"—a record of the surface of the bark. The bump-map is then algorithmically wrapped around the trunk and limbs of the tree.

The bump-map is not a three-dimensional contour of the bark although it will give that appearance in the rendering. It is used by the computer when the tree is "illuminated" with the shading algorithms. In order to give the appearance of a three-dimensional texture, the bump-map record is used to modify the surface-normals, in the shading procedure, so that the texture will scatter light *as though* it were a three-dimensional surface.

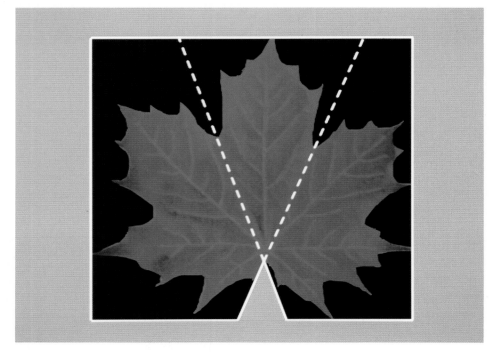

leaf The leaves were created by digitizing a photograph of a real maple leaf. A paint program was used to enhance color details such as the veining pattern. The dashed lines indicate imaginary "hinges" where the leaf can bend when wind is simulated.

a leaf cluster Actual maple leaf clusters were used to guide the design of this geometric model which utilizes the leaf shown at left. Notice that both sides of the maple leaf have been defined: the underside is lighter than the leaf's top side so that leaves facing away from the viewer are lighter.

Putting leaves on the maple tree presented its own problems. To produce a leaf form, Bloomenthal again decided to take a pattern from nature. The illustration (opposite) shows a single leaf that was digitized as a two-dimensional image from a video image of a real leaf. The leaf pattern was then enhanced through use of a paint system and texture-mapped onto invisible planes adjacent to the branches at angles derived from real maple trees. Other leaf configurations, again modeled on real maple trees, were placed at branch terminations.

The dotted lines in the figure indicate hinges around which the computer can bend the leaves in response to hypothetical "wind." By specifying the strength of the wind and its direction, Bloomenthal could thus simulate, to a certain extent, the way in which leaves on a real tree would move.

Since the model of the maple tree is three dimensional, we can visualize it from any viewpoint. Notice how, in the illustration on the next page, calculated from a point outside the tree, the shadows of leaves on the branches realistically indicate the direction of the sunlight. The "unreality" of the computer model is shown in the illustration below, which was calculated from a point *inside* the trunk looking up. It is evident that the trunk is merely a surface—the inside of the tree has not been defined.

inside a tree trunk A computer-graphics object can be rendered as an image from any point in space. Here, a viewpoint inside the tree's trunk was chosen—the resulting image reminds us that computer-graphics objects, however real they may appear, are defined only as surfaces. This image courtesy Jules Bloomenthal at Xerox Palo Alto Research Center.

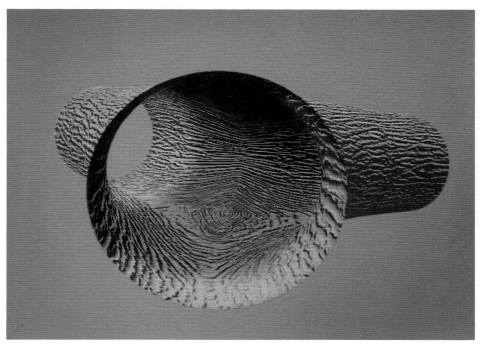

the fully rendered tree Notice that the tree casts shadows on itself. The clouds in the background are three dimensional.

An interesting feature of Bloomenthal's model is that it combines observational, synthetic, and transduced data. The model of the trunk and branches is synthesized procedurally but within limits derived from measurements of real maple trees. The bark texture is derived from an X-ray of a three-dimensional mold, a shortcut for making a digital record of its three-dimensional detail. The leaves are, in a sense, retouched digital "photographs."

Object-based computer graphics is just beginning to be used to model complex natural forms and Bloomenthal's methods are exploratory. The lengths to which he had to go, drawing on so many sources, points out the difficulties of making natural looking objects in the computer.

Bloomenthal's experiments are characteristic of the kinds of research going on in many computer-graphics laboratories. In attempting different methods for modeling the tree, Bloomenthal, and other researchers, find the eye to be very demanding. Creating a realistic bark pattern using procedural shortcuts was particularly difficult. Bark patterns produced in this way tended to look artificial, underlining the fact that the ultimate judge of the success of a given technique is the human visual system. Sometimes, as in the case of the bark, it is difficult to specify why procedural techniques produce forms that look false. Human beings are apparently very good at remembering qualities of textures. Whatever the reason, the bark problem is an example of the way in which computer-graphics techniques are influenced by the analytical strategies of the visual system.

Trees and plants are tantalizing subjects for computer graphicists because they are forms of great intricacy that grow. It is intriguing to try to reproduce their growth with data base amplification—techniques that, starting with a few instructions, "grow" large data structures.

A completely different method for generating tree structures procedurally is to conceptualize their branches as trajectories of imaginary particles. Within the computer, it is possible to define procedures that control the movement of particles. The famous Genesis sequence of *Star Trek II,* mentioned earlier, was produced by defining one kind of particle. By using different parameters for particles, it is possible to use them to grow tree shapes.

A program designed by William Reeves, of the Pixar Corporation, uses particles to "grow" whole forests of trees. With his program, tree height, branch thickness, the bifurcation angle of branches, and other qualities can be controlled. His program also introduces an element of randomness. The branches and sub-branches will not be identical because the algorithms automatically vary the controlling parameters. With Reeves' program a three-dimensional structure that looks very much like a real forest is created from a few instructions—a task that would be utterly impractical with the standard techniques of computer graphics which require combining individual geometric elements. Growing a whole, three-dimensional forest in the computer is vivid testimony to the power of procedural techniques.

computer, a hydrodynamic model was used and imaginary waves are actually breaking on an imaginary beach contained entirely within the computer. Here we see that as the waves break, the crests follow the shape of the shoreline. *Beach at Sunset* © 1986 Pixar. All Rights Reserved.

complex graphics This labyrinth of vines, *Inside a Quark*, designed by Ned Greene of the New York Institute of Technology, was constructed by repeating a single vertex, shown at right, over and over again to create a three-dimensional lattice. The capacity for repetition is one of the powerful features of computer graphics. The flowers and leaves were modeled as grids of extremely fine polygons (triangles) and then colored by texture mapping. The bark was created using Jules Bloomenthal's data (see "Modeling a Maple Tree"). The scene as a whole contains approximately 1.9 million polygons.

The final image (opposite) was rendered with Gouraud shading and texture mapping. The aerial perspective, involving the desaturation and hazing of the distant flowers in the center of the image, is difficult to achieve in computer graphics because the most distant objects would normally be rendered with the same degree of precision as the nearest. The computer had to be made to attenuate image contrast as an exponential function of the distance. Images courtesy Ned Greene, © New York Institute of Technology, Computer Graphics Laboratory, Old Westbury, New York.

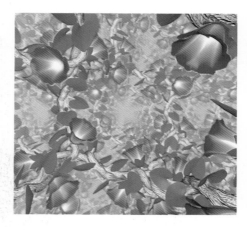

stereopair Since the data base is three dimensional, it is not difficult to generate the left and right perspectives required for the stereopair simply by horizontally shifting the viewpoint in a second rendering. Image courtesy Ned Greene, © New York Institute of Technology, Computer Graphics Laboratory, Old Westbury, New York.

The images can be seen in depth either by using a stereoscope or by crossing the eyes with a playing-card–size cardboard between them.

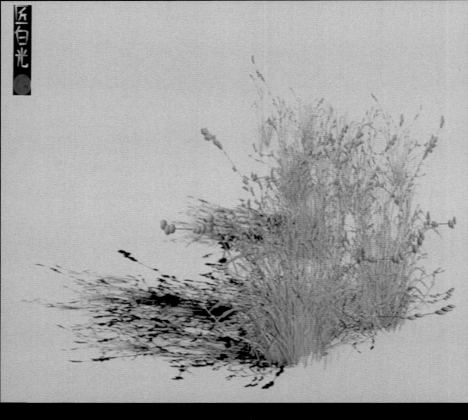

procedural model The flowering plants were "grown" in three dimensions using a procedural model for generating branching structures developed by Alvy Ray Smith. William Reeves provided the grasses, which were generated with a particle technique akin to the one used to create the fiery explosion in the Genesis sequence from the film *Star Trek II*. The particle technique lends the image a softness and delicacy that is often difficult to achieve with geometrically-based computer graphics. Image by Alvy Ray Smith © 1986 Pixar. All Rights Reserved.

procedural forest This three-dimensional forest was "grown" in the computer. The original data entered into the computer consisted of 21,000 characters (bytes). After data base amplification the data base contained 60,000,000 bytes—an amplification factor of about 3,000. From *The Adventures of André & Wally B.* Image courtesy of William Reeves, © 1984 Pixar.

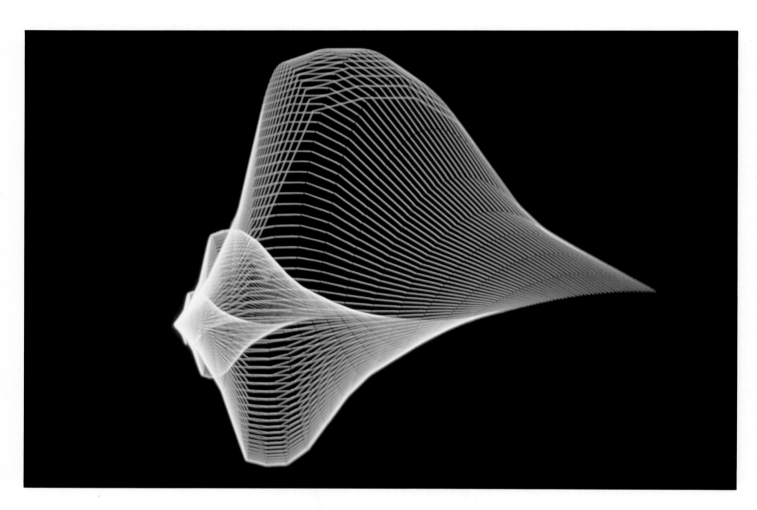

seashell Since a conch shell is "self-similar," its geometry can be modeled with a fractal technique. The structure shown was "grown" by the computer starting from a small "seed" form. Image courtesy Peter Oppenheimer, © New York Institute of Technology, Computer Graphics Laboratory, Old Westbury, New York.

fractals

Another strategy for creating certain classes of objects procedurally utilizes fractal geometry. Fractal geometry (the name is derived from the Latin *fractus*, meaning irregular or fragmented) was developed principally by Benoit Mandelbrot of the Thomas J. Watson Research Laboratories at IBM as a technique for studying complex or irregular systems. Computer graphics has borrowed some of its concepts to create objects in which the small-scale details have the same geometrical character as larger-scale features.

A cloud, for example, has, to a great extent, the same visual appearance whatever its size or however far we are from it. The small details of the clouds, the small parts we can see at close range, are similar to the cloud as a whole that is seen at a distance. If we were to take this small feature and enlarge it, the enlargement would resemble a full-sized cloud (at least to the non-meteorologist).

This quality of clouds, and some other objects, suggested a possible shortcut for object-based visualization of certain forms. If the large-scale features of an object resemble its smaller-scale details, the technique for generating the overall form of the object might be reapplied, perhaps over and over again, to produce the medium- and small-scale details of its shape and texture.

In geometry, "similarity" specifically means that two forms have the same shape even if different in size. "Self-similarity" means that the smaller details of a form have the same geometrical character as the larger form. Fractal techniques are used when objects are geometrically self-similar.

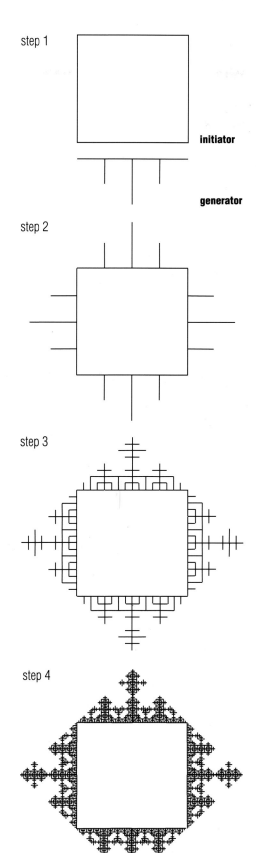

step 1

initiator

generator

step 2

step 3

step 4

generating a fractal

One way to generate a fractal is to start with a simple geometrical figure and to modify it in successive steps. In this example, the starting figure, called an "initiator," is a square. The square is modified by replacing each of its sides with another figure which is called the "generator." After this first step, the resulting shape is modified by having each of its segments replaced by the generator. As this process is reiterated, the shape becomes more and more detailed. The resulting figure has a high degree of self-similarity because of the iterative procedure by which it was created.

FRACTAL MOUNTAINS Although many two-dimensional figures are generated with fractals, it is also possible to create three-dimensional self-similar objects recursively. The sequence of images seen here depicts a fractal technique for generating a mountain, which was developed by Loren Carpenter of Pixar Corporation. The process begins with a simple geometric form, a triangle, positioned in three-dimensional space. The midpoint of each edge of the triangle has been connected to the other midpoints dividing the original triangle into four triangles. The midpoints are then deflected randomly upward or downward to give volume to the form. This process is repeated with the midpoints of the new triangles so that, in the third step, there are 16 triangles. The process can be repeated recursively, as many times as one likes, to produce an increasingly detailed mountain that will be made of smaller and smaller triangles.

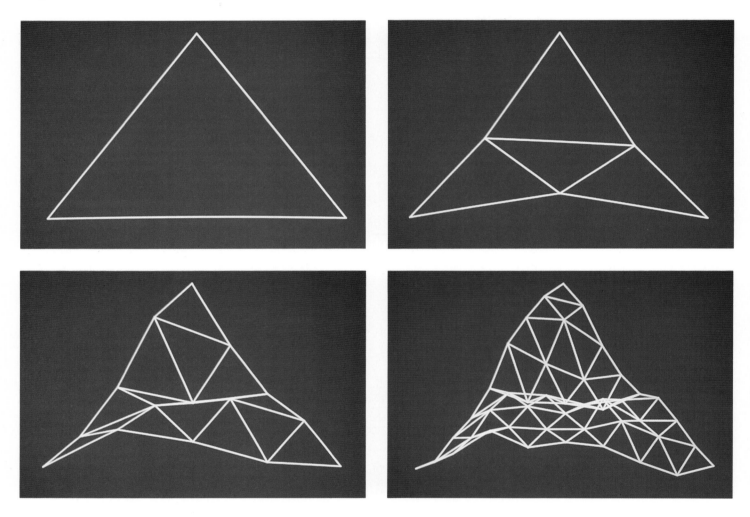

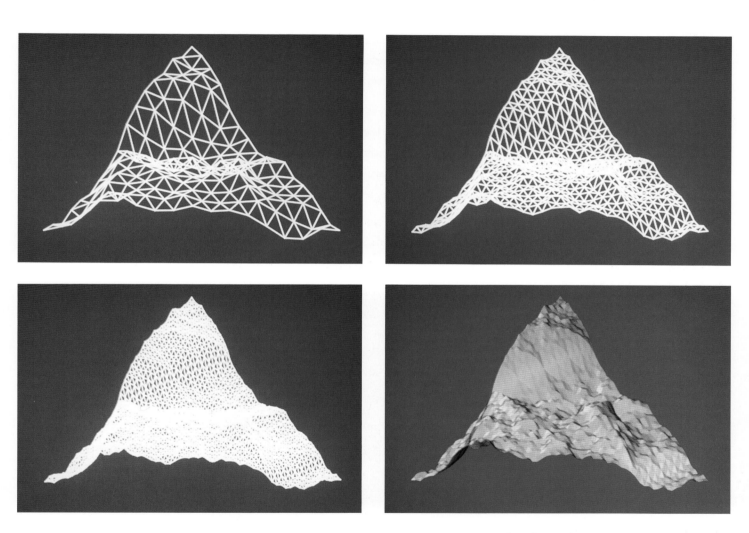

fractal mountain This sequence, *Fractal Demo* by Alvy Ray Smith, shows how a mountain form can be generated recursively with a fractal technique. The process begins with a single triangle that is divided into four smaller triangles. The new triangles are defined by connecting the midpoint of each side of the triangle as shown in the second image. This procedure is reiterated on each new triangle, until the desired degree of detail has been obtained. As the process is continued, the midpoints of the line segments are randomly displaced upward or downward to produce a more realistic effect. The final image has tiles added. Image sequence © 1986 Pixar Corporation. All Rights Reserved.

flight simulators

flight simulators Flight simulators are used in pilot training to provide flight experience without risking either pilots' lives or aircraft. A simulator consists of a fully instrumented cockpit that is hydraulically mounted and moves in response to the pilot's controls to give the sensation of a moving plane. Computer graphics are used to create the view from the cockpit windows. The images respond to the aircraft's controls so that the pilot can take off, maneuver, and land in the synthesized "airspace." The mountains in the distance, most likely fractal mountains, will appear more and more detailed as the plane approaches. The plane "flies" through clouds, over plains, rivers, and deserts and lands at an airport visualized by the computer.

Since the plane can be directed anywhere over the landscape, and because it moves in three dimensions, the computer must synthesize the images from a three-dimensional model of the terrain. In a sense, the object-based graphics system functions as a camera moving over a scale model, a method of flight simulation often employed before the advent of computer graphics.

Planes move very quickly so the data base from which the images are generated must be very large. Distant objects anywhere on the landscape can be approached quite closely, requiring that the computer be able to quickly fill in realistic details. Fractal algorithms play an important role in simplifying the job of making convincing looking terrain. Even with efficient algorithms, flight simulation requires some of the most powerful, and expensive, computer-graphics systems.

flight simulation This sequence of images depicting a carrier landing was generated in real-time. Flight simulation is one of the most computationally intensive forms of computer graphics because the images must be updated 30 times per second in response to the pilot's controls. Here a U.S. Navy T-45 trainer comes in for a landing on the U.S.S. *Enterprise*.

Weird events, impossible in real life, are sometimes possible with simulation programs under development. If the plane flies too low, it can pass into the ground or through mountains. The computer will happily calculate these impossible perspectives. Since these areas are not defined in the data base, the computer screen goes blank and the user is likely to become disoriented passing through undefined space at great speed. He must rediscover the defined surfaces of the data base to emerge back into the world. Such "catastrophes" are powerful reminders of the ethereal nature, despite the extraordinary realism, of the three-dimensional objects in the computer. Of course, simulators actually set up for training treat collisions with the ground as crashes.

In standard computer animation, in which frames may be rendered much more slowly, individual frames are transferred to videotape or are photographed one at a time (from a high-resolution monitor) with motion-picture film. The computer is not directly involved in the playback process. Flight simulators must produce 30 or 60 frames a second in response to the pilot's controls. A system that produces images so quickly that the visualization appears to respond directly to the user's controls is said to be operating in *real time.*

The illustrations here cannot fully convey the extraordinary realism of "flying over" a computer-generated terrain in a sophisticated simulator. Since depth perception by stereopsis is not important at a distance, the view from a real cockpit window is very much like a two-dimensional image and simulators *do* provide aerial perspective and motion parallax.

animation The techniques that produce computer-graphics images can be adapted to make the sequence of images required for animation. Two-dimensional systems have been adapted to partially automate drawing of individual frames, but the real potential of the field lies in animation with three-dimensional systems. When the objects defined in the computer are three dimensional "camera angles" can be chosen just as though the objects and the camera were real. Animators sometimes think of this computer as a "soft studio." The soft studio is in a sense equivalent to a movie sound stage but simulated entirely with software. Three-dimensional object-based animation is also having a significant impact on the visualization of complex scientific phenomena (see *Visual Experiments*).

ANIMATION WITH TWO-DIMENSIONAL

SYSTEMS In traditional animation, images are painted on clear acetate sheets called "cels." Every gesture of the characters must be reduced to tiny advancements of movement from cel to cel. (A background will be painted on a separate cel so it does not have to be repainted for each small change in position of the characters.) So much drawing is required that animation studios are organized so that the work can be divided efficiently. There is usually a principal animator who draws the keyframes, the definitive moments in the sequence, while intermediate frames are drawn by others, the so-called "in-betweeners."

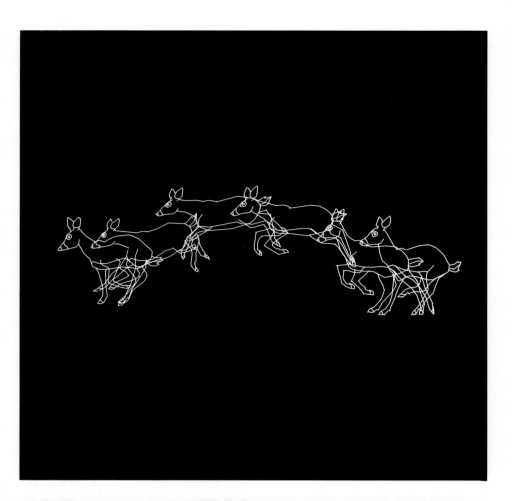

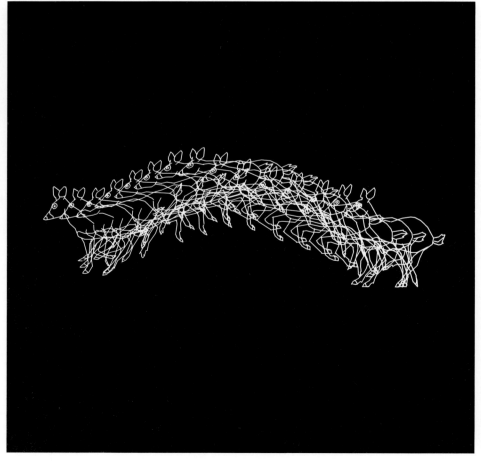

Two-dimensional object-based systems have been adapted to partially automate in-betweening. Key-frames are traced with a stylus. Computer algorithms then automatically generate frames in-between the key-frames. When intermediate forms have been created, the forms can be colored with the methods used in pixel-based paint systems.

One problem with these systems is that the computer cannot, in any sense, recognize the forms when it is in-betweening. In order for it to produce in-between frames, the animator must relate points in one key-frame to comparable points in the next drawing. The computer will then calculate, by mathematical interpolation, the intermediate shapes that turn the first form into the second. More key-frames are required for automated in-betweening and the resulting animations have a characteristic appearance due to the method of interpolation.

in-betweening In motion-picture animation, a chief designer draws only intermittent "key-frames" to define the motion of the character. "In-betweeners" traditionally draw the frames representing the motion connecting the key-frames. In recent years, computer programs have been designed to partially automate this process by interpolating frames between key-frames with algorithms.

The first illustration (left top) shows superimposed key-frames representing the movements of a deer. The second illustration (left bottom) superimposes the in-between frames created by the computer. The third image (right) is a frame from final animation.

Although computer in-betweening can be an aid to animators, it has not displaced human in-betweening. The computer, because it does not recognize the content of the image, in-betweens on the basis of interpolation. Points in one image are linked to points in a subsequent image and the computer interpolates intermediate shapes which do not necessarily correspond to the physical characteristics of the animated character or object. To make the interpolation method work, many more key-frames must be defined for the computer than would be necessary for a human in-betweener. Image sequence courtesy of Computer Graphics Laboratories, Inc. Roslyn Heights, New York.

ANIMATION WITH THREE-DIMENSIONAL

SYSTEMS With a three-dimensional object-based system, each frame is a visualization of a three-dimensional data base from a viewpoint specified by the user. In a sense, it is more like photography than drawing because, essentially, one chooses a camera angle and the lighting appropriate for the scene even though it exists only in the computer. A simple kind of sequence can be created just by shifting the viewpoint slightly from frame to frame. When the frames are put together, the effect can be similar to a crane shot in motion pictures except for the fact that a crane-mounted camera is much more limited in its movements.

In computer graphics, the viewpoint can be moved in a 360-degree loop or in a spiral around an object giving the object apparent movement in the resulting animation. The spiraling logos of the television networks and of "movies of the week" are often created by moving the viewpoint in this way. The logo may also be given an interesting surface, perhaps transparent or metallic. Moving the "light sources" from frame to frame also contributes to the overall dynamic appearance of the presentation.

ANIMATION WITH

PROCEDURAL TECHNIQUES It is usually desirable in animation not only to move the viewpoint but to move objects from frame to frame so that there is motion within the scene. There are a number of methods for changing the position of objects procedurally. Using special animation control languages, the animator can write a "script" that repositions objects automatically from frame to frame. The commands in the script will specify when a motion begins and ends, the path through space along which the object moves, how fast the object travels and whether or not it rotates in space while traveling. The script specifies the movement of each object. Once the commands have been organized as a script, the computer calculates the positions for the objects for each frame.

The animation script might simply be a list of commands but, in more sophisticated software packages, the script is represented as a graphic image in which the sequence for each object is represented as a horizontal bar where time is usually understood to move from left to right. Graphic symbols are used to indicate an aspect of an object's motion. Organizing the script in this way as an illustrated time line, makes it easier to coordinate the simultaneous motion of many objects.

In addition to script-based animation, there is a great deal of research being done to try to "teach" the computer the typical movements of certain kinds of objects so that it can produce animation automatically. Consider, for example, the motion of a falling row of dominoes. By programming the computer to model the force of gravity, and the forces of one domino knocking into another, the whole chain reaction of a falling row could be simulated.

Modeling gravity and motion is not any different, in principle, from modeling the interaction of light and surfaces: it requires the development of algorithms based on insights into the real phenomena. Of course, some subjects prove to be more difficult to model than others. A basic aspiration of computer graphicists is to model human movement. To work toward this goal, a number of researchers are developing algorithms that control the movements of a robot-like object. The movements of the robot (which exists, of course, only in the computer) are constrained by the algorithms to those movements that are possible with human limbs. Eventually, it might be possible to animate characters without drawing them, simply by guiding their movements procedurally, telling them where to go and what to do. This sort of modeling is a long way off, but it is interesting to see computer scientists studying human anatomy in order to get programming ideas.

the graphic interface In the early 1970s, Alan Kay, then a young computer scientist working at the Xerox Palo Alto Research Center (Xerox PARC), developed a new way of interacting with computers that was to have widespread significance for the coming explosion of computer technology. Kay was searching for ways of making the interaction between the user and the computer—the man–machine interface—simpler. The traditional way of interacting with large mainframe computers, typing complex commands onto computer punch cards had not changed much even with the ever-increasing availability of computing. The computer user, at best, was forced to communicate with the computer by typing statements in complex computer languages on a keyboard.

Kay was impressed with several attempts to make the computer more accessible by making it more visual. For example, Ivan Sutherland, as a doctoral student at the Massachusetts Institute of Technology, had developed Sketchpad, one of the first computer-graphics programs. Although primitive by today's standards, it was a significant turning point in computing and Sutherland went on to become a leading influence in the now-burgeoning computer-graphics industry. Sketchpad permitted the drawing and manipulation of simple geometric figures directly on a computer screen with the use of a specially developed light-pen. Sutherland had adapted the digital computer for the convenient handling of visual forms.

Kay was also influenced by two innovations made by Douglas Engelbart, then at the Stanford Research Institute. Engelbart created a way of pointing to areas of the computer screen with a "mouse." A mouse is a small device generally used to move an arrow pointer from place to place on a computer screen. As it is moved across a table-top, a pointer on the computer screen moves in the same manner. The mouse may also have a click switch or two. The computer user makes a selection from an option menu simply by moving the arrow and clicking the switch. As routine as this technique may seem today, it was a significant innovation because it was a way of eliminating both the need to remember arcane commands and the requirement that they be typed.

Engelbart's system also included "windows." In computing, a window is a region on the computer screen that is dedicated to one application or file. By windowing, the computer can be turned into something like a television control room where each screen shows a different camera angle. By using many windows, a user can simultaneously follow several different applications or files and move freely from one to the other without having to load and unload different programs.

A final influence on Kay was the Rand Corporation's Grail system in which the user was able to interact with the computer directly by using a graphics tablet and a graphic language. Complex computer programs could be developed, essentially, by drawing a flow-chart of Grail symbols. The Grail system demonstrated that a very intimate connection between computer and user could be achieved by making the interface visual.

Kay brought all of these influences together at Xerox PARC where, a few years later, Apple Computer co-founder Steven Jobs saw it on a visit. Jobs was deeply impressed with the technology and wanted Apple to market it. Apple's first version of the interface was the Lisa computer, which was an innovative business product but a commercial failure. The great success came with the Macintosh, a direct descendent of the Lisa, which included mouse control, graphics, windows, and control with "icons" (simple visual images used to represent different applications and files). These innovations are now found in many personal, business, and scientific computers.

procedural graphics in two dimensions
An example of procedural graphics of interest to graphic designers is a system conceived by Donald Knuth to design typefaces and other two-dimensional graphic forms. As with other computer languages, the user directs the computer by writing a program, a sequence of commands that will not only specify the shape of a letter or punctuation mark but render it with a specific style.

By changing the values of parameters, as simple as turning control knobs up or down, the whole character of a typeface can be altered. Strokes can be widened, serifs can be generated at stroke ends, the letter can be slanted. The height of the ascenders or descenders (the strokes in lower case letters that extend above or below the body of the letter) can be increased or diminished. Stroke-ends can be rounded or squared off. Thus, the program can be used to quickly produce variations of a typeface or different sizes of the same design with the numerous adjustments of proportion that might be required.

Knuth's program is procedural because the user never actually draws the character. The computer, directed by the user, creates the form. With a non-procedural technique, changing a typeface even slightly is almost as difficult as designing a new one. With Knuth's system, the designer, in effect, designs not characters but a system (program with subroutines) for generating them. This system then acts as a draftsman executing designs, and modifying them, in response to the designer's directions.

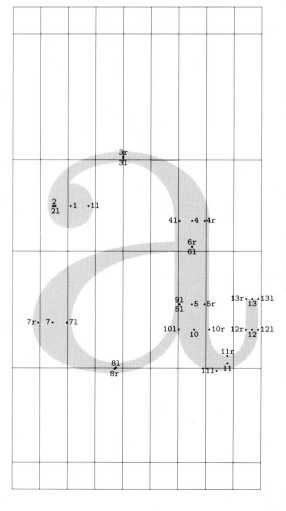

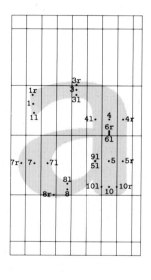

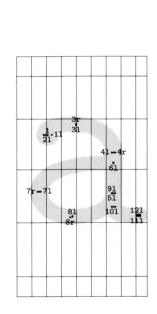

two-dimensional procedural graphics
Procedural graphics techniques can be used to partially automate graphic design. The letter forms here were automatically generated on the grids by Donald Knuth's METAFONT program from the numbered control points. Letters are rendered with specific styles, three of which are shown, depending upon how the program interprets the control points.

The METAFONT program permits the gradual modification of parameters utilized by its algorithms. This series shows how graded changes in two parameters can influence the design generated by the computer. The bowl shape is a portion of the letter b.

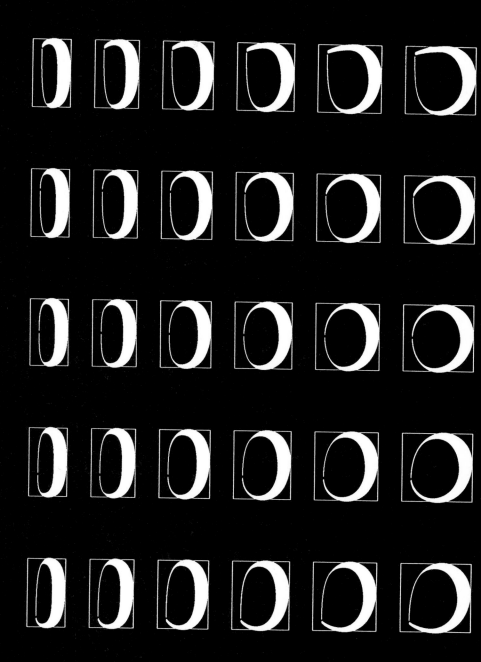

DESKTOP PUBLISHING

Desktop publishing systems are two-dimensional graphics programs that adapt home and business computers for graphic design and typesetting. They are used to typeset word-processed text in a variety of typefaces and type sizes, produce illustrations, and design page layouts. In conjunction with a high-resolution laser printer, layouts can be prepared for reproduction. These systems dramatically reduce the cost of preparing publications, making it possible for small organizations with access to a personal computer to produce high-quality graphics.

In word processing, it is not uncommon for the document to include codes that indicate underlining, boldface, or italics. All characters, whether or not they may ultimately be converted into headlines or headings, are initially the same size. Desktop publishing software, on the other hand, is based on the so-called WYSIWYG, or "What You See Is What You Get," interface. The document on the computer monitor appears the same as the printed page with all the different size typefaces, the illustrations, and the organization of columns.

The important feature of desktop graphics systems is that they treat the page as a graphic form rather than as a string of letters. The alphanumeric characters within a document are converted into a graphic format, an image, which is displayed on the screen. Since the system is graphics-oriented, there is no barrier to incorporating other graphic forms with text, such as digitized photographs or graphics produced on the computer.

The high-resolution laser printer is an important component of desktop publishing. Some systems function in full color and are used with color ink-jet, thermal transfer, plastic ink, or electrostatic printers. Desktop publishing systems can also be used in conjunction with digital typesetting machines to produce extremely high-resolution reproduction-quality master copies suitable for commercial printing.

desktop programs With programs that combine text, graphics, and images, the desktop computer can be used as a graphic design studio.

vision and algorithms

Of course, the ultimate test of all of these methods, the algorithms for shading, fractal, particle, and other procedural techniques for creating complex geometry, is the appearance of the image itself. Sometimes despite enormous effort, the visualization falls short and we know it at a glance.

It is interesting to consider the way in which we are making use of the eye's sensitivity when we evaluate algorithms in this way. When the visualization looks good, it means that the algorithm successfully models those features of the phenomenon that are important to our visual system. In this sense, a successful algorithm is a discovery not only about the world, but about perception. If fractal mountains are aesthetically satisfying despite the lack of true self-similarity in real mountains it must be because our eyes, at least when we view mountains from a distance, do not generally relate larger-scale details to smaller features. On the computer, the large-scale qualities reiterated in miniature will serve as an acceptable substitute, particularly in a moving image.

On the other hand, Bloomenthal found that he had to use real-world data for the bark of his maple tree because procedural methods did *not* produce a satisfactory appearance. Perhaps this is because, unlike mountains, we can get very close to trees and we have a more intimate knowledge of the details of bark structure. When objects are viewed at close range, the eye apparently requires a certain variety of detail so that fractal self-similarity simply does not suffice.

The process of evaluating a texture is rooted in the feverish activities of preconscious visual analysis. It tells us something about visual processing that, as computer graphicists routinely find, one kind of texture can appear realistic while another, closely related by algorithm, seems unrealistic. The same can be said about shading algorithms and algorithms for modeling motion. The visual machinery demands that algorithms of visualization create those qualities, whatever they may be, which are critical to its own methods of analysis. Thus, the schemata of visualization are discoveries not only about objects and light but about vision. Whatever its basis, the use of aesthetic criteria to judge what are essentially computer simulations is another indication of the diminishing distinction among art, perception, and science in visualization.

visual experiments

The words or the language, as they are written or spoken, do not seem to play any role in my mechanism of thought. The psychical entities which seem to serve as elements in thought are certain signs and more or less clear images which can be "voluntarily" reproduced and combined . . . this combinatory play seems to be the essential feature in productive thought before there is any connection with logical construction in words or other kinds of signs which can be communicated to others.

Albert Einstein in a letter to Jacques Hadamard

Images that appear on the screens of computer-graphics systems are deceptive. Where else is it possible to find a tree trunk that only has an outside surface? Fly into a mountain on a flight simulator and you might just disappear into "unspace"—a place that has no characteristics at all. Computer objects look real but, unlike objects in the physical world, have no qualities other than their visual appearance. Genuine objects have an inside as well as an outside. They have mass and hardness. Computer-graphics objects, tangible as they might appear, are pure surface—visible equations.

On the other hand, it is with the computer that we have absolute dominion. We can, if we wish, design algorithms to advance the capabilities of the computer beyond simply modeling light and surfaces. Computers are already used to simulate the forces binding molecules, the support structures of buildings, manufacturing processes, astrophysical systems, theoretical mathematics—and the list is growing. There is no foreseeable limit to the kinds of phenomena that can be modeled.

Only a few years ago, the common way of interacting with computers was with paper punch cards. Stacks of cards with programs and data encoded with machine-readable holes were fed into the computer and a printed output, usually rows and columns of numbers, was returned. This method, which required a great deal of time between cycles, was inadequate for guiding large complex computations such as are commonly found in visualization. Apart from the time factor of repunching cards, the form of the output was not congenial to understanding complex phenomena. Our ability to recognize a pattern, or to make a comparison, in numerical data does not compare with the eye/brain's fantastic ability to recognize and compare graphic forms.

Although computer-graphics simulations involve many diverse fields, it is apparent in reviewing a wide variety that there is a common quality to the man/machine interaction wherever one looks. The graphics interface facilitates the systematic consideration of a wide range of alternatives in areas in which it was not previously possible because of the complexity of the required computations. It seems appropriate to call these kinds of simulations "visual experiments" because they are, in so many ways, similar to the experiments of empirical science. Both kinds of experiments are attempts to uncover a hidden relationship by manipulating one set of variables and observing the effects on another. In both endeavors, in simulation and in the formal scientific experiment, problems are solved by repeating this process until a relationship is fully discerned.

The visual experiments framework proposed here applies as well to activities usually thought of as artistic and beyond the realm of formal empiricism. When the computer is used by an architect to visualize design alternatives, for example, it becomes apparent that designers, very much like scientists, are trying to isolate and understand a relationship between variables. Without the computer, the architect deals in a handful of "snapshots." When the computer is used, the same designer is permitted to explore fully the implications not only of isolated inspirations but of all the variations in between. In this sense, the computer is serving the same function as it does for the scientist.

images instead of calculations

To understand the role of visualization it is not even necessary to refer to the computer. Consider a game in which two players take turns choosing numbered chips from a hat. The chips are visibly numbered 1 through 9 and the goal of the game is to be the first to draw three chips that total 15. Each player must also keep in mind the need to block the opponent from arriving at the sum of 15 first.

Note that the game requires a series of *computations* for each round. In order to evaluate alternative choices, a player must determine not only which chip will bring the total to 15 but must also consider the value the remaining chips would have for the opponent. A series of arithmetic calculations must be performed to make each move.

The game can also be played another way—visually. The arrangement of numbers 1 through 9 shown here has the special property that each row, column, and diagonal sums to 15—the critical value required for victory.

$$
\begin{array}{ccc}
6 & 7 & 2 \\
1 & 5 & 9 \\
8 & 3 & 4
\end{array}
$$

Since the rows, columns, and diagonals represent every possible combination that sums to 15, the square can be used to eliminate the computations needed to make each move. To win the game, a player simply picks three numbers within a single row, column, or diagonal. Instead of calculating arithmetically, the players choose boxes in the grid visually.

A convenient way of recording the player's choices is for one player to mark the boxes with x's and the other with o's. Played this way it immediately becomes apparent that the game can be simplified even further if numbers are forgotten altogether and choices are made by marking a clean grid. In this form, of course, the game is recognizable as tic-tac-toe. In the grid form, the game is more "intuitive" since it simply requires the completion of horizontal, vertical, or diagonal lines. The important point is that, in the second form, arithmetic calculation is exchanged for visual comparisons.

This example captures the essence of visualization: a successful visualization removes computational barriers so that we may proceed with strictly visual comparisons. (Much of the information processing required to solve a problem is moved from conscious intellection to the preconscious processes of the visual system.) In tic-tac-toe, the computations required are simple and the game can be played satisfactorily in either form. In science, engineering, and design, however, computational barriers to alternative testing can be much more formidable. In these cases, visualizing the problem can change the whole nature of the "game."

SIMULATING MOLECULES One discipline that is literally being transformed by visualization is biochemistry. Contemporary biochemical problems are so complex that traditional ball-and-stick molecular models are rapidly becoming inadequate. Biochemists today need to know more than simply the idealized form of a molecule that can be represented with a wood model. Molecules twist, turn, and vibrate continuously. Biochemists need to know how a molecule, especially if it is made of tens of thousands of atoms, *behaves*. It is only by understanding these dynamic processes, that the molecule's interaction with other molecules, its reactivity, can be predicted.

structure and function To understand the role digital visualization plays in biochemistry, we must appreciate that the function of a molecule is intimately related to its structure. A given molecule can assume many different structures, technically called *conformations,* some of which are stable and others which are not. A molecule's conformation is determined by many different kinds of forces. The great majority of biomolecules are chains of amino acids, which in turn are made up of small numbers of atoms. The amino acids and their component atoms have both attractive and repulsive forces that constrain the molecule's movements. A long molecule might be thought of as a chain of diversely shaped magnets that attract and repel each other and that cause the chain to assume a shape, often spherical, which maximizes attractive forces and minimizes repulsive forces.

Chemists evaluate various conformations in terms of their *potential energy.* Before a molecule folds in on itself it is said to have a high "potential energy," much as a stretched spring has potential energy that is released when it shrinks to its collapsed form. When a molecule folds up it gives off this energy and becomes more stable. The biochemist, for example in designing a drug, seeks to produce a molecule with a particular conformation. A sequence of amino acids is chosen to form the molecule and then an evaluation is made to see whether the molecule conforms, folds in on itself, to the desired shape.

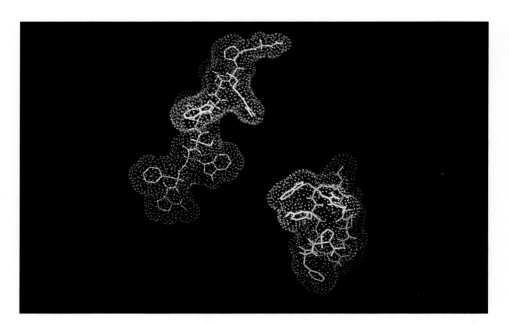

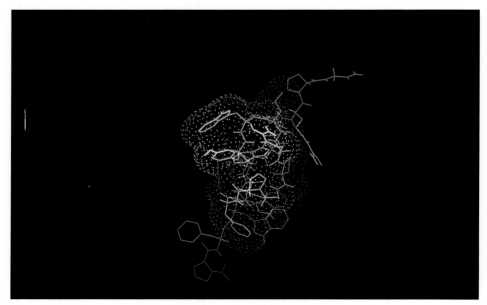

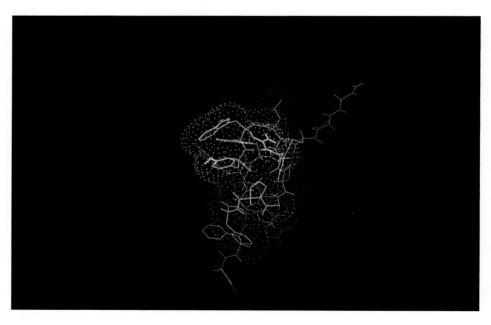

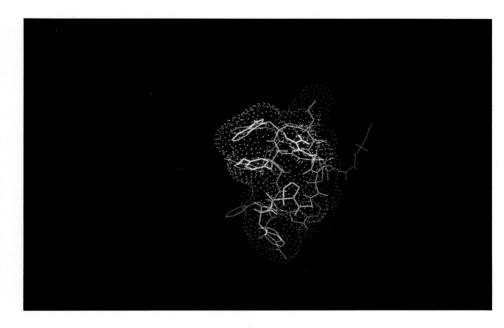

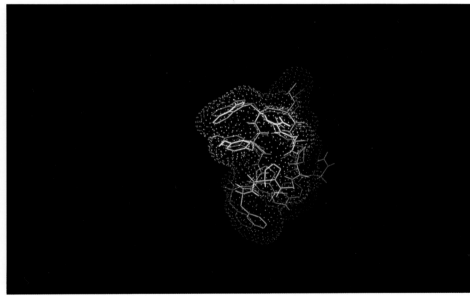

template forcing The red structure is an extended conformation that is being template forced to match the structure of the blue molecule. As the shape of the molecule is changed, the computer calculates changes in potential energy. In the final image, the red molecule assumes a structure similar to the blue molecule and has a low potential energy indicating that it would be stable in that form.

To predict the conformation, biochemists calculate the attractive and repulsive forces for each of the atoms. It is a little bit like predicting the shape of a string of magnets except that, of course, it is vastly more complicated because there are a number of different kinds of forces, possibly thousands of atoms, and because chemical bonds vibrate. With larger molecules, the complexity of the problem grows exponentially because every interaction between every atom in the molecule must be considered. For a biomolecule composed of one hundred atoms, for example, the minimum number of calculations required is 100^2 or 10,000.

Computer visualization facilitates the process not only by automating the complex computations but by providing a way of comparing different geometries visually. Here, as in the simple tic-tac-toe example, visualization eliminates the computational barrier in favor of visual thinking.

The sequence of five images shows how computer visualization can be used in the design of a drug molecule. Scott Struthers and Arnold Hagler at the Agouron Institute and Jean Rivier at the Salk Institute, La Jolla, California, were interested in designing an antagonist for Gonadotrophin Releasing Hormone (GnRH). A hormone molecule acts by binding to molecules called receptors which are found in the membrane of cells where the hormone will have its effect. The hormone molecule, essentially, fits into the receptor molecule because the two molecules have reciprocal geometries—the hormone is a kind of key and the receptor is a lock. An antagonist is simply a molecule that has structural similarities to the hormone so that it will also bind to the receptor but without producing the response normally triggered by the hormone. It is the same in its general geometric form but different in detail so that, in essence, it blocks the keyhole but does not unlock the lock. Technically speaking, an antagonist blocks the action of the hormone by taking the hormone's place at the receptor. The goal of the biochemist, therefore, is to design a structure that is similar, but not identical, to the hormone. In this case, an antagonist for GnRH would be expected to be useful as a contraceptive and as a drug for controlling some kinds of cancer.

The blue rendering in the illustration depicts the structure of a weak form of a GnRH antagonist that was discovered in the laboratory. Since the molecule shown in blue is known to bind to the receptor, it is assumed that other antagonists would generally have a comparable shape. The red structure is an extended conformation (the extended chain of amino acids with a very high potential energy) of a proposed antagonist. The structure is said to be extended because the chain of amino acids has not yet folded in on itself: the computer uses the extended conformation as a starting point.

Since the molecule must have the shape of the known antagonist, the computer is used to calculate the change in potential energy as the molecule is forced into that shape. This process, known as *template forcing,* is a method for determining if the proposed amino-acid sequence would, by itself, conform to the shape of the known antagonist.

In the sequence shown, the computer calculates the change in potential energy as the conformation is forced into a shape resembling the known antagonist (blue). The basic question is whether, when the molecule is in a form that would make it function as an antagonist, it has a higher or a lower potential energy than in other conformations. If the potential energy is higher, the conformation will be unstable. If the potential energy is low in the target conformation (relative to other conformations), the molecule can be expected to be stable in that form.

Using this method, the scientists can evaluate many possible amino-acid sequences to find one that would naturally conform to the desired shape. In the last images, the two molecules have almost identical structures. In the simulation, the computer indicated that the red structure would have a low potential energy in this form, indicating that the molecule is a good candidate for testing in the laboratory.

a continuum from pictorial to symbolic

In visualization it is useful to define a "symbol" as an image that can only be understood after learning a convention. The letters of the alphabet, chemical notations, and stop signs are symbols. A "picture" on the other hand is an image that can be understood without special learning. A traffic sign depicting children crossing the street can be said to be "pictorial" in this sense, as is a photograph, because neither requires specialized knowledge.

If the distinction seems artificial, consider that there are certain kinds of neurological disorders whose victims can see but who cannot understand symbols or signs. To these individuals, newspapers, for instance, would seem to be printed in a foreign alphabet. They recognize the photographs but cannot read the captions. They are not blind in the normal sense but are unable to use certain associative processes needed to recall the meaning of symbols. Symbols are gone but pictures remain.

Many images, such as magnetic resonance images, fall in between these two formal categories. Major anatomical features are recognizable but the colors used to denote differences in the distribution of hydrogen atoms can only be understood by someone familiar with the conventions.

One of the fundamental goals of visualization is to make the representations of phenomena as "pictorial" as possible. In magnetic resonance imaging, this might mean that body organs should be denoted by their true colors. In such a scheme, venous blood would be blue while arterial blood would be red. Grey and white matter of the brain might also be so differentiated in visualization.

The problem of using a pictorial style becomes more difficult when the phenomenon itself lacks a visual dimension. Metabolic disorders, for example, cannot usually be directly observed by a change in color or the appearance of an organ. In these cases, visualization with a pictorial style becomes an aesthetic and artistic question in which color and form are used suggestively, as in positron tomography, where areas of high metabolic activity are generally labeled with hot colors. The pictorial technique is effective in calling our attention to areas of intense activity even though, of course, there is no significant temperature change.

Computer visualization is superior to ball-and-stick modeling in several critical respects. For one thing, accurate physical models require a great deal of time to construct. It is just not possible to evaluate large numbers of conformations when a physical model must be constructed for each one. Furthermore, when it comes to comparing the geometries of molecules, for example the proposed and the known antagonists, the computer is superior because it can overlap the two structures in three dimensions with great accuracy. Physical models cannot be superimposed in the same space and provide no automatic way of measuring differences between structures quantitatively.

The most important benefit, however, is that the process is interactive. On the computer, the dynamic relationship between potential energy and conformation can be discerned by slowly changing the form of the molecule and watching the way in which it affects the value of potential energy. This kind of understanding, actually seeing one variable influence another, is quite difficult to obtain by manual methods which are encumbered by computation and, inevitably, a limit on the number of models that can be built. Without the computer, the biochemist must preconceive individual conformations likely to be of interest. Physical models provide only a handful of "snapshots" of the phenomenon, giving no real sense of the molecule's dynamics or unanticipated conformations.

With graphics, the biochemist can see the model move and gradually becomes aware of advantages and deficiencies of certain groupings of amino acids. It is possible, by testing amino-acid substitutions, to work toward a sequence that will conform in the desired way. This process, which may involve hundreds of millions, or billions, of computations, is thus qualitatively changed with the use of a graphic interface.

The dynamic properties of molecules are so important to the biochemist that it is often desirable to produce a movie showing the way in which the molecule moves from instant to instant. Chemical bonds constantly jiggle, stretch, and shrink, causing the molecule to move continuously. The molecule has both high- and low-frequency vibrations. The high-frequency vibrations correspond to the movements around the individual bonds. The low-frequency vibrations correspond to the overall bending of the molecule. To produce an animation that shows the full cycle of movement, perhaps 20,000 conformations will need to be calculated. If 10,000 computations are required for a single conformation, then 200 million computations are required to depict a complete cycle. The computer visualization makes it feasible to perceive a dynamic that would otherwise be impossible to see.

Visualization is also important in biochemistry as a communications tool. Before these techniques became available, it was much more difficult to communicate subtle ideas about the dynamics of molecules to other biochemists. Now, however, the digital data describing molecules is easily transmitted to other computers. When a molecule's shape has been determined, it is customary to transmit the information to a depository such as the Protein Data Bank at Brookhaven National Laboratories in Brookhaven, New York, where it becomes available to scientists all over the world.

The essential function of visualization in biochemistry remains, however, the same as in visualizing tic-tac-toe. Conformations are simply alternatives, analogous to tic-tac-toe moves, that need to be compared. The principal difference is in the quantity of computations required to make the comparison. In tic-tac-toe, the computations are easy enough so that one can play the game with or without visualization. In biochemistry, on the other hand, comparing alternatives can require millions or billions of calculations—a sufficient number to discourage the undertaking before it begins, if it could not be managed visually by a computer.

Theoretical biophysical chemistry formally uses mathematics so that it is easy to recognize the computational barriers that are eliminated with the computer. We are less accustomed to thinking in computational terms when it comes to art and design where the comparison of alternatives might not have an obvious mathematical basis. In using the computer for many artistic and design projects, however, it becomes evident that the computer can, with visualization, remove computational obstacles to comparing alternatives in these areas too.

CAD, CAM, and CIM Computer-aided design, or CAD, is used in an ever increasing variety of applications in the appliance, automotive, aerospace, and many other industries. It is used to design whole buildings as well as individual machine parts and other products. CAD can be used to test the interaction of moving parts in a machine, for example, making sure that the gears in an automobile transmission mesh properly, or that the wheels have room to turn. As in architecture, stresses can be evaluated within the computer without construction of a prototype, making design testing faster and more economical.

CAD is also used extensively in the electronics industry in the design of electronic circuits and microchips some with millions of components. CAD is used in textile design and manufacture and, recently, even clothing manufacturers have begun exploring the use of CAD in fashion design. This requires computer programs that can realistically display the draping of fabric on the body. Interior designers are using CAD to design furniture, furniture placement, and lighting.

An important goal of using CAD in manufacturing is that design information can, at least theoretically, be used to control manufacture. When CAD is linked with computer automated manufacturing, CAM, the acronym generally used is CAD/CAM. In principle, the three-dimensional data base created by the designer can control manufacturing directly, leading to important gains in efficiency. Design data can be used to control robotic machine tools such as looms, lathes, drills, and milling machines. Computer driven machines are said to be *numerically controlled*. In textile manufacture, for example, patterns can be created on CAD workstations and then executed on numerically controlled looms.

The goal of CAD/CAM is to move from design to finished product with little or no human intervention. This ideal is often referred to as computer-integrated manufacturing, or CIM. In practice, it is quite difficult to do this with any complex product and CIM is more of an ideal than a reality.

ARCHITECTURAL MODELING

Computer visualization has been advancing very rapidly in architecture. The most sophisticated applications are usually found in large architectural firms where it is used in the design of office complexes, commercial centers, factories, terminals and other large-scale projects. It is having a profound impact on both the methods by which designers of these projects work and the structures they are creating. The computer is used throughout the process: to create designs, to satisfy zoning ordinances, to assess environmental impact, to manage construction, for promotion, and, in some cases even for interior decoration.

The computer is introduced as soon as the architect has created preliminary sketches and is ready to produce more precise plans. The designer uses a stylus on a graphics tablet or a light-pen on a monitor to draw. Drafting tools are unnecessary because the computer-aided design (CAD) system has automatic functions that take the place of protractors, rulers, templates, and other instruments. Drawings can be printed with a variety of different devices including conventional computer printers. A digital "plotter," which draws lines with a pen, is used to produce large-format drawings that are similar in appearance to standard architectural plans.

Since the CAD system contains a three-dimensional representation of the structure, perspective drawings from any point in space either outside the building or within it can be rendered automatically by choosing coordinates for that specific viewpoint. A few commands generate a freshly plotted perspective rendering. The illustrations on pages 142–43 are computer renderings of Worldwide Plaza, a block-long residential and commercial center at Eighth Avenue and Fiftieth Street in Manhattan, designed in part by Skidmore, Owings & Merrill. In the drawings, the proposed building is placed among existing buildings that surround the site. Drawings such as these are very important in understanding the way in which a building will function. The computer is especially useful when interior perspectives are critical as, for instance, when a theater is incorporated into the base of a skyscraper. In this case, the computer can be used to create perspective drawings that test whether supporting structures block the view of the stage from any of the hundreds of seats.

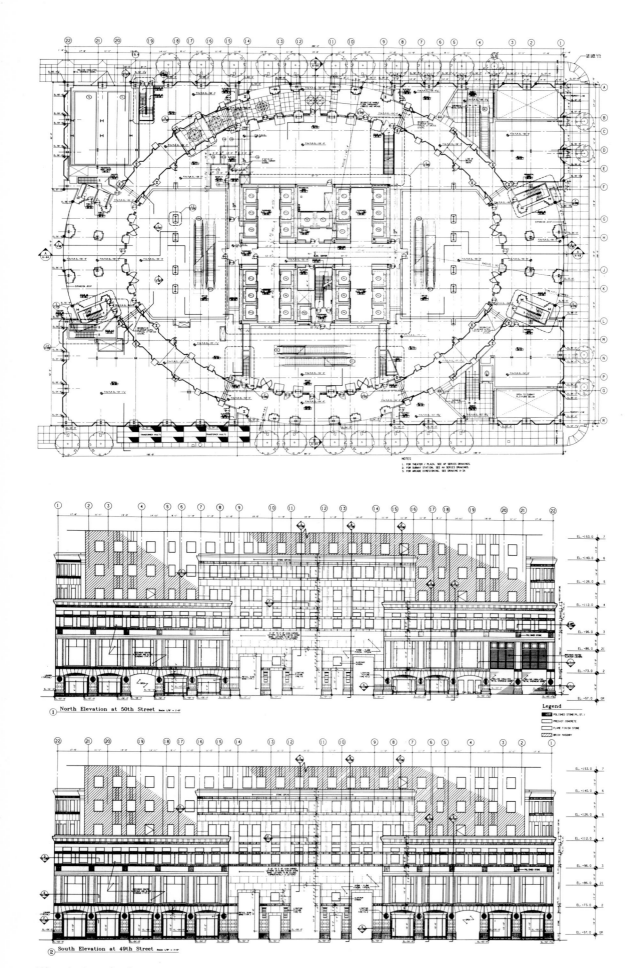

① North Elevation at 50th Street

② South Elevation at 49th Street

Legend

Notes
1. FOR THEATER / PLAZA, SEE AP SERIES DRAWINGS.
2. FOR SUBWAY STATION, SEE AA SERIES DRAWINGS.
3. FOR ARCADE DIMENSIONING, SEE DRAWING A-3A.

140   visual experiments

plotter drawings Left top: Section of the Worldwide Plaza Lobby floor plan. Left bottom: Detail of elevation drawing. Below: Elevation drawing. Courtesy Skidmore, Owings & Merrill.

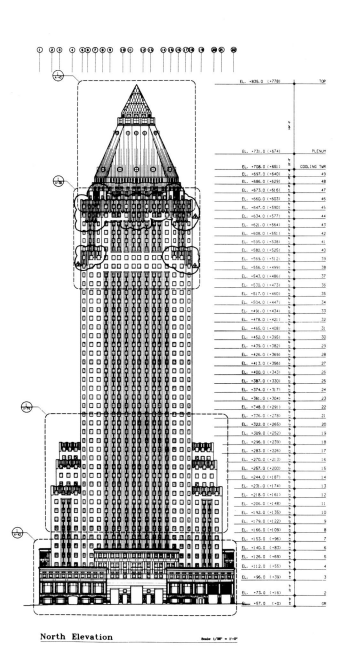

North Elevation

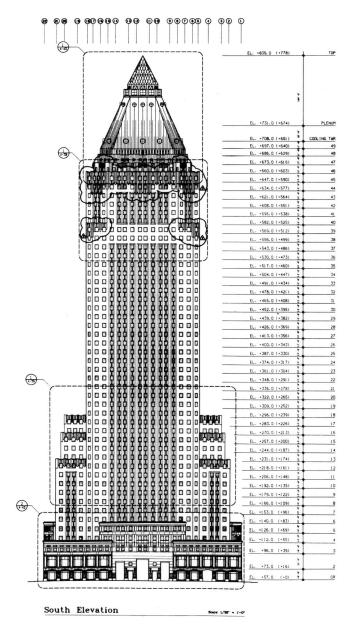

South Elevation

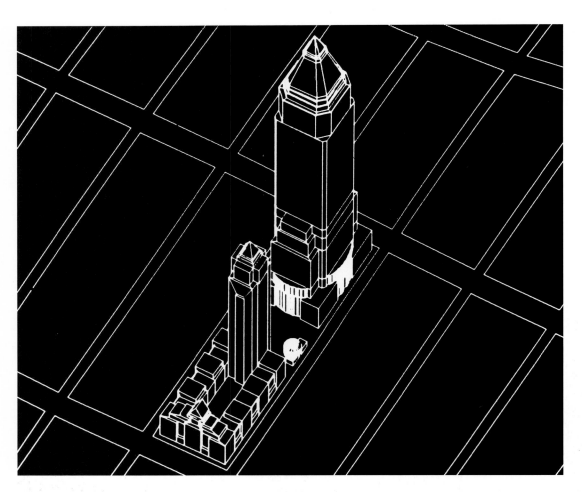

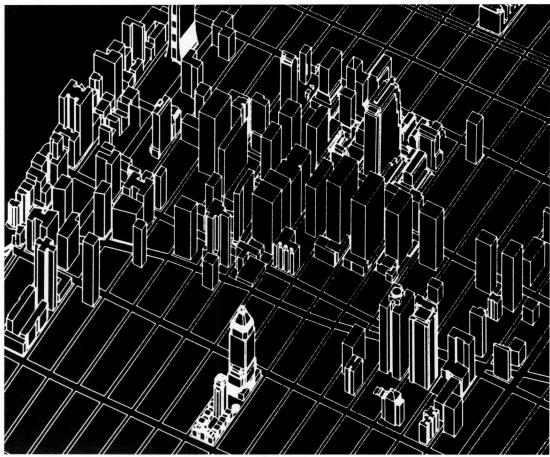

Three perspective drawings of Worldwide Plaza generated automatically by the architectural CAD system. The difficulty of producing such drawings conventionally has traditionally meant that they are used to document an already completed design. One of the great advantages of CAD systems is that they can readily provide such renderings *during* the design phase to help the architect understand the function and visual impact of a design in progress. Perspective renderings are also quite useful for communicating alternative design ideas to clients. The architects have produced data bases of major cities so that they can readily visualize designs in context. Here they surround Worldwide Plaza with the buildings of Manhattan. Courtesy Skidmore, Owings & Merrill.

High-quality renderings are very useful for communicating design ideas to clients and to others, for example community leaders, who might be inexperienced in interpreting architectural plans. Increasingly, architectural systems are being equipped to produce full-color renderings by ray-tracing. The advantage of ray-tracing is that light and surfaces are represented accurately (see *Computer Graphics*). As expensive as ray-tracing is, it can be very useful since the surface of a building is so important to its appearance. With ray-tracing, renderings can show, for instance, the way in which anodized aluminum or glass walls will reflect sunlight. Ray-traced images can also be incorporated into actual photographs of the site so that a highly realistic image of the building *in situ* is created.

The greatest advantage of rendering with the computer, however, accrues to the architect. When a design is created on the computer, the architect is able to produce perspective drawings and more sophisticated renderings while still experimenting with different ideas. Traditionally, realistic renderings are reserved for documenting the appearance of a completed, or nearly completed, design. With the computer, realistic visualizations of design ideas, since they can be produced so conveniently, can be used to guide the evolution of a design to its final form.

CAD systems can also be used to automate analyses that are otherwise quite costly and time consuming and this, too, contributes to the design process. Architects are often faced with complex safety codes or zoning ordinances that must be carefully considered in the design process. In New York, for example, there are limits on how much sunlight a building can block from the street. Every proposed design must be subjected to a complicated "lighting study" to ensure that it complies with city regulations. Codes in other cities, for example Los Angeles and Tokyo, require the architect to analyze the way in which a design would withstand earthquake shocks. Compliance with these restrictions often inhibits design experimentation because evaluating an innovative design can be so difficult and costly. Too often, it is easier to modify an existing plan than to start with a radically new design.

lighting study New York City zoning laws regulate the amount of light a building may block from reaching the street. The regulations require that a "sky exposure plane" be calculated. The portion of the building above the plane blocks light that would otherwise reach the street. In this lighting study, the portions of the building above and below the sky exposure plane are rendered in contrasting colors. Courtesy Skidmore, Owings & Merrill.

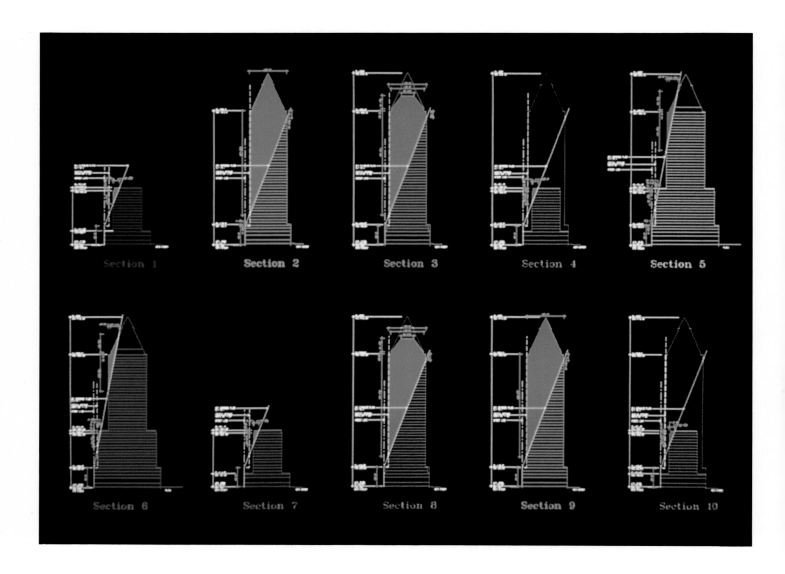

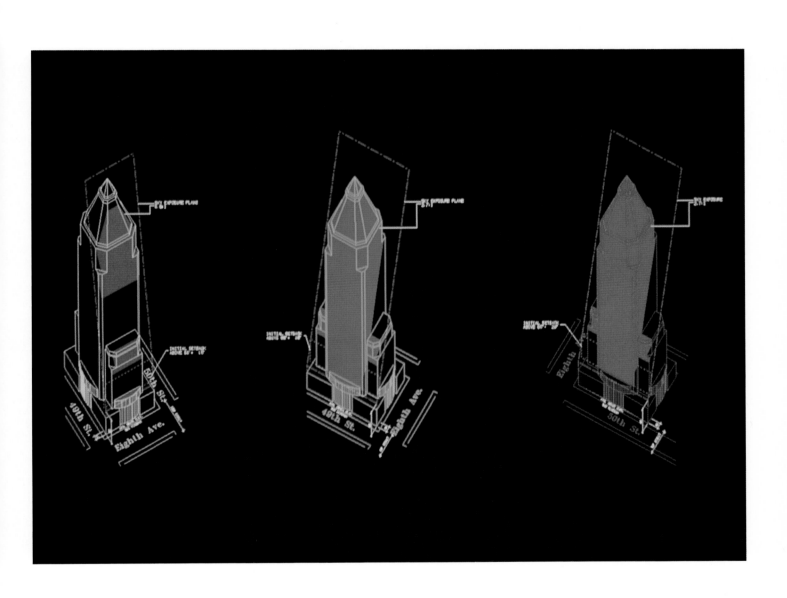

An important advantage of working with the computer is that algorithms can be used to perform these kinds of analyses using the working plans that already exist as a data base. The illustrations on pages 146–47, for example, show a lighting study performed by the computer on plans for the Worldwide Plaza. Since the time and expense required to evaluate designs drop dramatically, it becomes possible to experiment with a greater range of ideas. Thus, a long-term effect of visualization may be to increase architectural diversity because it facilitates experimentation.

Another advantage of the computer is that it partially automates the building of scale models. Models, traditionally built by special craftsmen, are time consuming and costly to produce but are invaluable for showing three-dimensional spatial relationships between components of a design. As with high-quality renderings, the cost and difficulty of building models have usually meant that they functioned to document a completed, or nearly completed, design rather than as tools for evaluating a work in progress.

With computer visualization, model building becomes much simpler since the machine can be connected to a laser device that cuts cardboard, plastic, and wood parts in scale directly from the design data base. The model of Worldwide Plaza shown here was produced automatically in this way. The parts were produced in a scale chosen by the architect and then assembled by hand. If changes are subsequently made in the design (perhaps as a result of studying the model) a new model is easily produced. The architect can thus utilize, as part of the creative process, an evolving three-dimensional model.

Another important feature of the CAD system is that a single data base can serve as the definitive source of information for everyone involved in the design and construction of a building. The same data base that is used to produce ray-traced architectural renderings can be used with other computer programs to help organize the physical construction phase of the building. The computer can be used to automatically prepare lists of the required materials—everything from concrete to doorknobs. The computer can even specify the required construction personnel and propose a schedule for completion of the building. Such lists and schedules are traditionally derived manually by inspection of building plans. The computer is usually much more accurate than the manual preparation and can produce schedules that, because they are all derived from the same data base, have a high degree of concordance. Furthermore, should the architect have last minute changes, all the lists can be automatically recalculated.

As different as the two fields are, there are important parallels between visualization in architecture and in biochemistry. In both fields, a centralized digital data base provides a consistent medium through which members of a design team, whether or not they are at the same location, interact with a minimum of ambiguity. In both fields, the removal of computational barriers makes it possible to consider a much wider range of alternatives than would otherwise be possible. In both cases, the effect of visualization is not simply an increase in efficiency. Visualization is important because it lets the designer, of a drug or a building, steer toward an optimum result by exploring many alternatives and intermediate values *during* the design process.

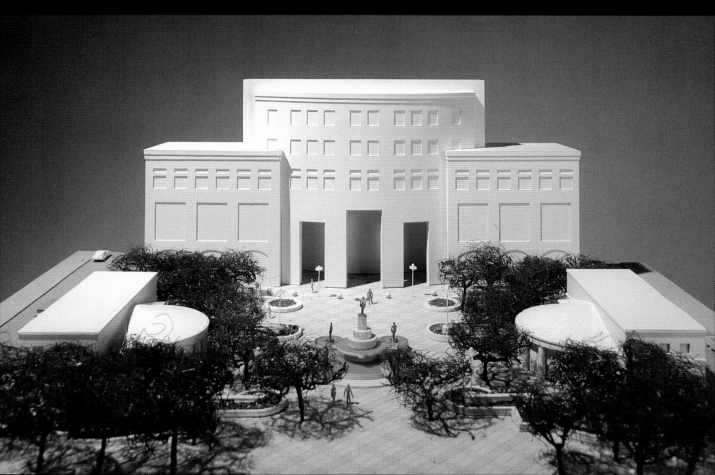

computer-produced model The component parts of this scale model were shaped by a computer controlled laser cutter. Courtesy Skidmore, Owings & Merrill.

sculptural design The sculpture *Skyharp* by Robert Fisher, commissioned for the atrium of the Osaka International Hilton, was designed using a specially created CAD program by Ramon Masters. The intricacy of the large-scale sculpture made ordinary models of doubtful value for giving a sense of how the sculpture would appear to spectators.

This illustration near right shows the CONTROL program menu. CONTROL is a custom designed user-friendly software package created by Ramon Masters for Robert Fisher for the design of *Skyharp*.

The left window shows the position of the plates on the cables schematically. The right window portrays the three-dimensional structure on a two-dimensional screen by using rotation—making use of motion parallax—which the artist found highly satisfactory. In the far right image, plates are added to the design, raised and lowered along the cables, and subtracted by moving a stylus, permitting the artist to work directly with the design unencumbered by the need to type commands. Perspective renderings, on screen or plotted, are readily produced of designs in progress so that, according to Fisher, "...transitions from the moment of creation to working drawings become instantaneous." The CAD program was also able to generate a simulated walk-through of the sculpture placed in the building.

computer-aided sculpture design The speed and ease with which CAD permits consideration of many design alternatives change the artistic design process in much the same way they change scientific problem solving. Because the designer can readily perceive the effects of design changes, a fuller understanding of the relationship between critical variables is achieved than would be possible otherwise.

Robert Fisher uses CAD to design large, highly intricate sculptures. Because ordinary CAD software is not well suited to the kind of playful experimentation used in developing his sculptural ideas, he turned to programmer Ramon Masters of Pennsylvania State University for special software. Masters developed the CONTROL program, specifically for the design of Fisher's *Skyharp,* commissioned for the atrium of a Japanese hotel.

According to the artist, Masters' program completely eliminated the need for elaborate scale models which, in his experience, are problematic because they tend to fix the design idea at too early a stage and do not represent detail effectively. Above all, the program was designed with the aim of encouraging freedom of experimentation. Commands are intuitive and easily mastered and correspond directly to the design elements. Using CONTROL, Fisher was able to experiment with a wide range of designs for the sculpture, which is made from metal plates attached to vertical cables. The software is designed to give a schematic of the sculptor's current arrangement as well as a three-dimensional view by rotating the sculpture around its vertical axis. Fisher found that motion-parallax information provided in this way was a very satisfying equivalent, in his opinion, to viewing a hologram of the design. CAD was especially useful in this particular project because the sculpture was designed concurrently with the building. As the building design changed, Fisher was able to quickly adapt the sculpture to fit. The software renders perspective drawings from any vantage point, which can be viewed on-screen or plotted. The program allows the storage of a sequence of views that can be "in-betweened" to create an animation showing the sculpture as a spectator walking around the balconies of the hotel atrium would see it.

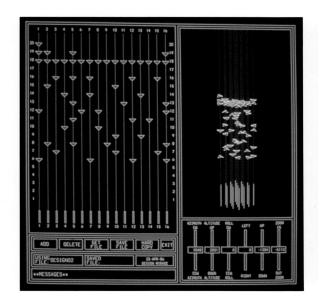 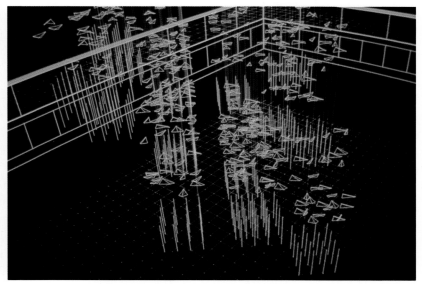

This is not to say that the computer does not have its limitations. At first, the team depicted as much information about the hotel atrium as they could. They found that rendering the walls and floors proved confusing and eliminated it in favor of just showing the balcony railings. Fisher also asked for an aerial perspective algorithm, not generally part of CAD packages, to adjust line weights (sharpness) so that cables in the simulation seemed to be at their true distances.

Fisher does not use the computer to model lighting or color. Despite the development of highly sophisticated shading algorithms, he finds too great a discrepancy between the "luminescent" colors of video and the "...passive, receptive quality of an actual paint surface." Color simulations can be used effectively to find a "solution realm," a range of possible color relations that is then evaluated with real surfaces and light sources. Fisher feels the ideal approach, used on the *Skyharp* commission, is to balance the CAD simulation with a full-scale model of a small section of the sculpture.

Whatever the limitations of the computer, Fisher notes that his experiences contradict the conventional notion that the computer might inhibit artistic expression. Perhaps because the software was designed to specification the "...computer became transparent in the design process, imposing little while exposing much that would have remained unimaginable."

NUMERICAL EXPERIMENTS The most sophisticated application of computer simulation is in so-called numerical experiments. In numerical experiments, powerful computers are used by scientists and mathematicians to model the interaction of forces or entities which cannot, because of either their complexity or remoteness, be tested in a laboratory. Astrophysicists, as just one example, use the computer to simulate the forces surrounding so-called "black holes," the concentration of matter that follows the collapse of a star. Mathematicians use numerical experiments to study, among other things, irreducible systems—systems that cannot easily be characterized with equations. In these experiments, the computer becomes a kind of test chamber in which entities are defined and then permitted to interact. By replaying simulations over and over again, by systematically modifying conditions in order to observe their effects, the scientist hopes to understand the dynamics of the real phenomenon.

The method of numerical experimentation is not without controversy. Traditional scientists and mathematicians point out that the computer can be deceptive. The laws controlling simulations are determined by the programmer, not by nature, and there is a persistent danger of being misled. Furthermore, the more elaborate the simulation, the greater the chance of mistaking the imagery of the simulation for the real thing. The preconscious visual processes that analyze color, form, depth relations, texture, motion, and other visual qualities are not subject to the same kinds of critical analysis as quantitative numeric data from an experiment.

Traditional scientists and mathematicians also argue that simulations are, at best, poor substitutes for so-called *analytic solutions*. An analytic solution is a mathematical formula or principle that fully quantifies the relationship between two or more variables. For example, Newton's laws of motion, an analytic model, predict the trajectories of the planets around the sun. It is not necessary to actually simulate the motion of the planets to predict their location at a given time—one simply uses the mathematical formulae. A numerical experiment designed to produce the same result would involve describing the orbits of the various planets and playing them out in the computer until reaching the moment of interest. In numerical experiments, predictions about future states are made by reproducing all the intermediate phases leading to that moment.

Some argue that in numerical experiments the computer is being used as a crutch, that these complex simulations are a substitute for genuine insight. Advocates of numerical experimentation respond that simulation is a kind of explanation and that the inherent complexity of certain kinds of systems, perhaps because their behavior emerges from complex interactions of large numbers of elements, is inherently irreducible to simple laws. According to this view, there are whole classes of problems for which no amount of imagination or insight will conceivably yield an analytic solution. They also argue that simulation is a useful way of searching for analytic solutions when they *are* possible.

visualizing the computer The world of computing is an intensely visual one. Visualization is important both in hardware and software design and in interfacing computer functioning with visual perception.

The figures show two different algorithms for "sorting," for example, arranging a list in alphabetic or numerical order. The items to be sorted are represented by a row of colored chips at the bottom. Each row represents the completion of a step in the sorting process. The visualization chronicles the sorting process as it occurs, step by step. A glance at the two visualizations makes it obvious that the sorting procedures are quite different. Visual programming languages are under development that will enable the programmer to draw the structure of a program rather than, as is currently done, by typing lines of code.

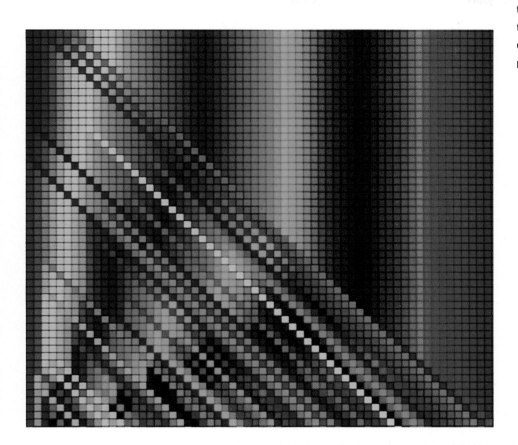

visualizing algorithms Computer programs are often so complex that it is difficult to understand exactly how a program functions. Visualization can be used to show the dynamic relationships between algorithms and data structures, sometimes while the program is actually working. These two images show different algorithms for sorting. The process is represented by the sorting of colors in successive rows from bottom to top to achieve the spectral color order, and it is apparent that the two algorithms function differently. It is easier to compare the operation of the algorithms with these visualizations than to compare the computer programs themselves.

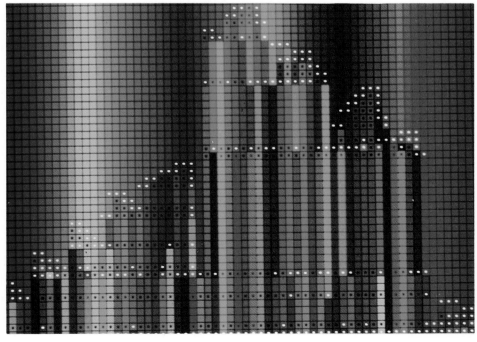

cellular automatons These one-dimensional cellular automatons by Stephen Wolfram are designed to model the behavior of "unpredictable systems." A cell can exist in any of five states indicated by the colors red, blue, yellow, green and black. In each of the figures, the top row depicts the starting status of the cells. The rows below show the status of the cells for each cycle of computation.

The three figures on these pages start with one colored element and the rest black. The three figures on pages 156–57 begin with a random distribution of initial states. As is evident in the figures, some automata establish regular rhythmic patterns while others seem to be unpredictable indefinitely—never settling into a discernible pattern. Others, not shown, go to black in a few cycles of computation.

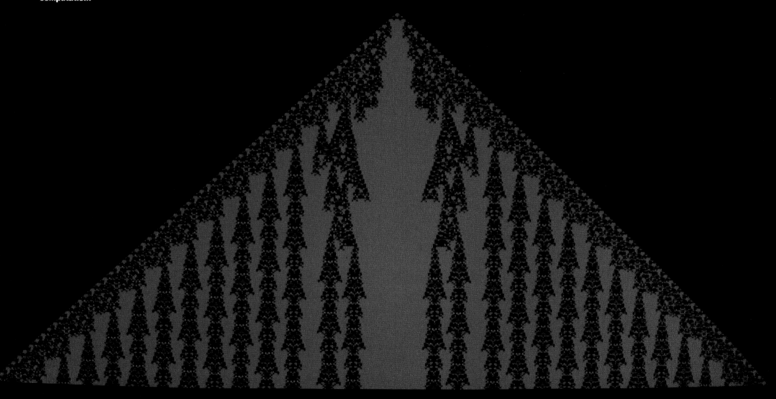

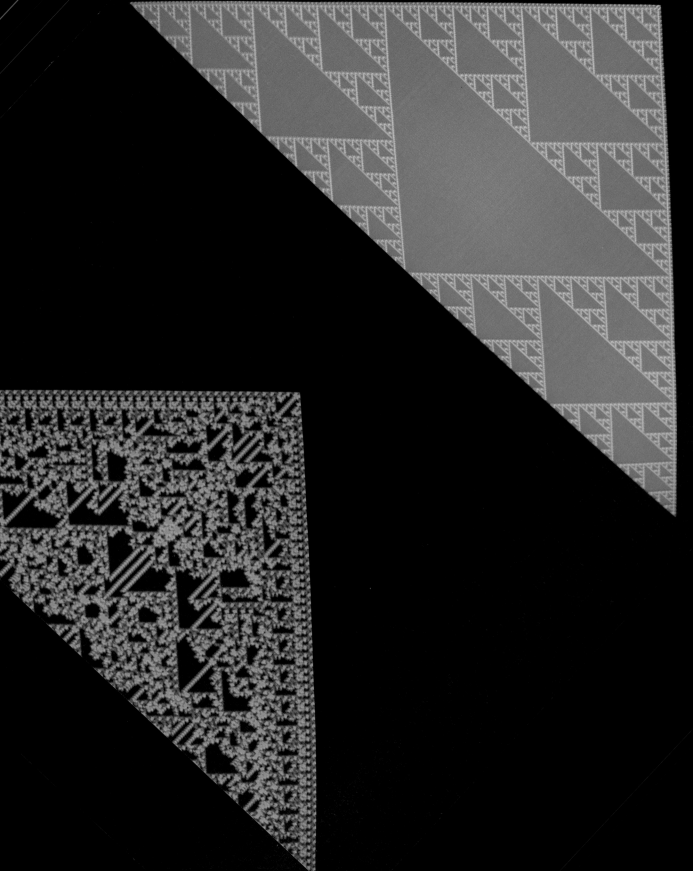

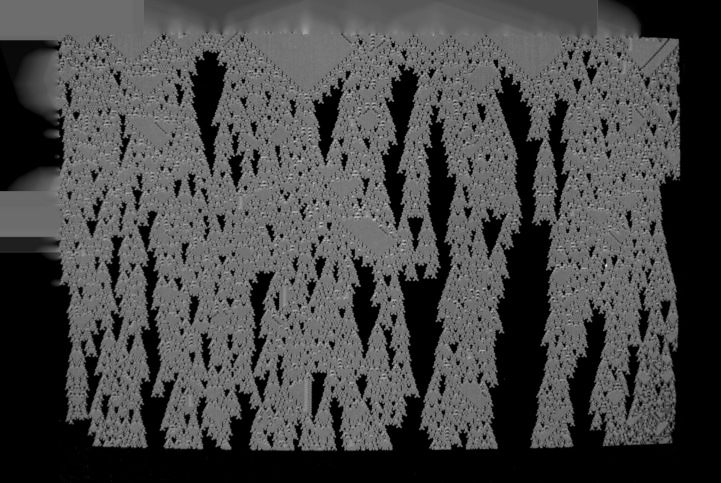

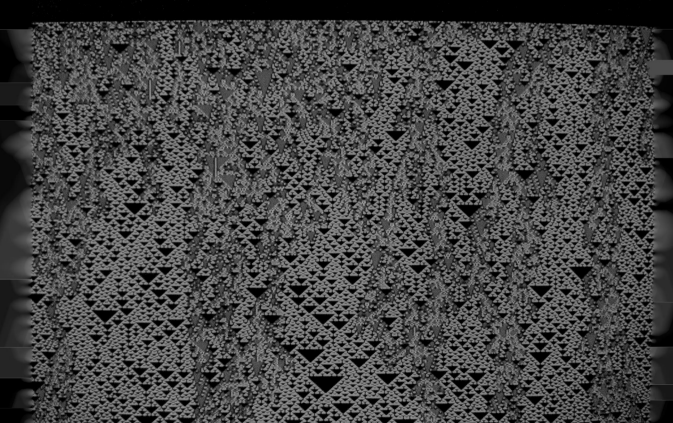

simulating a snowflake pattern with a cellular automaton

The formation of a snowflake pattern is a simple example of a numerical simulation. Snowflakes are formed as cooled water molecules lose kinetic energy. At lower temperatures, the molecules vibrate less, move closer together, and organize into a crystal. The pattern that is formed is determined by the interaction of molecules as they settle into the growing crystal structure. Slight differences in the conditions under which the water molecules are incorporated into the crystal lattice ultimately produce large-scale differences in the snowflake.

One way of studying complex systems such as a snowflake is by creating a *cellular automaton* on the computer. In a cellular-automaton simulation, a large number of simple and identical units called cells are defined within the computer. The behavior of each of the cells is governed by the status of its immediate neighbors. The behavior of the automaton—the system as a whole—depends upon the interaction of the individual cells.

In the illustration, a simulation of snowflake formation created by Stephen Wolfram, using a program developed by Norman H. Packard, is represented on a two-dimensional hexagonal grid. Cells labeled with the value of 1 are ice and those represented by 0 are water vapor. A simple algorithm governs the cells: a frozen cell does not thaw. Cells adjacent to a frozen cell will freeze unless they are surrounded by frozen cells. (In this case the cell cannot dissipate heat.) Starting with the single frozen cell in the center of the figure this simple algorithm is applied over and over again and a snowflake-like pattern emerges. The model is not meant as a true portrayal of snowflake formation but does show how the interaction of elements, defined by a set of rules, can be simulated on the computer.

Theoretically, a cellular automaton can be made to model any phenomenon since any kind of rules can be devised to control its behavior. The one-dimensional cellular automata designed by Wolfram, for example shown on pages 154–57, are used in theoretical mathematics to study "unpredictable" systems.

snowflake cellular automation A snowflake pattern produced by a "cellular automaton" simulation in which the cells have been programmed to interact in a way that parallels the interaction of freezing water molecules. Cellular automatons permit the simulation of complex phenomena that emerge from the interactions of many sub-units.

supercomputing The definition of a supercomputer continues to change as faster and more powerful computers are designed, and as ordinary mainframe and desktop computers also become more powerful. One way of characterizing the power of a computer is by the number of floating-point operations (arithmetic calculations with a moving decimal point) it can perform in a second. Present supercomputers are rated in gigaflops, or billions of floating-point operations per second. For example, the Cray-2 supercomputer is capable of 1.7 gigaflops and future models are expected to be capable of 10 gigaflops. The growth of supercomputing is linked to visualization simply because visualization is so often computationally intensive.

Since supercomputers are expensive to build and to operate, they are, for the most part, found in special supercomputing facilities. In the mid-1980s, the National Science Foundation, recognizing the importance of supercomputing for scientific and technological competitiveness, established five facilities—at the University of Illinois, Cornell University, Princeton University, University of California (San Diego), and in Pittsburgh at Carnegie-Mellon University and the University of Pittsburgh. (Several states have also been involved in the establishment of important supercomputing facilities, including Minnesota, Ohio, and Kentucky.)

Among those who played an important part in bringing about the establishment of these supercomputing centers is Larry Smarr, who founded the Illinois center and who has been an important advocate of scientific visualization. (Kenneth G. Wilson, the Nobel Prize laureate in physics, now at Ohio State University, and William H. Press, a physicist at Harvard University, also played important roles.) Smarr, a professor of physics and astronomy at Illinois, had become a proponent of scientific visualization in the mid-1970s while working on computer simulations of Einstein's theory of relativity. He recognized that computer technology itself was advancing much faster than the technologies designed to help understand the computer's output. Smarr had, in his own work, developed a computer simulation of relativity but, in the age before sophisticated computer graphics, was obliged to represent it with three-dimensional models made from paper strips. Smarr recognized that computer graphics could ultimately be used to create a far better interface—a window into the computer.

The supercomputing facility at Illinois, under Smarr's direction, has been important in advancing scientific visualization. Smarr was interested, from the very beginning, in creating an environment in which scientists with little or no experience in computational science could come and collaborate on visualizations. He brought together experts in computational science, computer graphics (including artists working on motion-picture special effects), and programming in order to develop multidisciplinary teams that could collaborate with visiting scientists to solve the various scientific and aesthetic questions that arise in visualization.

A current priority of the Illinois facility is to improve the hardware and software used in real-time interactive simulations. Since one of the important features of visualization is that it accelerates the process of exploring and comparing alternatives, ideally this would be done interactively, even with the most computationally intensive simulations. Smarr would like to develop user-friendly software and networking capabilities, so that scientists in any part of the country could interact with a supercomputing facility using a desktop computer. The ultimate goal is to make it possible for individuals in all areas of science and technology, even those with little training in computer science, to marshal the extraordinary power of the supercomputer.

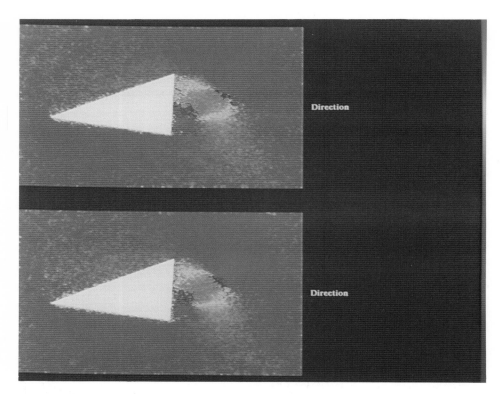

Direction

Direction

fluid dynamics Fluid dynamics is an area of physics that deals with liquids, gases and plasma. This image shows two moments in the flow of fluid around a wedge. Notice the build-up of turbulence immediately to the right of the wedge. Visualization is essential for gaining insight into fluid dynamic simulations which are often so computationally intensive that they require the most powerful computers existing.

simulating a black hole In the case of snowflake formation, it is not difficult to compare the computer simulation with the real phenomenon. In other instances of numerical experiments, it can be much more difficult. In the simulation of the astrophysical entity called a "black hole," for example, the real thing is quite small, remote in space, and invisible because it does not reflect light. Indeed, there are astrophysicists who insist that black holes do not exist at all.

Whether they exist or not, black holes have been beautifully visualized on the computer in some of the most computationally intensive simulations ever undertaken. In theory, black holes are formed as the final phase in the life of very massive stars. When a large star loses its radiant energy, matter collapses inwardly, creating a small central core of extreme density. The increasingly dense system is called a black hole because its gravitational field does not let light escape, preventing direct observation with a telescope.

An alternative to telescopic observation is to perform numerical experiments using fluid dynamics to simulate the collapse of matter (gases) into the black hole. Fluid dynamics is the area of physics that deals with entities in which the constituent particles have attractive forces too weak to form a solid. In addition to liquids, this includes gases, and plasma (a condition in which electrons are not bound to protons and neutrons to form atoms). Plasma is particularly important to astrophysicists because much of the matter of the Universe is in this form. (Aerodynamics, hydrodynamics, and meteorology are other disciplines that utilize fluid dynamics.) As might be expected, predicting the behavior of fluids is tremendously difficult, which is why fluid dynamic modeling often requires computer visualization.

Once the black hole is established, it feeds on the low-density matter that occupies the space surrounding it. The visualization created by Larry Smarr here shows the way in which a new supply of matter would fall into a black hole that had already consumed all the matter in its vicinity. False color is used to show 73 different densities of matter as it converges on the hole, with blue representing the lowest density and red the highest. In the course of the simulation, 1.28 billion data points are calculated: five separate values for each of the 25,600 sections at ten thousand or more instants in time.

black hole density Simulation showing a black hole at center. To simulate the black hole system, the region around it was divided into 25,600 separate sections. The colors portray the density of gas as it flows toward the hole with blue being the lowest density and red the highest. The rectilinear edges near the periphery of the image are the boundaries of the individual sections that make up the simulation.

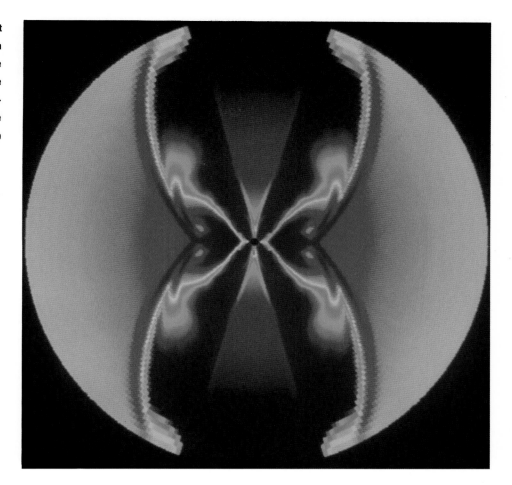

black hole pressure It is often fruitful to visualize and compare different aspects of a phenomenon, in this case pressure rather than the density of gases surrounding the black hole. Dark blue is the lowest pressure and red is the highest. Shock fronts, important to understanding black hole dynamics, are apparent as color changes. Shock fronts are easier to identify in this visualization because they are characterized by larger changes in pressure than in density.

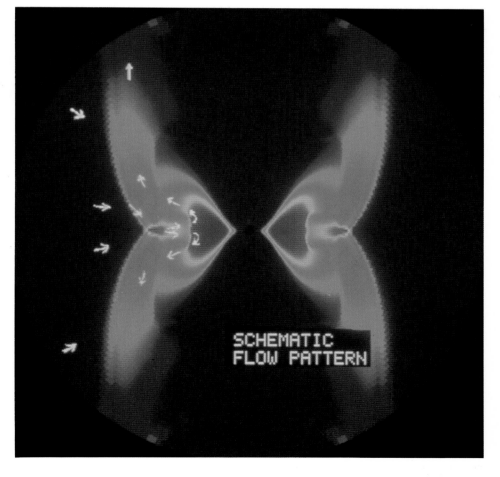

SCHEMATIC
FLOW PATTERN

Since the simulation is designed to elucidate the *dynamics* of the system, the way in which matter moves toward the hole, thousands of individual images representing separate instants in time are compiled into an animation. The animation may be studied dozens of times before another is attempted with different parameter settings.

It is characteristic of numerical experimentation that many simulations are performed to explore the way such a system would behave under a variety of theoretical conditions. In the repeated trial simulations we see something akin to the alternative testing of architecture and biochemistry. The astrophysicist is not trying to produce a single result but to reveal causal relationships. Here as in the other applications, discerning causal relationships without the graphic interface would be, practically speaking, impossible.

As mentioned earlier, one of the controversial aspects of numerical experimentation is that it is not so easily regulated by the traditional safeguards used in scientific research. Data from laboratory experiments is normally subjected to statistical analysis which helps to differentiate chance artifacts from real experimental effects. Such controls are difficult to apply to experiments performed wholly in the invented universe of the computer because the simulation derives directly from assumptions made by the investigator. Unlike standard empirical experiments, it is difficult to formalize methods, statistical or otherwise, for assessing the degree to which it matches the natural phenomenon it represents. Astrophysical computer simulations are particularly troublesome because they have great aesthetic beauty. They are so compelling that it would be easy to forget that black holes may not really exist at all.

Additionally, as Smarr points out, proper procedures for peer review, the normal method by which scientific papers are criticized before publication, have not been developed for numerical experiments. It is very difficult for scientists, remote from the site of an elaborate simulation, to know precisely how a simulation was carried out (which equations were used) or what it really looked like.

simulating a tornado Weather phenomena are often so complex that visualization is essential for understanding them. These images are frames from a supercomputer simulation of a tornado that hit Del City, Oklahoma. The "quilt-like" pattern is an artifact of the visualization technique.

numerical experiments
in theoretical mathematics

Numerical experiments are increasingly used in theoretical mathematics to investigate a variety of phenomena such as the Mandelbrot set, which was discovered by Benoit Mandelbrot who is also important to visualization as the principal exponent of fractal geometry (see *Computer Graphics*). The Mandelbrot set is a sub-set of the so-called complex numbers. It is used to understand "chaotic" systems—systems whose long-term behavior is highly sensitive to minute differences in initial conditions.

The complex numbers belonging to the Mandelbrot set are identified by an iterative process: a simple equation is used to calculate a value that is then inserted back into the equation in order to obtain the next value. Starting with a given complex number, the iteration is repeated over and over again. As it proceeds, the value of the equation will, with some complex numbers, begin to grow very large, eventually increasing to infinity. With other complex numbers, it does not. The Mandelbrot set is defined as the set that includes all complex numbers that do not go to infinity when evaluated in this way.

Complex numbers have two components and can thus be plotted on Cartesian coordinates as has been done in the illustration. The black areas correspond to numbers included in the Mandelbrot set while the colored areas correspond to numbers which are not. The colors of surrounding areas are assigned to indicate the rate at which the complex number at that location iterates to infinity. The image can be calculated with any degree of resolution and has been shown to have a fractal quality: some small regions, when enlarged, are geometrically similar to the larger scale forms.

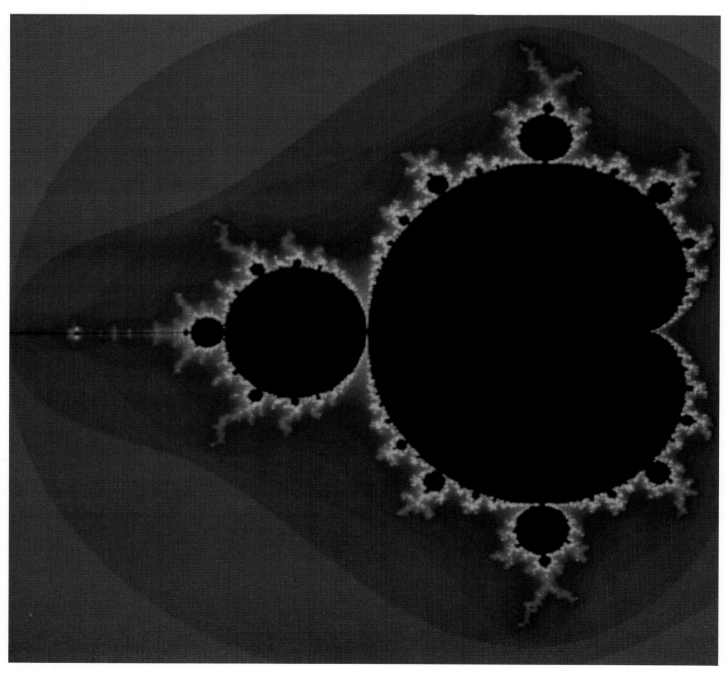

the mandelbrot set Because complex numbers have two components they can be located on the x,y coordinates. The complex numbers that do not increase to infinity when evaluated with the Mandelbrot technique are located in the black areas. Complex numbers not in the set are shown in color where color indicates how rapidly they tend toward infinity.

Below: A sub-region of the Mandelbrot set.

Other regions of the Mandelbrot set indicate the variety of shapes found in the set. Images can be produced with any resolution and have been helpful in identifying some of the important properties of the set, for example, that all members are connected.

Visualization of the Mandelbrot set has helped to reveal some of its important features, suggesting, for example, that all the clusters are connected. When the image is enlarged sufficiently there are no isolated islands. Fine filaments invariably connect the black areas if the image is produced with sufficient resolution. For mathematicians, this was an important discovery, which was made by visualizing the set on the computer, although the discovery had to be confirmed by mathematical proof.

While the use of computer visualization is controversial in other areas of science, it is especially so in mathematics. Numerical experimentation, the idea of exploring simulations visually in order to discover important relationships, is inherently foreign to mathematicians who are accustomed to the method of the logical proof. For this reason, it remains to be seen whether visualization, specifically numerical experimentation, will have the importance in mathematics that it is beginning to have in some of the other sciences.

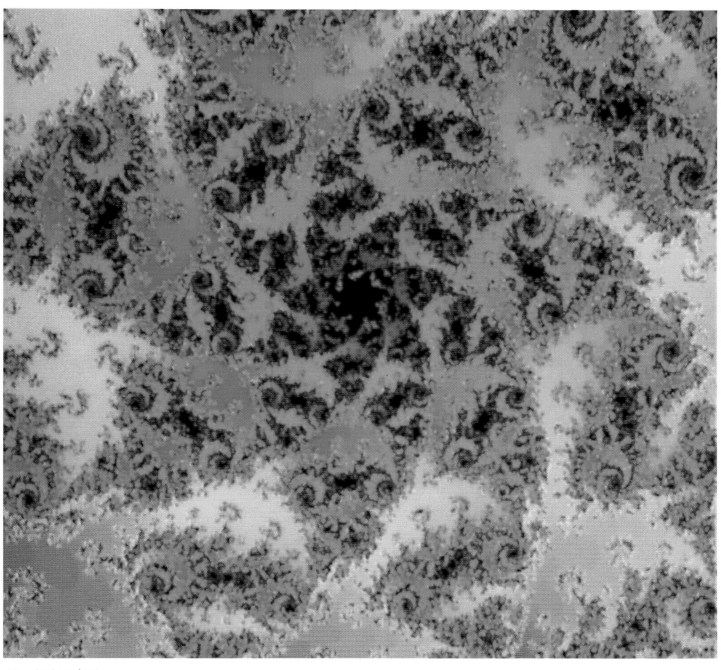

simulations as visual experiments

It is well worth considering in detail both the similarities and the differences between simulations and more traditional kinds of laboratory experiments. It is only by making this comparison that we can clarify the proper role of the computer and guard against confusing one kind of investigation for the other.

A good place to start is with a simple distinction that is always made in empirical science—the distinction between independent and dependent variables. In laboratory experiments, independent variables are the conditions we set up and control directly. Dependent variables are the quantities we seek to measure—the response we cannot predict but which is assumed to be determined in some way by the independent variable. A successful experiment reveals the relationship between the two.

In simulations, as in laboratory experiments, there are factors that can be controlled directly and one or more unknowns that are being evaluated. In designing a molecule with template forcing, for example, conformation is varied to determine its relation to potential energy. Conformation can be thought of as analogous to the independent variable and potential energy as analogous to the dependent variable. Similarly, in black-hole simulation, the initial state determined by the astrophysicist can be thought of as the independent variable and the resulting "flow of matter" into the black-hole system as a dependent variable. It is interesting to make this distinction even when thinking about non-scientific simulations. In architecture, a change is made in a design in order to determine its effect on either aesthetic, economic, or engineering values. The design change can be thought of as an independent variable and its effects can be thought of as changes in dependent variables.

The advantage to formulating even non-scientific simulations in this way, even when it might seem somewhat artificial, is that it clarifies the role of the computer. A problem should be visualized both 1) when there is a formidable computational barrier to calculating values of a dependent variable, and 2) when the dependent variable is either inherently visual or so complex (as in black-hole simulations) that visualization is required to perceive the way it changes.

Without the computer, attention must first be directed to computation and only secondarily to comparison of values of the dependent variable. All too often, in both science and design, the complexity of the computation limits our view of the dependent variable to a few "snapshots." With visualization, however, it is possible to get an unobstructed sense of the behavior of the unknown for many, perhaps all, values of the independent variable. Indeed, if the visualization can be made interactive, it is sometimes possible, as in template forcing, to "steer" toward a desirable value of the dependent variable.

Simulations follow the form of an experiment, testing one kind of variable against another, but only as they have been defined to the computer. Although this distinction is widely appreciated, it is still difficult not to be "taken in" by the visualization. Once a full-color, shaded, three-dimensional (perhaps presented stereographically), animated image of the movement of a complex biomolecule is seen, for example, it is difficult to conceptualize it in any other way even if the equations used to create the visualization are wrong. The advancement of visualization in the future cannot, therefore, only be based on technological discovery. It is equally important to come to grips with the whole problem of conducting experiments in the invented universe within the computer.

objectification Visualization takes advantage of the fact that the eye and the visual brain are powerful information processors. Unlike a computer, however, the eye/brain is not equally adaptable to every kind of task. It is specifically adapted to recognizing and differentiating objects on the basis of two-dimensional patterns that are projected to the retinas. Whether we are speaking of color vision, stereopsis, form perception, or other aspects of vision, the visual mechanisms are designed to analyze the patterns on the retinas specifically for features that are useful for categorizing objects.

To take full advantage of the capabilities of the eye/brain, therefore, the goal of visualization should be *objectification.* By "objectification," it is meant that a phenomenon, whether it is inherently visual or not, should be represented as something that has form, color, texture, motion, and other qualities of objects. Visualization often serves the purpose of objectifying a relationship between an independent and a dependent variable. For example, the template forcing animation objectifies the relationship between conformation and potential energy. In reality, there is no way of controlling conformation in the way that it is done on the computer. The animation does not depict a real process; it objectifies a relation between independent and dependent variables. It turns it into a visible thing.

It is sometimes more difficult to recognize this objectification outside of science. We have to remind ourselves that even aesthetic questions are answered by experiments, by a trial-and-error process, which gradually reveals a relation of one kind or another. Designers may protest that they do not require so many intermediate values for a "dependent" variable. An architect, given the way things are traditionally done, may not feel an urgent need for a system that permits modification by degree. It can be argued, however, that if systems become available to permit objectification of variables usually inaccessible to the designer it will have a significant impact on the design process. It is reasonable to assume that if an architect could "walk through" a realistic ray-traced rendering of a building (not a floor plan, but a real looking environment) during the earliest phases of the design process it would have an effect on the outcome of the design. In that case, the architect would be objectifying independent-dependent variable relations that were previously unavailable only because of logistical and computational barriers.

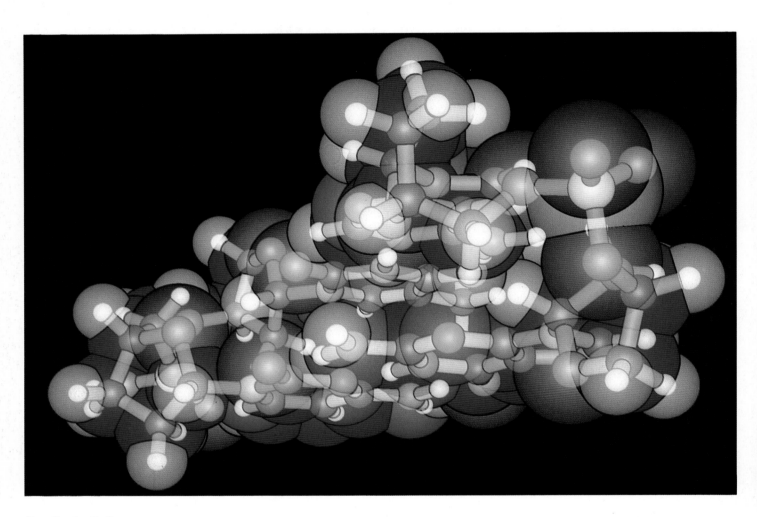

alternative visualizations This double exposure overlays two methods for representing biomolecules such as the DNA shown. The inner representation is a conventional "ball-and-stick" model in which atoms are represented by balls and atomic bonds by sticks. The surrounding representation is a "space-filling" model in which atoms are represented as energy fields. These superimposed models, which would normally be shown separately, demonstrate that the conventions of pictorial realism can be employed in different ways to show different aspects of a non-visual phenomenon.

surrealism in visualization Since details of molecular structure are smaller than the shortest wavelength of light, and molecules are not objects in the conventional sense, they do not have the smooth surfaces, highlights, or shadows depicted in the rendering of DNA shown here. This image has been rendered with these qualities to facilitate perception of the all-important three-dimensional structure of the molecule. Shadows, highlights, obscuration, and other monocular depth cues can be useful in visualizing the molecule even though they are not meant as literal features.

In a sense, this is surrealism as it applies to visualization. For instance, in Yves Tanguy's *Indefinite Divisibility,* the schemata of realistic painting are used to depict imaginary objects. Linear perspective, sourced light and shadows, and other conventions are used to create a sense of reality in this otherwise unreal scene. It is the contrast between the exaggerated realism and the fantasy subject matter that creates the unsettling effect. In scientific visualization, the schemata of realism can be very useful in communicating information although they must be used with great discretion since they can also be misleading.

surrealism Yves Tanguy, *Indefinite Divisibility*. 1942. Oil on canvas, 40 x 35". Albright-Knox Art Gallery, Buffalo, New York. Room of Contemporary Art Fund, 1945.

emergent technologies

I will found my enjoyments on the affections of the heart, the visions of the imagination, and the spectacle of nature.
Etienne Louis Malus

In science, the word *emergent* has come to have a more specific meaning than it does in ordinary usage. In evolutionary biology, for example, a feature is said to be emergent if it seems to have arisen from a combination of already existing features. For example, the first cells with a defined nucleus, the eukaryotes, had emergent qualities which resulted from the fact that they were formed from the association of a wide variety of non-nucleated cells, the prokaryotes. In some fashion, diverse kinds of prokaryotes combined to form a new kind of single-cell organism that would, eventually, be capable of evolving into multicellular animals due to its ability to differentiate into diverse tissues. The new eukaryotic cell had emergent qualities.

The word emergent is not, however, limited to use in evolutionary biology. In neuroscience, as another example, consciousness is sometimes characterized as an emergent phenomenon because it arises, again in some complex way, from an interaction—in this case among neurons. There are many other phenomena that may be called emergent. Indeed the word should be used whenever the interaction among different elements produces something new and unanticipated.

Using this definition, the field of visualization can be thought of as emergent. The ideas and technologies that have been brought together under its banner, as we have seen, come from many different sources including vision research, art and art history, remote sensing, image processing, diagnostic imaging, holography, computer graphics, mathematics, and other disciplines. Until recently, there were no compelling reasons to think beyond these disciplines—to consider what would result from their commingling. Specialists tended to stay within their own fields and ideas rarely jumped from one application to another.

The boom in digital computing changed all that. Computer scientists sometimes use the expression "digital is forever" to describe the transcendent quality of digital data. When data is in a digital form, it can be processed by any kind of digital computer. This means that machines developed for one application can be easily linked to digital machines designed for a different purpose. The algorithms, furthermore, developed in one field are easily adapted, or used directly, in other fields.

The technologies presented in this chapter are emergent because they have been ingeniously devised from technologies already in use. Since they are new, they do not necessarily produce the best images and, sometimes, it is difficult to judge their ultimate importance or how they might evolve in the future. Whatever happens, they are very important because they are the very first technologies that are entirely unique to the new discipline called visualization.

synthetic fly-over: combining image processing and computer graphics

The images shown on the following pages appear, at first, to be ordinary aerial photographs of Los Angeles. In fact, they demonstrate the capabilities that can result from combining image processing and computer graphics. The video from which these images have been taken creates the impression that we are in an airplane flying over the city at a low altitude. Ahead, we see mountains and the landscape changing in perspective as we fly over. The remarkable thing about the images is that they were produced from a two-dimensional satellite image. The computer was used to build, in its memory, the three-dimensional model we see in the pictures. Unfortunately, still images do not convey the remarkable sensation of flying over hills, and other features, that one experiences seeing the movie.

To produce the animation, a single image from a Landsat satellite was combined with a topographical map. First, prominent features common to both were used to geometrically conform the Landsat image to the topographical map. To produce an individual frame of the animation, a viewpoint was chosen over the scene. Algorithms similar to those used for ray-tracing were then used to calculate the color and the altitude of every point visible in the image. (For discussions of geometric processing see *Images from Energy;* for ray-tracing see *Computer Graphics.*) A "line" was drawn from the viewpoint through a plane of pixels to the topographical map that gave the color from the Landsat image and elevation at that point.

The animated sequence, which was created by Kevin Hussey, Bob Mortensen and Jeff Hall at the Digital Image Animation Laboratory (DIAL) at Jet Propulsion Laboratories, was made by producing video frames one at a time from sequential viewpoints. Over 3,000 frames were produced for a three-minute movie that required five-and-a-half days of computer time on a machine capable of 4 million computer instructions per second. The final animation has approximately 2.6 billion bytes of data—the equivalent of 1.3 million pages of alphanumeric text.

The simulated fly-over has many applications, the most obvious of which is in the interpretation of satellite reconnaissance data for espionage and arms control verification purposes. Many features that are camouflaged in still images are revealed when a movie is made, particularly if the viewer can choose viewpoints freely. Because of this, the fly-over technique can also be used to show fighter pilots inaccessible enemy territory as a method for pre-programming drone planes.

combining techniques **Following pages: One new hybrid technology combines techniques of remote sensing, telemetry, image processing, and computer graphics, in this case to synthesize a three-dimensional fly-over of the Los Angeles area from a two-dimensional satellite image. The technique combined topographic data supplied by the United States Defense Mapping Agency with a Landsat image (page 174) to calculate viewpoints from an imaginary freely moving airborne camera. The two other images are frames from the animation,** *L.A.: The Movie.* **The elevations are exaggerated by a factor of two.**

combining image processing, computer stereopsis, and computer graphics

In the preceding example, the elevation data used to transform the two-dimensional Landsat image into a three-dimensional fly-over was derived from geological surveys. It is impressive that the computer can be used to combine these two different kinds of information, but there is an easier way of producing elevation information that requires only image data. This should not be too surprising because, after all, the eye/brain builds up a three-dimensional world utilizing only the two-dimensional images that are projected to the retinas. Depth perception is complex, but one visual subsense, stereopsis, yields depth information simply by measuring disparity, the difference in horizontal position, of identical forms in the retinal images of the left and right eyes (see *We Create the World We See*). The computer can similarly be used to identify identical elements in left and right images and can use the difference in their horizontal position to estimate their relative distance.

In *computer* stereopsis, a pair of images, left and right views, are made with a stereo camera or by other means. The computer searches the image pair looking for areas that are similar by a method of statistical correlation. When two areas in the image correlate statistically, they are judged to represent the same object. Those areas of the image are then measured for their horizontal disparity, which indicates their distance relative to other forms in the image.

computer stereopsis A pair of radar images made from two points in the orbit of a space shuttle was analyzed by the computer for disparity. The computer, mimicking human stereopsis, then generated a three-dimensional model in its memory which can be used to produce virtually any view of Mount Shasta. The elevation of the mountain has been exaggerated to enhance topographical features.

The illustration on pages 176–77 shows twenty views of a three-dimensional model of Mount Shasta in northern California that was created with computer stereopsis. The computer was used to analyze a pair of radar images made from two points in the orbit of the space shuttle. The two images, of course, were separated by a distance much greater than the two inches between the left and right eyes. This, however, does not matter as the stereoptic method can still be employed. The computer searched the pair of images for areas that were identical and then measured their disparity relative to the background. It was thus able to determine the relative distance of various features. This information could then be used to "build" a three-dimensional model of the terrain in the computer's memory.

The original space shuttle images were, of course, from a top-down perspective. The remarkable thing about the false-colored images seen here is that Mount Shasta is shown from a side view. The computer produced this image by deriving the depth information in a top-down image pair and then building a three-dimensional object in its memory. This object was then rendered as an image with computer-graphics methods. Of course, any "view" of the computer model could have been produced just as easily.

In this visualization technique, the computer mimics an aspect of visual perception by generating a three-dimensional model from two flat images—an achievement that again underscores the increasingly intimate relationship between vision science and visualization.

miranda fly-over: combining image processing, computer graphics, computer stereopsis, and animation

In the preceding example, still images are described, but it is also possible to create an animated fly-over with the same technique simply by producing a series of renderings from sequential viewpoints. This possibility has been realized dramatically by the Jet Propulsion Laboratories group which has synthesized a fly-over of Miranda, a moon of the distant planet Uranus. Unlike the Los Angeles Basin, there was no existing data base of topographical information that could be used to synthesize a fly-over. Instead, the depth information was derived from images, in a manner similar to the Mount Shasta example, sent back from the space probe Voyager II.

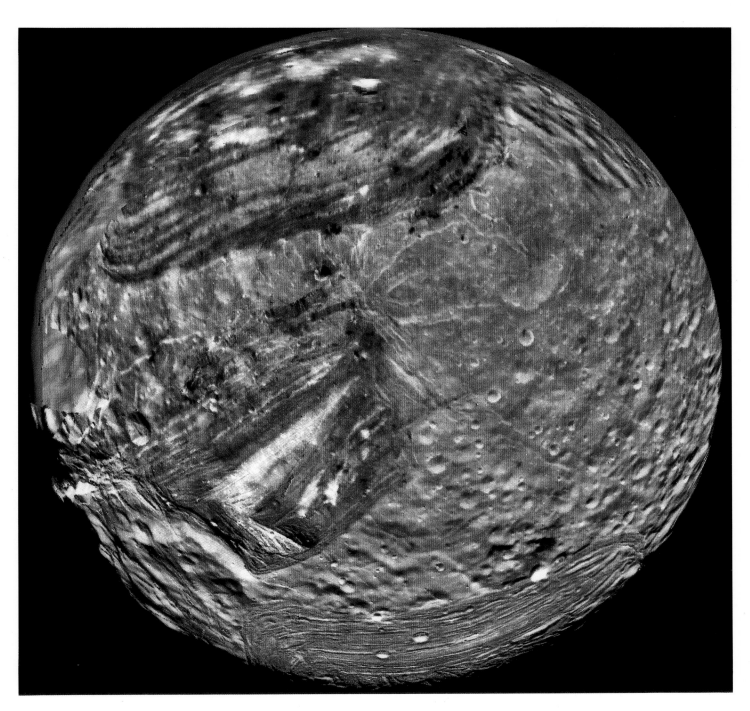

stereoptically generated movie Above and following pages: Computer stereopsis was combined with the fly-over technique to synthesize this fly-over of Miranda—a remarkable feat since Miranda is a moon of the distant planet Uranus, which is more than a billion and a half miles from Earth. Elevation data were calculated from the disparity in overlapping images transmitted from Voyager II. The illustration above is a composite of Voyager II images. The following illustrations are frames from the fly-over movie. Elevations are exaggerated by a factor of three. The elevation data were calculated by the United States Geological Service, Flagstaff, Arizona, and then combined with image data by Jet Propulsion Laboratory and NASA.

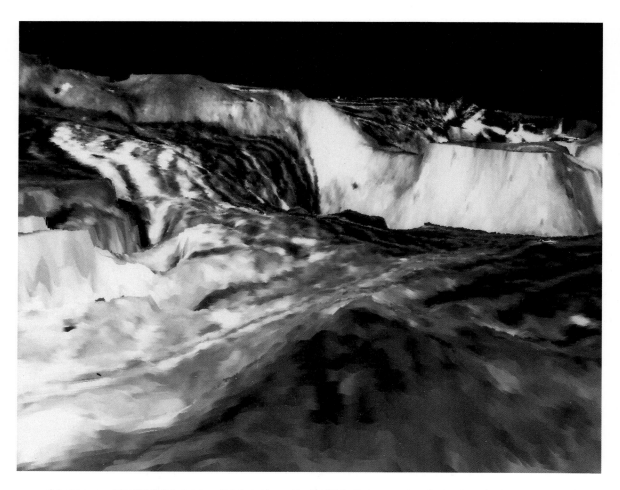

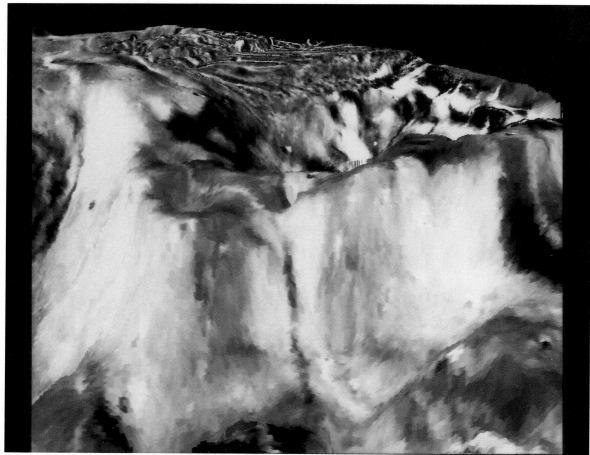

Voyager transmitted a sequence of images that, for this visualization, was assembled in the computer into a composite with overlapping areas. The overlapping images could then be used as stereopairs since they provide two perspectives on the same terrain. The computer then found matching areas in pairs of images and used their disparity to determine relative distance. The moving sequence was produced a frame at a time and creates the impression of flying over Miranda at an altitude of 3 to 20 miles. The apparent detail in the fly-over is all the more remarkable given that Uranus is the third most distant planet in the solar system—more than a billion and a half miles from Earth.

The DIAL group is currently producing a fly-over of an area of Mars produced from data returned from the Viking Orbiter in 1975. The simulated Mars fly-over is a prelude to a hoped-for manned mission which would require detailed knowledge of possible Martian landing sites and their surrounding areas.

The DIAL group is also involved in intensive research on methods for generating these kinds of animations more conveniently at a lower cost. One of the most important areas of research is in improving the stereopsis algorithms that are computationally very intensive. New methods will accelerate the process and provide more precise depth information with greater resolution. Ultimately, it would be desirable to simulate such fly-overs in real time, as is done with flight simulators, although the required rate of computation exceeds the capabilities of current computers (see the section on "parallel computing").

The techniques described above, computer stereopsis and computer fly-overs, properly belong to the field of visualization rather than to remote sensing. This is because they can be easily adapted for many different applications far afield from satellite or space probe reconnaissance. The fly-over technique could just as easily be adapted to visualize data from scanning-electron microscopy, such as the surface of a micro-organism. Computer stereopsis can, and should, be used whenever it would be desirable to create a three-dimensional model from two-dimensional image pairs.

volume visualization: combining image processing, computer graphics, and tomography

Another technique that properly belongs to the discipline of visualization is a hybrid of image processing and computer graphics called *volume visualization*. In volume visualization, which has come out of medical diagnostics, a three-dimensional form is defined in the computer from a sequence of cross-sectional images such as those produced by tomography (see *Images from Energy*).

The example here shows how this has been done with laser scans of a puff of smoke. The laser beam was used to cut through the puff in successive planes to provide a series of photographic cross-sections. The cross-sections were then compiled in the computer to produce a three-dimensional representation of the whole puff. Once represented in three dimensions, the puff can be rotated, enlarged, and examined interactively in real time.

A series of cross-sections of this smoke puff were made by "slicing" the puff with a laser. The cross-sections were then used to assemble a volume image in the computer. Volume visualization is becoming an essential tool in medical diagnostics. Imagine trying to form a mental model of the whole smoke puff from a series of cross-sectional slices. This is, essentially, what a physician must do to understand the structure of a three-dimensional lesion from tomographic cross-sections without volume visualization. Created by Pixar. Data courtesy of Professors Juan Agüí and Lambertus Hesselink, Department of Aeronautics and Astronautics, Stanford University. © 1987 Pixar. All Rights Reserved.

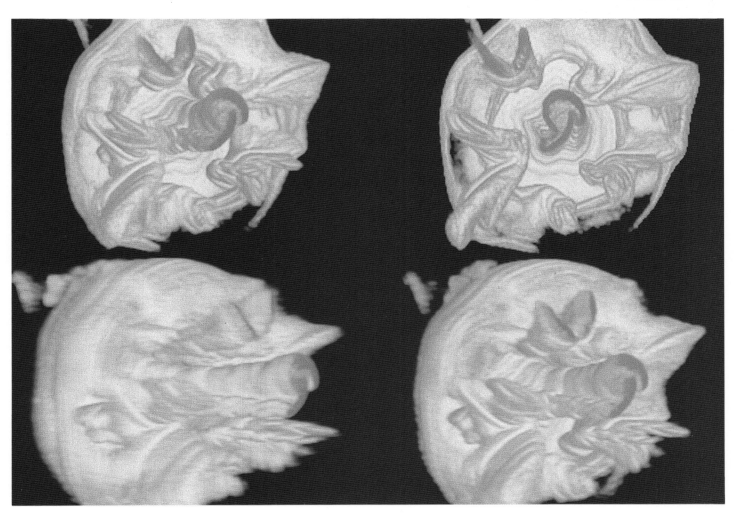

volume visualization of
computer tomography

Fifty-nine CT scans were compiled to create this three-dimensional model which is rendered with computer-graphics shading techniques. In four of the images, bone is rendered as solid white, muscle and organs are rendered semi-transparent in red, and fat tissue is rendered as transparent green. In the others, skin and fat tissue are rendered transparent (invisible) and soft tissue is shaded to reveal its surface structure. The protruding filaments are blood vessels. Data courtesy of Elliot Fishman, M.D., Johns Hopkins Hospital. Created by Pixar.

© 1987 Pixar. All Rights Reserved.

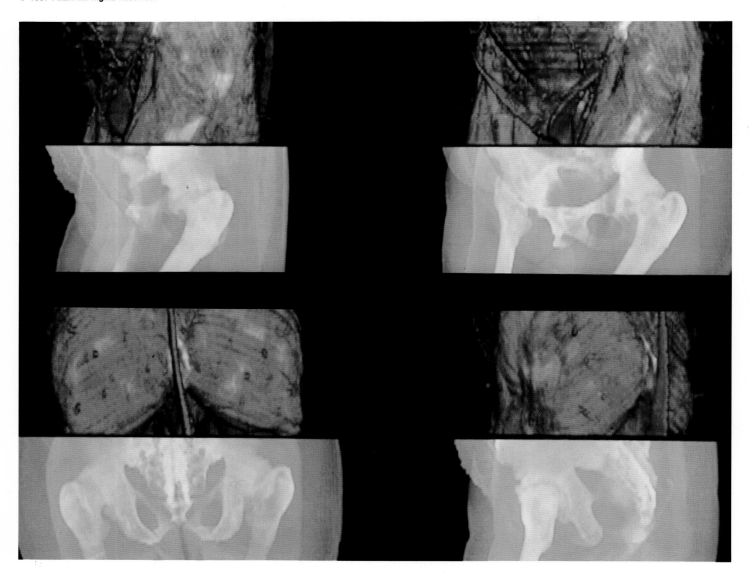

volume visualization of a head This fibrous dysplasia patient suffers from abnormal bone tissue growth on the right side of the face and deformation of the skull. In these images, volume visualization utilizing computer-graphics shading techniques visualizes structures of interest. The top image visualizes the skin surface while in the middle image the skin and interior soft tissue have been made transparent to portray bone structure. At bottom, the top and back half of the skull have been edited out to give a cross-sectional view of the abnormal bone tissue. Data courtesy of Hugh Curtin, M.D., and David W. Johnson, M.D. Department of Radiology, University Health Centers of Pittsburgh, Pittsburgh, Pennsylvania. © 1987, Pixar.

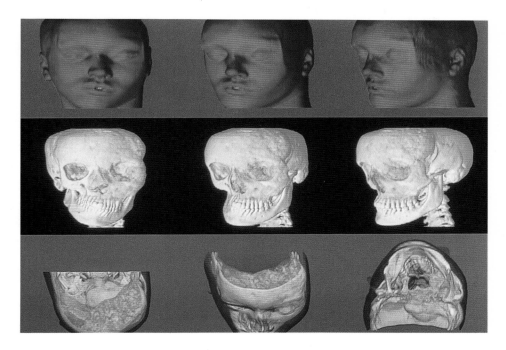

In the illustration at left, the same kind of volume visualization has been made from X-ray tomography images. Standard X-ray tomograms represent slices through the body and are generally viewed as a series. A computer-graphics system can be used to compile such slices into a three-dimensional model just as has been done with the puff of smoke. The method of volume visualization can also be used with other tomographic techniques such as PET and MR or any other process that yields sequential slices. The three-dimensional object can also be displayed on a special stereographic terminal so that the three-dimensional form can be seen with stereopsis.

Volume visualization in medical diagnostics is much more informative than sequential cross-sections because the physician does not have to *infer* three-dimensional structure. Imagine trying to mentally construct a model of the puff of smoke given only the cross-sectional images. This would be extremely difficult but is analogous to what is expected of a physician who must discern the form of a tumor from a series of tomographic cross-sections. Two important visual subsenses, stereopsis and motion parallax (the depth sense that relies on motion), cannot be used at all unless the object is volume visualized on a stereographic terminal. This particular application is an excellent example of the

way in which visualization technology can shift information processing from higher levels of the brain, conscious processes, to the preconscious processes of the visual system. Instead of using reasoning to infer the shape of a tumor, for example, the physician simply *sees* it on the screen as a three-dimensional object. Eventually, surgeons will be able to rehearse procedures that require great precision with the help of volume visualizations. Before an actual operation they will be able to "operate" on the computer model. Indeed, it may eventually be possible to pre-program numerically controlled surgical instruments giving greater exactitude to surgical procedures.

Volume visualization is another example of a technique that transcends disciplines. It can be used whenever a transduction technique yields two-dimensional cross-sections. Although the technique is still very new, it has already been used in a number of areas outside of medicine such as in the visualization of weather systems, fluid and gas dynamics, and for terrain mapping.

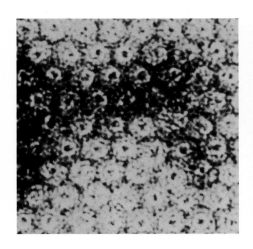

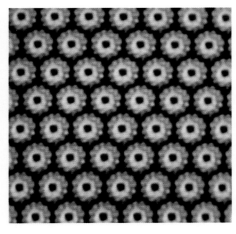

visualizing the bacteriophage: combining electron microscopy, image processing, and computer graphics

visualizing a bacteriophage The process of visualizing the three-dimensional structure of the bacteriophage, a virus that infects bacteria, begins when a crystal is made. In this electron micrograph, each hexagonal structure is one "neck" region. The sample has been stained to enhance structural details.

Image processing removes visual "noise" in the micrograph. Data from 30 micrographs, each taken at a different angle, are analyzed by the computer to develop a three-dimensional representation of the density of the virus.

The visualization of the details of a bacteriophage, a virus that infects a bacteria, demonstrates how certain visualization techniques can be combined to solve a particularly difficult problem, in this case visualizing the smallest actors in the biological microworld. The bacteriophage is molecular in scale. To visualize it, a number of different techniques including electron microscopy, Fourier analysis and edge-detection (image-processing techniques), and interactive computer graphics were combined.

Even though a virus does not have morphological structures that compare with those of multicellular organisms, the researchers decided to visualize a narrow portion of the bacteriophage which can be referred to as the "neck." They did this by first crystalizing the bacteriophage. In a crystal, molecules come together to form a repeating structure. By

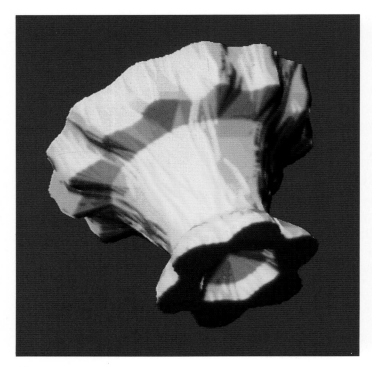

making a cross-section of the crystal, we can discern repeating patterns that are a clue to the organism's three-dimensional geometry.

First, however, electron micrographs of the cross-sections must be made in order to see the patterns. By tilting the stage of the electron microscope a few degrees between each exposure, electron micrographs are made at different angles. Fourier analysis is then used on the set of micrographs to clarify them. Although it is difficult to interpret, the two-dimensional micrographs taken together contain information about the densities within the three-dimensional geometry of the bacteriophage. An analogy can be made to computerized tomography (see *Images from Energy*) in which the densities within a volume are reconstructed from a series of readings made at different angles circumscribing the body.

Unfortunately, this tomography-like process does not, alone, reveal the *structure* of the bacteriophage neck. It is just a rough reconstruction of its density. To begin to delineate structure, the rough three-dimensional form was "sliced" on the computer into adjacent planes. In this way, edge-enhancement-type techniques (see *Images from Energy*) could be used to make a well defined stack of cross-sections.

Once this has occurred, three-dimensional computer-graphics techniques can be used to create a cleaner model. All the previous steps were designed to give the computer graphicist an outline of a form. This outline is used as the basis for synthesizing a computer-graphics object. This last step is partially subjective. The computer graphicist uses judgment in creating an idealized structure.

The visualization of the bacteriophage is interesting because of the variety of techniques used. The original data were obtained in two dimensions by electron microscopy—a transduction technique. Image processing was used in a tomography-like process to create a three-dimensional data base. Edge-detection techniques were used to identify boundaries in two-dimensional cross-sections of the three-dimensional data base. A final rendering was then made with computer graphics. The whole process is an example of the remarkable possibilities created by combining the basic tools of visualization.

Again, although it was developed for this special application, we can think of this technique as emergent and as belonging to the discipline of visualization. It can be applied to a wide variety of problems in which the structure of a microscopic entity must be determined from two-dimensional electron micrographs.

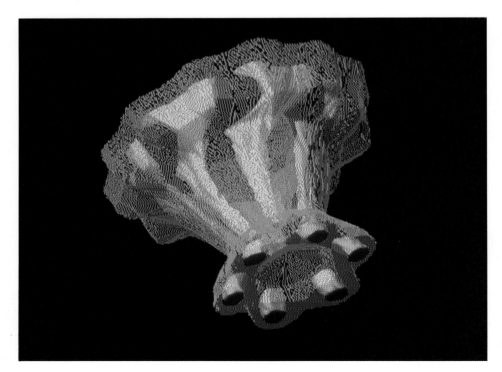

The representation of density was cut into planes, in the computer, and two sets of contours were defined for the resulting cross-sections. The first set of contours followed regions of low-staining densities and were compiled, with a technique akin to volume visualization, to form this three-dimensional image which emphasizes the outer surface of the virus.

The second set of contours, which traced higher density areas of the micrographs, was compiled into a three-dimensional form that emphasizes structures within the virus.

The two images have been superimposed to yield a visualization combining all the identified features.

combining computers with holography

The holographer's ideal, the full-color, wide-angle realistic holographic movie, remains a technological challenge but there are some indications that the digital computer may play a very important, and somewhat unanticipated, role in bringing it closer to reality.

Holography is a difficult medium with which to work because traditional holograms must be exposed with laser light in vibration free environments, which seriously limits the kinds of subjects that are suitable. Holograms must also be displayed under congenial conditions, often with laser light or at least point sources of white light arranged at precise angles. If the computer is used in the holographic process, however, the problems normally encountered in production can be, at least theoretically, bypassed.

computer-generated holographic

stereograms

The holographic stereogram is a hybrid of holography and stereophotography which uses holography to display series of stereographic images without the need for a special viewer or polarized glasses (see *Images from Energy*). We have already seen that object-based graphics systems can produce a stereopair simply by rendering images from two viewpoints separated horizontally by a couple of inches (see *Computer Graphics*). The computer can also be used to create the thousand or more perspectives required for a holographic stereogram. Once the images have been rendered, they are used to make strip holograms and assembled into a holographic sterogram. The result is that a holographic stereogram can be made of a scene that has been synthesized entirely within the computer.

computer-generated full-color holographic stereogram State-of-the-art computer-graphics techniques were used to create this holographic stereogram of a still life by Wendy Plesniak and Michael Klug. A holographic stereogram requires a series of two-dimensional perspectives which can be easily generated with object-based computer graphics. It displays the imaginary computer-generated objects in color and in three dimensions without a stereoviewer and thus has great significance for visualization. It could be used to produce a three-dimensional record of a computer simulation or of a design, for example an architectural structure, that was created with the computer.

computer-generated laser-transmission

holograms We have already seen earlier that the computer can be used to model light (see *Computer Graphics*). The computer-graphics technique called ray-tracing, for example, uses algorithms based on the classical formulae of optics to simulate reflection, refraction and other phenomena in order to render images with photographic realism.

Ray-tracing, however, does not model every aspect of light. Light has a dualistic nature—it can be considered both as particles that travel in straight lines or as waves (see *Images from Energy*). Ray-tracing is based only on the particle model which is sufficient for conventional renderings since the wave properties of light are not usually apparent.

In order to imitate the holographic process with the computer, the *wave* properties of light need to be modeled. As computationally intensive as ray-tracing is, it is dwarfed by the complexities of modeling the wave interactions that produce the interference patterns that are the basis of holography. Nonetheless, in the last few years, a number of holographers have been at work on the problem and have synthesized some simple holograms. They have found that, in addition to the problems inherent in modeling the wave properties of light, they also face difficulties in the physical production of the hologram, since interference patterns are microscopic and must be reproduced within exact tolerances. The hologram is made by exposing a photographic plate with a digitally controlled laser, although producing high quality holograms in this way has proved difficult.

Given the rate at which visualization is advancing, perhaps it will not be too long before computer-synthesized holograms comparable to those made in the holography studio will be produced. Such advancements would make it possible to produce holograms free of the restrictions of the studio such as the requirement that it be free of vibration (a restriction which, except for pulsed holograms, excludes living subjects). Computer-synthesized holograms could be produced from image data from virtually any source. Holograms could be produced from volume visualizations, from astrophysical simulations—from any digital data base. Indeed, the time may come when it is possible to produce a hologram from a stereograph. The computer could conceivably use stereopsis to create a three-dimensional model (see earlier section) which could then be rendered as a hologram. Thus, one could "take" a hologram as simply as taking a stereophotograph.

mit media lab One of the most exciting institutions involved in the development of new media technologies, some of which are directly relevant to visualization, is the Media Lab at the Massachusetts Institute of Technology. Co-founded and directed by Nicholas Negroponte, a professor of computer graphics at MIT, and Jerome Wiesner, MIT's President Emeritus, the Media Lab has attracted some of the greatest innovators in media technology, computer science, music, optics, psychology, and holography. Among them are Seymour Papert, a leading advocate of computerized education, Alan Kay, an innovator of personal computers (see "The Graphic Interface"), Stephen Benton, a leader in the field of holography, and Marvin Minsky, an expert in artificial intelligence.

The Media Lab focuses on twelve general areas, which include interactive and high-definition television research, electronic publishing, movies of the future, spatial imaging, music and cognition, human interface research, computer graphics and animation, computer speech understanding, education technology, vision science, and experimental film and video technology. These areas are, however, loosely defined—the idea of the Lab is to bring diverse experts together to collaborate and to invent.

One has only to look at the spatial imaging group (holography), headed by Benton, to see the advantage of cross-discipline collaboration. In addition to pioneering research on existing categories of holography, the spatial imaging group is involved in developing new techniques, some of which utilize the computer. They are improving the quality and ease of production of computer-generated holographic stereograms and developing the computer-synthesized equivalent of the transmission hologram. Their research team is made up not only of artists and holographers but also of computer scientists. The Media Lab was created to foster precisely this type of collaboration and, because of it, is becoming an important center for technological innovation.

parallel computing: combining computers with computers

A different kind of emergent technology results when multiple computers are linked together. A conventional computer has only one central processing unit and so can perform only one operation at a time. A new breed of computer, however, links many central processing units together so that many computational tasks can be performed simultaneously. The result is not only the acceleration of the rate at which computing can be done, but also the possibility of a new kind of computing of special relevance to visualization.

A conventional computer-graphics system with a single central processing unit renders different components of an image in separate stages. It might break up the rendering task into four steps: first determining which surfaces need to be rendered and then calculating the image's red, green, and blue components. A process such as this is said to be *sequential*.

A new kind of computer, which uses separate central processing units to tackle portions of the computational problem simultaneously, is said to process information in *parallel*. While relatively inexpensive commercial parallel computers have only a small number of processors, other parallel computers have considerably more—sometimes tens of thousands. Such "highly" parallel computers promise to revolutionize computing but also present formidable programming challenges.

parallel vs. sequential computing

The typical computer, whether a desktop model or an industrial mainframe, has three central components. It has a memory that stores instructions and data. The memory is connected through a "bus"'—a switching device—to a central processing unit. Data and instructions are sent through the bus to the processor where the data is operated upon and then returned to the memory. When it comes time to print, to output to a monitor, or to communicate in some other way, the bus is used to direct information to the proper device.

The underlying idea of the computer is that any task can be broken down into basic arithmetic and logical operations that can be performed one at a time in a sequence. Thanks to a hierarchy of programming languages, the user is usually unaware of the tremendous number of sub-operations involved in the simplest tasks. Even in word processing, which is not computationally intensive, millions of operations are performed to do something as simple as a spelling check of a document. The tremendous speed with which these individual instructions are executed often gives the impression that the computer is performing at a higher level of complexity than is actually the case.

All traditional computers with a single central processing unit are based on this same design. A supercomputer is similar in its basic elements to a personal computer except for its speed, its memory, and the variety of operations its processor can do. In both cases, problems are reduced to small steps that are performed in a sequence as data and instructions are shipped back and forth from the memory to the central processing unit.

Since the first electronic computers of the 1940s, there has been a staggering acceleration of processing speed—averaging a ten-fold increase every seven years. The first gains were made with transistors. Silicon microchips that increase speed because they dramatically reduce the distance electronic signals travel within the computer soon followed. Today's so-called supercomputers are so fast that their speed is measured in millions of floating-point operations per second or *megaflops.* Floating-point operations are arithmetic operations with a moving decimal point that allow a great deal of precision and little rounding. The Cray–2 supercomputer runs at 1,200 megaflops and it is said that 10,000 megaflops (ten billion floating point operations/sec) is about to become a reality.

Although great things can be done with such fast computers there are a number of compelling reasons to consider parallel processing as an alternative. As powerful as supercomputers are, visualization makes incredible demands. Real-time ray-tracing and animation; simulations with thousands of equations and thousands of variables; procedural graphics; fly-overs; computer stereopsis—these processes are so computationally intensive that they can tax even the fastest existing computers. Furthermore, supercomputers are very expensive to build and to operate and are nearing the speed limit theoretically possible. This is because the distances signals travel within the computer are already so minimal they cannot be reduced much further. One possible way of producing a computer that would be more economical and provide more computing power is to use parallel architecture.

A source of inspiration for parallel computing is the nervous systems of animals, visual systems in particular, which clearly process information in parallel. The retina accepts input all over its surface and generates output in parallel through a million fibers of the optic nerve. David Hubel and Torsten Wiesel's work suggests that processing up to and including the visual cortex is accomplished by small functionally autonomous analyzers. Indeed, the nervous system could hardly accomplish what it does without parallel organization because the neuronal components are, individually, quite slow when compared with man-made devices. The fact that neurons working in parallel but operating at relatively low response rates can quickly accomplish complex analyses encourages the designers of parallel computers. Individual units each performing simple operations seem to have, when functioning as a group, an emergent power.

Although it is evident that parallelism is important in the visual system, it is far from clear how it exploits its "parallel architecture." Similarly, although most computer scientists agree that parallel computing is very important, it is not entirely clear how to connect the individual processors together or what kinds of algorithms will need to be developed to make parallel machines useful in a wide variety of applications. There are a number of competing designs that differ principally in the way in which individual processors are connected together.

Some parallel computers have been designed with a "tree" structure so that computational products flow downward to an expanding number of processors. In other designs, a given processor is connected with every other processor in the system. In still other parallel machines, processors are connected only to their immediate neighbors. With each type of machine, programming is quite different.

The hardware and software of parallel computing are now undergoing rapid development and, in the next decade, it is anticipated that relatively inexpensive parallel computers will be available with capabilities, for some applications, comparable to supercomputers.

Parallel computing is expected to have great importance in visualization because both image processing and computer graphics often involve repetitive computations that parallel computers can perform in a much shorter time. Consider contrast stretching, for example. With this technique, the contrast in an image can be improved simply by recalculating the brightness for each pixel. A constant is subtracted from each pixel's brightness and the result is multiplied by a second constant (see *Images from Energy*). With a conventional computer, the calculations would be done sequentially, one pixel at a time. The computer would probably move in a raster sequence, pixel by pixel, row by row. A parallel computer with a large number of processors could contrast stretch an image much faster by calculating all the new pixel values simultaneously. One current parallel computer has 65,536 processors—a sufficient number so that a black-and-white image of medium resolution could be contrast stretched in one step, or roughly 65,000 times faster than by the sequential method.

There are many other ways in which parallel computers can be used in image processing. The 65,536-processor computer, for example, can perform a kind of stereoptic procedure (see earlier section) in real time. The computer creates a topographic map from a stereopair. The whole process involving 500 million computer operations is accomplished in just half a second. With this technique, moving one's hand under a pair of video cameras produces a real-time "animated" topographic map: the hand is shown as an elevation that moves.

Parallel computers can also be used for visualizations of phenomena that are themselves constituted of many processes occurring simultaneously. For example, the behavior of a fluid can be predicted using a model based on the collisions of particles. Each computer within the parallel computer can be programmed to model the behavior of a single particle, or a few particles. The simulation involves letting the computers interact as the particles would—obviating the need for a more complex mathematical model. Parallel computers are also beginning to be used in artificial intelligence. Here, it is assumed that human thinking involves many processes occurring simultaneously and is therefore better modeled by a parallel computer than by sequential methods. In all of these applications, however, the designers have the considerable challenge of creating algorithms that exploit the full potential of parallelism. It remains to be seen how problems are best reduced to the kinds of small procedures that can be done simultaneously on a computer with tens of thousands, or potentially millions, of processors.

modeling with parallel computers This is a frame from an animation depicting the thermal motion of an enzyme (triosephosphate isomerase). Modeling the dynamics of complex biomolecules is one of the most computationally intensive kinds of simulation (see *Visual Experiments*). Parallel computers can speed the process by performing separate components of the computation simultaneously.

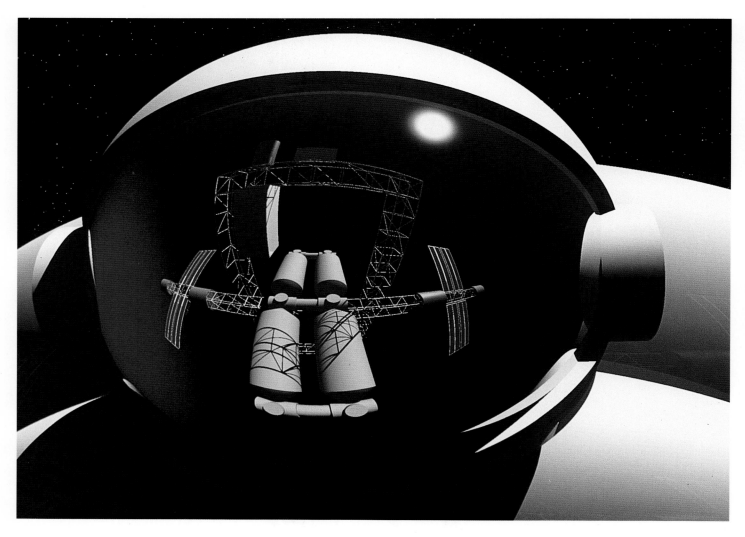

"artificial realities"

While graphics has revolutionized computer output, there has not been a comparable improvement in the way in which we control or input data to the computer. Except in special cases, such as flight simulators, we most often communicate with the computer by typing on a keyboard. In recent years, there have been efforts to make the human/computer interface more intuitive and natural. One of the pioneers has been Myron Kruger of the University of Connecticut. Kruger coined the term "artificial reality" to describe a computer interface that seemingly surrounds the individual. In one of Kruger's artificial realities, for example, sophisticated image processing and computer graphics are used to insert a live image of an individual (who is moving in a darkened room) into an object-based computer-graphics environment. On a large projection television, one sees oneself moving (much as on a closed-circuit television), in real time, among the objects in the computer. Kruger's technology was conceived primarily for artistic and aesthetic exploration but suggests a new way of interacting with computer-generated objects.

VISUALIZING A SPACE STATION

Perhaps the most audacious experiment with artificial realities is being planned by the National Aeronautics and Space Administration (NASA) in partnership with its contractors working on the design of the space station. The space station, a permanent orbiting habitation, will be visualized more thoroughly and with a wider variety of technologies than any structure or phenomenon heretofore. Visualization will be utilized at every step from preliminary designs, already underway, to the manufacture of the station's modular components, their assembly in space and finally to the space station's operation.

space station reflection This ray-traced image shows a proposed space station design reflected on the face mask of an astronaut. Both the helmet and the space station models are represented in three dimensions in the computer. *Shuttle Stop Space Station* by Randy Bradley **RPI/CICG** © 1987.

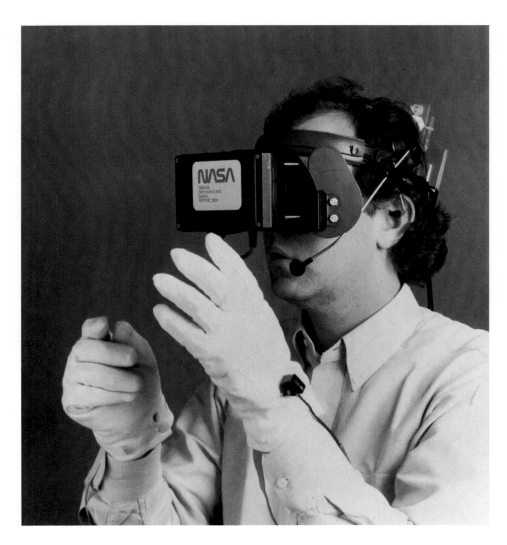

"dataglove" An exciting new interface technology for use with artificial realities is the "dataglove," developed by Thomas G. Zimmerman and L. Young Harvill at VPL Research, which uses special fiber-optics embedded in the fabric to detect finger movements. The position and orientation of the hand are detected by a separate sensor made by the Polhemus Navigation Sciences division of the McDonnell Douglas Corporation. The viewer, created by Scott Fisher at NASA Ames Research Center, presents stereoptic views to the left and right eyes. The combination of viewer and dataglove creates the potential for a new kind of computer interface with which the user can directly manipulate objects in a computer synthesized world.

The space station presents unique challenges since it will be manufactured on Earth in modular components which will then be transported to orbit on the space shuttle. With the requirements for structural integrity, airtightness in space, and size, as well as optimal efficiency in weightlessness, design problems are formidable. With visualization, it is possible to place a simulated figure in a rendering made from the design data base and to have the figure move in three dimensions. Indeed, a stereoview can be generated to provide the designer with the experience of moving within the structure even though it exists only in the computer.

Many of those working on the space-station design are hoping to create an artificial reality on a grand scale using new interface technologies that will co-evolve with the space station program itself. One prototype technology utilizes digitized hand movements. When the hand in a "dataglove" moves, the movement is imitated in the object-based computer.

With this glove, it should eventually be possible to interact with the computer by shaping and moving objects directly instead of, as now, indicating x, y, and z components. Instead of building complex objects with typed commands on a keyboard, one will be able to sculpt them just as objects in the real world can be modeled with clay. The same technology has been used to make an entire suit so that whole body movements can be directly input to the computer. Eventually, the designers of the space station hope to be able to explore their designs by putting on the suit and moving within a three-dimensional computer rendering.

space station A ray-traced image of a space station design. *High Frontier* by Randy Bradley RPI/CICG © 1988.

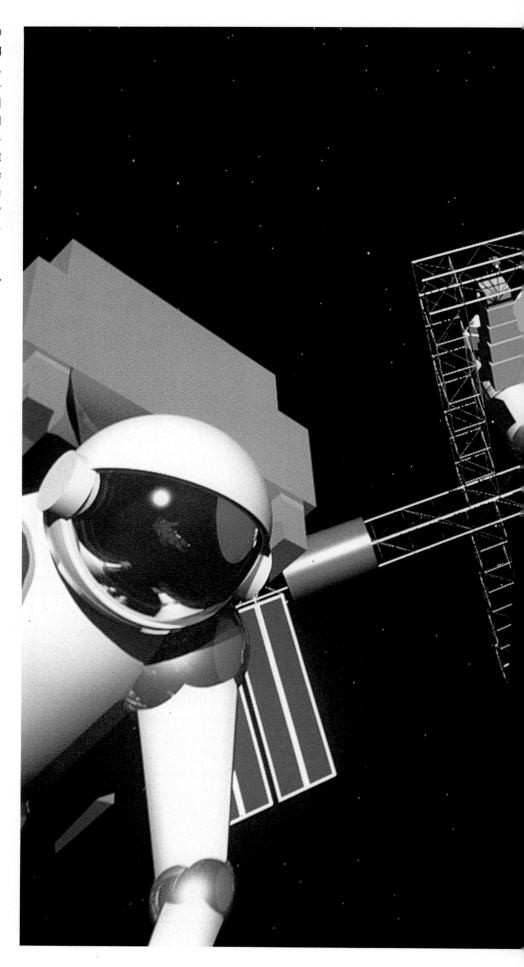

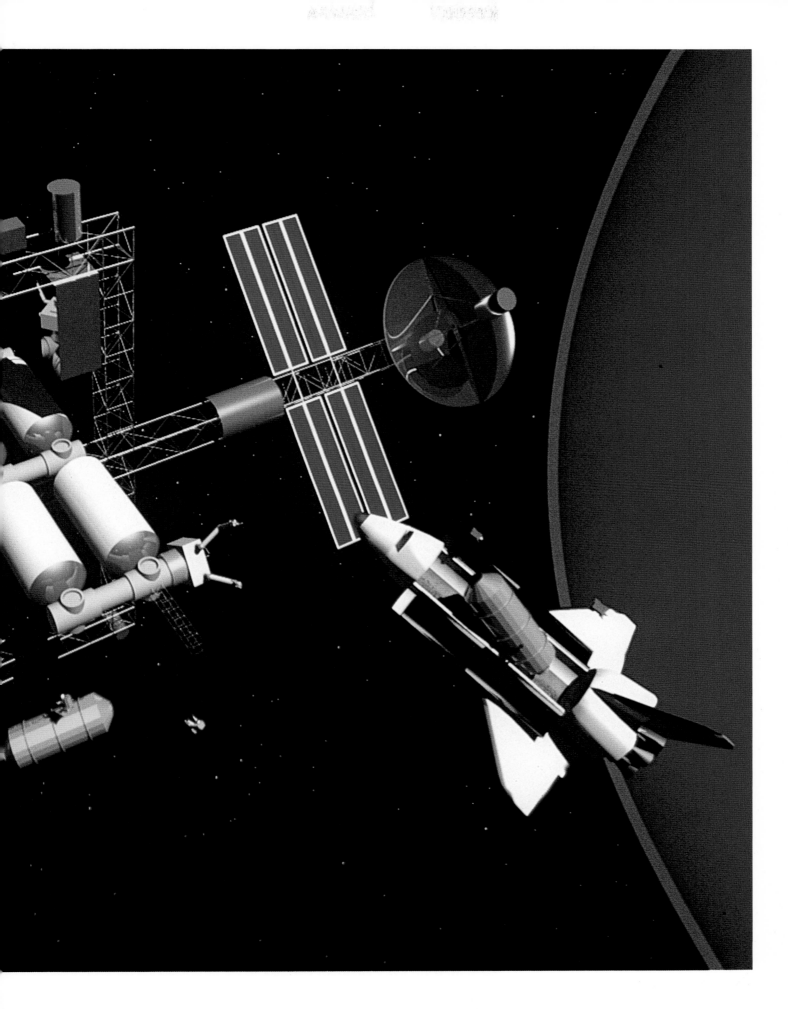

This emphasis on visualization will not end with the physical construction of the space station. It is expected that these technologies will also be on board to help in the management of this "macromachine" and to direct maneuvers in space. Three-dimensional interface units within the space station could be linked to robots outside. With head movements, an astronaut will be able to control the movements of the robot's cameras while with dataglove devices he could control the robot's hands. A real-time simulator aboard the space station would permit the occupants to rehearse a maneuver, such as retrieving a satellite, which would then be executed automatically by the robots.

Visualization of the space station will advance visualization technology enormously and many of these techniques will rapidly find their way into the design and management of other macro-machines such as nuclear reactors, large-scale computers, and industrial plants.

Visualization is an incipient field and these hybrid technologies are only a suggestion of what may yet emerge. It is easier to speculate, of course, than to actually solve the technical problems inherent in developing new technologies. In considering the progress of the last decade or two, it is interesting to see that the imperative for advancing visualization is not always practical or commercial. Many of those involved in visualization have a strong desire to try ideas for their own sake, without knowing where their new technologies will lead them or what kinds of applications will ultimately be possible. The very idea of combining technologies to achieve never-before-possible illusions is, for many, irresistible. Perhaps the reader too, in considering the offerings of this volume, has also felt that impulse, really an invitation, to ask: What if?

perfect illusions: a final note

Having surveyed the technologies of visualization in this book, it is fair to ask: Why do we invest so much to develop these techniques? Beyond the obvious practical considerations, thinking of these technologies as solutions to specific problems, is there something to be observed about human nature in the flowering of visualization as a bold new field of endeavor? It seems insufficient simply to point to the massive proportion of the human brain devoted to vision, because it raises the equally puzzling question of why the brain should be so designed. What is the deeper imperative expressed in this relentless search for more and more perfect illusions?

There is, of course, no single answer but perception research suggests something about our relationship with our environment which may be relevant. Wherever we look, in the retina, in the mechanisms of color perception and stereopsis, in the "wiring" of the visual cortex, we find the visual system organizing. The visual brain is not a passive machine but a creator that sorts through all that is ephemeral in search of enduring signs.

In his book *What is Life?* the great physicist Erwin Schroedinger, one of the creators of quantum mechanics, tries to come to grips with the chemical improbability of organisms and his analysis has some bearing on our problem. Organisms, Schroedinger asserts, are supremely organized systems which, at first glance, appear to defy the fundamental physical principle that all systems move toward disorder and decay. Schroedinger argues, however, that organisms are not exempt from this universal law but that they differ from non-living systems by utilizing the order around them to, at least temporarily, counteract it. Organisms literally and figuratively feed on the orderliness around them. Food, for example, has molecular order which, by virtue of metabolism, is used to maintain the order of the organism.

Is it so surprising, then, to discover that the visual system itself is so masterful at finding order even when this order is concealed in considerable disorder? The whole activity of the visual system, at whatever level we choose to study it, is designed to find significant discontinuities, pockets of order in the ordinary tumult of light. Color vision in the three retinex systems discovers reflectance regularities that cannot be found within a single channel. The stereopsis mechanism discovers depth order by comparing patterns supplied by the left and right eyes. In the visual cortex, analyzers are attuned to another kind of order—departures from randomness known as lines, movements, and blobs.

In some sense, the technologies of visualization are an outer reflection of this organizing imperative of our sensory systems. Their own evolution shows that we endeavor to utilize more and more subtle aspects of this organizing process. To remain utterly objective, we might dismiss this phenomenon with the well-worn cliché that visualization merely "extends vision into unseen worlds." As we enlarge our ability to perceive, however, and as we learn more about the visual system itself, it is tempting to see visualization as more than merely an extension of a sensory system. Perhaps it is a manifestation of a very deep organizing imperative expressed through vision but one that is more fundamental.

acknowledgments

This book began forming in my mind in the early 1980s when I was consulting for the Polaroid Corporation. At that time, I was lucky enough to be granted interviews with many distinguished individuals about imaging technologies, computer science, and related areas of vision and perception, and who, in a sense, are responsible for my initial exposure to these fields. Special thanks go to Edwin H. Land (now at The Rowland Institute for Science), for his many kindnesses then and more recently; Stephen Benton (now of the MIT Media Lab); Bela Julesz (Bell Laboratories and California Institute of Technology); Torsten Wiesel (then at Harvard University Medical School); David H. Hubel (Harvard University Medical School); Richard L. Gregory (University of Bristol); Joseph Weizenbaum (MIT); E.H. Gombrich (The Warburg Institute); William H. Oldendorf (UCLA Medical School); and Richard Wollheim (University of London).

The theme of this book could not have been properly developed without the interest of the individuals in many fields who were kind enough to be interviewed at their institutions or, in exceptional cases, by phone, during its preparation and to share detailed information about their work and, frequently, their visions of the future. Appreciation, in the order in which they were contacted, to: Alan Kay (Apple Computer, Inc., and the MIT Media Lab); David Childs and Natalie Leighton (Skidmore Owings & Merrill); Larry Smarr, Craig Upson, and Bill Allen (National Center for Supercomputing Applications at the University of Illinois); Tom DeFanti and Maxine Brown (University of Illinois, Chicago); David Sturman, David Seltzer, Walter Bender, Muriel Cooper, and Tim Browne (MIT Media Lab); Randy Bradley and Patricia Search (Rensselaer Polytechnic Institute); Ned Greene, Michael O'Rourke, and Peter Oppenheimer (New York Institute of Technology); Jules Bloomenthal (Xerox PARC); Kevin Hussey, James Blinn, Bob and Helen Mortensen, and Jeff Hall (Jet Propulsion Laboratories); Judson Rosebush (Judson Rosebush Company, Inc.); Alex Weil (Charlex, Inc.); Homer Smith (Art Matrix Corporation); Irving Geis; Brad Stringer and David Luther (Evans and Sutherland Molecular Sciences Division); Ken Anderson (Anderson Report); Rob Fisher (Design Mirage); Robert McGill (Bell Laboratories); Richard Weinberg (Cinema/Television Computer Animation Laboratory, USC); Scott Fisher and Craig

Reynolds (Symbolics, Inc.); Alyce Kaprow (The New Studio); David Waltz (Thinking Machines, Inc.); Tom Dewitt; Greg Panos (Rockwell International); and Kristina Hooper (Apple Computer, Inc.).

The authors retain responsibility for the contents but would like to thank the following individuals who reviewed the portions of the manuscript which concern their particular fields: Holly Perry (The Rowland Institute for Science); Margaret Livingstone (Harvard University Medical School); Julie Walker and Tim Browne (MIT Media Lab); Ned Greene (New York Institute of Technology); Larry Smarr, Stephen Wolfram, and Bill Allen (National Center for Supercomputing Applications at the University of Illinois); Bob Mortensen (Jet Propulsion Laboratories); Keira Bromberg (Thinking Machines, Inc.); Homer Brown (Art Matrix Corporation and Cornell National Supercomputer Facility); Scott Struthers (Salk Institute); and Tom Waite (Vicom Systems, Inc.).

Many other individuals were kind enough to supply specific information about their work or their institutions, or to check concepts and facts: Ben Krose (California Institute of Technology); Thomas Banchoff (Brown University); Murray Lerner (MLF Productions); Sheila Blake (Polaroid Corporation); Thompson Webb III (Brown University); Stephen M. Kosslyn (Harvard University); Nancy Flower and Katy deBus (National Computer Graphics Association); Carl Machover (Machover Associates); Jim Thomas (Battelle Northwest, Inc.); Susan Nickelsen (Evans and Sutherland); Karl-Heinz Winkler (Los Alamos National Laboratories); Art Hoffman (UCLA); Geoffrey Goldbogen (Rensselaer Polytechnic Institute); Fred Aronson (Association for Computing Machinery).

Others helped obtain the diverse images to be found in these pages, a number of which were specially produced. Pictures are credited separately but several individuals, not directly credited for images, deserve special mention, including: Jenny Adamiec (Siemens Corporation); Don Miskowich, Andy Kopra, Jeremy Schwartz (Symbolics, Inc.); Jay Scarpetti (The Rowland Institute for Science); Malcolm Blanchard (Pixar Corporation); Jurrie van der Woude (Jet Propulsion Laboratories); Pam Schippers (Spot Image Corporation); Lennart Nilsson (Karolinska Institute); and special thanks to Gina Carillo, Andrea DeMico, Malcolm McNeil, and Paige Wood (Charlex, Inc.); Paul Hubel (Oxford University).

Finally, a number of people should be thanked for their general interest in and support for this project including: Arnold Friedhoff; June Goodfield; Richard Fritzson (UNISYS); and David G. Hays. George Braziller is also thanked for suggesting the title for the second chapter.

I would also like to express appreciation to the American Association for the Advancement of Science for granting me a fellowship in its Media program. It was through this program that I first developed an interest in, and grew to see the importance of, communicating scientific ideas to the public. Thanks also to Jonathan Ward, then of the CBS News Program *Walter Cronkite's Universe,* for encouraging me, as a Media Fellow under his direction, to pursue my interest in these matters.

There are many people to thank at Abrams. Appreciation to Paul Gottlieb, the publisher, for taking a chance on a new topic *before* it heated up and for his kind consideration. I would also like to express my gratitude to my editor, Edith Pavese, for her patience, tactfulness, and editorial perceptiveness and for being prescient in recognizing the importance of visualization. Special thanks also to picture editor Sue Sherman for her fearlessness and for upholding the highest standards under difficult conditions; and to designer Elissa Ichiyasu, who worked with great artistry and sensitivity despite the complexity of this book and impending deadlines.

This book would not have been possible at all without the dedicated efforts of Denise Modjeski, who transcended her formal research duties and consistently made important suggestions as to the writing and subject matter. It would have been quite impossible to prepare a book of this scope without her brilliant assistance. Her presence is evident in every paragraph.

I would also like to thank my beloved wife, Livia Antola Friedhoff, for her unflagging patience and many sacrifices throughout this project. It is also impossible to completely express the gratitude I feel to my sister, Nancy Friedhoff, for her support and encouragement from the beginning of this project to its conclusion. Thanks for the encouragement of my parents, Arnold and Frances Friedhoff, as well as my brother, Lawrence Friedhoff. May all those who aspire to write books begin their long journey with such faithful relations.

Richard Mark Friedhoff

further reading

introduction:
visual thinking
with computers

Cooper, C.A. and R.N. Shepard. 1984. Turning something over in the mind. *Scientific American,* 251, no. 6: 106–14.

Gombrich, E.H. 1960. *Art and Illusion.* Princeton University Press.

Gregory, R.L. 1980. Perceptions as hypotheses. *Philosophical Transcripts of the Royal Society, London,* B290: 181–97.

Kosslyn, S.M. 1983. *Ghosts in the Mind's Machine.* Norton.

Livingstone, M.S. 1988. Art, illusion and the visual system. *Scientific American,* 258, no. 1: 78–85.

Sperry, R. 1982. Some effects of disconnecting the cerebral hemispheres. *Science,* 217: 1223–26.

we create
the world we see

Gregory, R.L. 1974. *Concepts and Mechanisms of Perception.* Scribner's.

———. 1979. *Eye and Brain.* World University Library/ McGraw-Hill.

Hubel, D.H. 1988. *Eye, Brain, and Vision.* Scientific American Library, W.H. Freeman.

Julesz, B. 1971. *Foundations of Cyclopean Perception.* University of Chicago Press.

———. 1986. Texton Gradients: Texton theory revisited. *Biological Cybernetics,* 54: 245–55.

Kihlstrom, J.F. 1987. The cognitive unconscious. *Science,* 237: 1445–52.

Land, E.H. 1959. Experiments in color vision. *Scientific American,* 200, no. 5, 84–99.

———. 1977. Six Eyes of Man. *Proceedings of the Society of Photo-Optical Instrumentation Engineering,* 120: 43–50.

———. 1977. The retinex theory of color vision. *Scientific American,* 237, no. 6: 108–28.

———. 1981. Color vision. In *Encyclopedia of Physics, Vision and Color,* R. Lerner and G. Triggs, eds. 1090–97, Addison-Wesley.

———. 1986. Recent advances in retinex theory. *Vision Research,* 26, no. 1: 7–21.

Livingstone, M.S. and D.H. Hubel. 1984. Anatomy and physiology of a color system in the primate visual cortex. *Journal of Neuroscience*, 4: 309–356.

Ornstein, R. and R.F. Thompson. 1984. *The Amazing Brain*. Houghton-Mifflin.

Poggio, G.F., and B. Fischer. 1977. Binocular interaction and depth sensitivity of striate and prestriate cortical neurons of the behaving rhesus monkey. *Journal of Neurophysiology*, 40: 1392–1405.

Wolfe, J.M. 1983. Hidden visual processes. *Scientific American*, 248, no. 2: 70–77.

Glassner, A.S. 1984. *Computer Graphic Users Guide*. Howard W. Sams.

Haber, R.N. 1986. Flight simulation. *Scientific American*, 255, no. 1: 96–103.

Kunii, T.L., ed. 1987. *Image Synthesis*. Springer-Verlag.

Rogers, D.F. and R.A. Earnshaw, eds. 1987. *Techniques for Computer Graphics*. Springer-Verlag.

Seybold, John W. 1987. The desk-top publishing phenomenon. *Byte*, 12, no. 5; 149–54.

van Dam, A. 1984. Computer software for graphics. *Scientific American*, 251, no. 3: 146–59.

images from energy

Benton, S.A. 1985. Display holography. *Proceedings of the Society of Photo-Optical Instrumentation Engineering*, 532: 8–11.

Cannon, T.M. and B.R. Hunt. 1981. Image processing by computer. *Scientific American*, 245, no. 4: 214–25.

Caulfield, H.J. with R.S. Jackson and R.P. Barilleaux. 1983. *Holography Works*. Museum of Holography, New York.

Gombrich, E.H. 1974. Standards of truth: the arrested image and the moving eye. In *The Language of Images*, W.J. Mitchell, ed. 181–218. University of Chicago Press.

————. J. Hochberg and M. Black. 1972. *Art, Perception and Reality*. Johns Hopkins University Press.

Gregory, R.L. and E.H. Gombrich, eds. 1973. *Illusion In Nature and Art*. Scribner's.

Newhouse, V.L., ed. 1988. *Progress in Medical Imaging*. Springer-Verlag.

Oldendorf, W.H. 1980. *The Quest for an Image of the Brain*. Raven Press.

Rosenfield, A. and A.C. Kak. 1982. *Digital Picture Processing*, vols. 1 and 2. Academic Press.

Saxby, Graham. 1988. *Practical Holography*. Prentice-Hall International.

Sheldon, K. 1987. Probing space by camera. *Byte*, 12, no. 43: 143–48.

Unterseher, F., J. Hansen and B. Schlesinger. 1982. *The Holography Handbook*. Ross Books.

computer graphics

Foley, J.D. and A. van Dam. 1982. *Fundamentals of Interactive Computer Graphics*. Addison-Wesley.

Fox, D. and M. Waite. 1984. *Computer Animation Primer*. Byte Books/McGraw-Hill.

visual experiments

Bowman, D.J. 1984. *The CAD/CAM Primer*. Howard W. Sams.

Check, W. 1986. A picture is worth . . . *Mosaic*, 17, no. 1: 32–41.

Dubois, J.E., D. Laurent and J. Weber. 1985. Chemical ideograms and molecular graphics. *The Visual Computer*. 1, no. 1: 49–64.

Groover, M.P. and E.W. Zimmers Jr. 1984. *CAD/CAM: Computer-Aided Design and Manufacturing*. Prentice-Hall.

Mandelbrot, B.B. 1983. *The Fractal Geometry of Nature*. W.H. Freeman.

McCormick, B.H., T.A. DeFanti, and M.D. Brown, eds. 1987. Visualization in scientfic computing. *The Siggraph Computer Graphics Newsletter*, 21, no. 6.

Peitgen, H.-O., and D. Saupe. 1988. *The Science of Fractal Images*. Springer-Verlag.

Simon, Herbert A. 1981. *The Sciences of the Artificial*. MIT Press.

Vida, J.A., and M. Gordon. 1984. *Conformationally Directed Drug Design*. American Chemical Society.

Wolfram, S. 1984. Computer software in science and mathematics. *Scientific American*, 251, no. 3: 188–203.

emergent technologies

Fisher, S.S., M. McGreevy, J. Humphries, W. Robinett. 1986. *Virtual Environment Display System*. Association for Computing Machinery Workshop on Interactive 3D Graphics.

Foley, J.D. 1987. Interfaces for advanced computing. *Scientific American*, 257, no. 4: 127–35.

Fox, G.C. and P.C. Messina. 1987. Advanced computer architectures. *Scientific American*, 257, no. 4: 66–74.

Kruger, M.W. 1983. *Artificial Reality*. Addison-Wesley.

Tello, E.R. 1988. Between man and machine. *Byte*, 13, no. 9: 288–93.

index

All references are to page numbers. Text references are in roman type; pages on which illustrations appear are in *italic* type.

A

Accommodation, visual, 32
Acuity, visual, 42, *43*, 44, *44*
  human responsivity to brightness, 50, 51
  limitations of, 13, *14*, 32
Advertising, paint systems in, 86
Aerial perspective, 32, *114*, 123, 151
Aerodynamics, 160, *162–3*
Aesthetics
  to judge visualization, 131, 136
  questions of, experimental attitude toward, 133, 137, 169
  See also Art
AI, *see* Artificial intelligence
Algorithms
  aerial perspective, 151
  defined, 50
  fractal, 122
  image-processing, 86, 88
  for in-betweening, 125
  imitating nature's geometry, 107
  optical, 189
  for parallel processing, 191, 192
  as schemata, 84
  for sorting, 152, *153*
  versatility of applications, 172
  vision as test of, 131
  visualizing, 152, 153
  warping, 86, 89
Al-Khowarizmi, 50
Alphabetizing, 152, *153*
Alternatives, exploration and comparison of, 150–51, 159, 169
  during architectural design process, 138, 143, 144, 148, 169
  in astrophysics, 152, 160, 162
  in biochemistry, 132–33
Ambiguity
  of three-dimensionality in images, *33*
  reducing, in communication, 137, 148
American Gothic, Wood, *87–9*
Amino acids, 134
Anaglyphs, 38
Analysis
  statistical, as opposed to visual experiments, 152, 162
  visual system's methods of, 12, 131

Anatomy, human, in modeling movement, 126
Animation, computer-graphics, 83, 124–6, 169
  black hole simulation, 160, 162
  modeling early forces of creation, *17*
  procedural techniques, *104–5*
  real-time, 191
  research on, 189
  in sculpture design, 151
  synthetic fly-over, 173, 178–82
Anti-logarithmic processing, 52
Architecture
  design experimentation process, 144, 148, 168
  visualization in, 138–49, *140, 141, 142, 143, 144, 145, 146, 147, 149*
Art
  commercial, 86
  creative exploration, in artificial realities, 194
  of false coloring, 53, 76, 81
  history, and visualization, 16
  and science, in interpretation and judgment of visualization images, 46, 53, 76, 81
  thinking computationally in, 133, 137, 169
  use of information about visual channels in, 13–14, 43–4
Artifacts, perceptual, 76
  chance, differentiation from real experimental effects, 162
  due to channel conflict, 13, *43, 44*
  in false coloring, 53
  in PET, 81
  visual, 13, 17, *43, 53*, 81
  See also Images, misleading aspects of
Artificial intelligence (AI), parallel computers in, 192
Artificial realities, generating, 46, 194–8
Artists
  computer graphicists as, 187
  computer use by, 151, 152
  conventions for representing, 82, 84
  designers, similarity to scientists, 133, 169
  diminished stereoptic perception in, 30, *36*
  and scientists, on visualization teams, 159, 189
Astigmatism, and stereopsis, 30
Astronomy, aperture synthesis radio, 60, 64
Astrophysics
  simulating complex or remote entities, *17*, 152, 153, 160–2, 168
Attention, conscious
  freeing of, by engaging preconscious processes, 13, 44, 45, 56, 131, 133, 185
  visual, directing, 40, 45
Automatons, cellular, *154–7*
  snowflake pattern, *158*

B

Bacteriophage, visualizing, 186–7, *186–7*
Bark, 108, *108*, 112, 131
  digitizing, 108
Beam splitter, 71
Benton, Stephen, 74, 189
Big Bang theory, *17*
Binocular parallax, *see* Disparity
Biochemistry, 134–7, 162
Biomolecules, modeling, *192–3*
  DNA, *170*, 171
  hormone, *134–5*, 135–7
The Birth of Venus, Botticelli, *87, 89*
Black holes, simulating, 152, 160, *161*, 162, 168
Bloomenthal, Jules, *106–11*, 107–9, 112, 114, 131
Brain
  active creation of visual world, 12, 18, 37, 45, 76, 132, 169
  hemispheres, 14, 40
  metabolic function (PET scan of), *66*
  preconscious, 12–13, 45, 56, 131, 133, 152, 185
  proportion devoted to vision, 12, 199
  topographic mapping of visual information in, 40
  visual, 12–13, 18, 40–5, 169, 191
Branching, models of, 107
  procedural, *116*
  as trajectories of imaginary particles, 112
Brightness, 26–9
  changes, revealing foreign elements, 77
  of color, as perceived through shape channel, *43*, 44, 53
  compared with reflectance, 26–7
  computer estimates of, 94, 95
  in contrast stretching, 50, 51
  human visual responsivity to, 50
  images as spatial changes in, 60
  in multispectral scanning, 58
  pixel, 48–51
  standing pattern, 68
Bronowski, Jacob, 12
Bruce, James, 84
Brush shapes, in paint systems, 86
Buildings, construction and deesign, centralized CAD data base, 148
Bump-mapping, *99*, 108
Bus, computer, 190

C

CAD, *see* Computer-aided design
Calculations
  basic techniques, 50
  communicating visually rather than with, 16, 132, 133, 135, 137, 152, 169, 185
  computer time required for, 52, 100, 132, 135, 137, 144, 159, 161, 168, 173, 190–1
  in dominant hemisphere, 14
  neuronal speed, working in parallel, 191
Calibration, and problems of interpretation, 76–81
CAM, *see* Computer-automated manufacturing
Carpenter, Loren, 120
Cartesian coordinates
  for complex numbers, 164, *164*
  to create a color space, 28, *28*
  to store images in computer, 90
Cathode ray tube (CRT), 49
CCD, *see* Charge-coupled devices
Cels, 124
Cells
  eukaryotes, 172
  neuronal, 191
  retinal, 24, 26, 40, *41*
Cellular automatons, *154–7, 158*
Central processing unit, 190
Channels, information, in the visual system, 18, 42–4, 199
  conflicts between, 13, *14, 43,* 44, 53
  variable acuity of, 13, *14,* 44
''Chaotic'' systems, 164
Charge-coupled devices (CCD), 48
Childhood Blue Slucid, O'Rourke, *91*
Christ of Gala, Dali, *38*
CIM, *see* Computer-integrated manufacturing
Cognition
  and music, 189
  and visualization, 16
Collimeter lens, *71*
Color, 18–25
  channels, in the visual system, 13, *14,* 18, *43,* 44, 53
  constancy, 21, 26, 29
  in holograms, *72*
  human ability to perceive, 13–14, 42–4, 199
  issues of interpretation, 46, 53, 76, 81
  in object-based computer graphics, 95
  perception, independent of wavelength, 21, *22–3,* 24, *27*
  in pixel-based computer graphics, 86
  pseudocoloring, *47,* 52, 53–5, 56, 76, 81, 160, *161, 176–7*
  reflectance profile unique to each, 25
  suggestive use, in pictorial style visualization, 136
  in two-dimensional animation, 125
  video, 151
  visual subsense, 13–14, 18–29, 42
  to visualize density or pressure, *161*

Color space, Cartesian coordinate system, *28*
Color vision theory, 19, *27,* 58
  retinex, 21–9, *27*
  trivariance, 19–21, 26, 40, 48, 49, 52, 76, 94, 95, 199
  Young-Helmholtz, 19, 21, 24, 26, *27,* 29, 58
Communication, visualization's facilitation of, 137, 148, 159, 172, 191, 194, 198
  See also Interface, human/machine; Language
Camouflage, and stereopsis, 36
Computed tomography (CT), 60, 63–7, *63, 65–7*
  on the pictorial/symbolic continuum, 136
  use in art, *65*
  to visualize Earth's inner structure, 64
  volume visualization, 182–5, *184–5*
Computer-aided design (CAD) system, 138, *139, 142–3,* 148
  applications, 138, 150–1
  centralized data base, in building construction and design, 148
  ray-traced rendering, *139, 144–5*
Computer-automated manufacturing (CAM), 138, 148
Computer graphics
  aesthetic criteria to judge, 131, 136
  animation, 83, 124–6
  combinatory uses in visualization, 16, 173–87
  computer object creation, 93–103
  in desktop publishing, 130
  fractal, *118,* 119–21, *120–1,* 131
  human/machine interface, 127, 132–3, 137, 148, 151, 159, 162, 186, 187, 194–6
  and image processing, 173–82
  light effects, 90–103
  to model complex natural forms, 103, 112
  object-based systems, 83, 86, 90–120, 122, 188, *188,* 194
  pixel-based systems, 86, *87–9*
  procedural techniques in, 103–21, *104–6, 116, 117,* 126, 128
  to produce stereopairs, 38
  research on, 189
  revealing causal relationships, 162, 168
  three-dimensional, 90, *91,* 93
  as tool for visual experiments, 13–16, 45, 132, 133, 135, 137, 152, 169, 185
Computer-integrated manufacturing (CIM), 138
Computers
  algorithms in, 50
  clarifying role of, in visual experiments, 168
  combined with holography, 72, 188–9
  communicating with, 194
  computation time required for problem solving, 52, 100, 132, 133, 135, 137, 144, 159, 161, 173, 190–1
  desktop, 159
  digital, linked to energy-pattern sensors, 46, 48–67
  geometric description of image, 90
  graphic interface, history of, 127
  as inhibiting artistic expression, 151
  parallel versus sequential, 190–3
  as test chamber, 152
  transcendent quality of digital data, 172
  visual nature of, 152
Conceptualization, visualization's power to shape, 46, 152, 168, 171
Cones, visual, 24, 26, 40, *41*
Conformation, molecular, 134–7, *134–5,* 168, 169
  extended, 134, *135,* 136

Connections
  among parallel processors, 191
Consciousness
  as emergent phenomenon, 172, 191
  engagement of preconscious processes, 13, 44, 45, 56, 131, 133, 185
  in problem solving, 12–13, 45, 56, 133, 152, 185
  visual system, relation to, 12–13, 45, 131
Construction, use of computers in, 138, 148
Context analysis, 76–7
Continuum
  of color, *see* Spectrum
  from pictorial to symbolic, 136
Contrast stretching, 50, 51, 191
CONTROL program, 150–1
Controls, scientific, 152, 162
  See also Variables
Conventions, visual, 82, 84–5, 131, 170, 171
Convergence, visual, 30–2
  versus disparity, 34, *36*
Cook, Robert, 102
Corpus callosum, 14
Cortex, cerebral, striate area (*i.e.,* visual), 27, 40, 42, 191
  processing power of, 12–13, 45, 131, 152–3, 185
Costs
  of design evaluation, 144, 148
  of ray-tracing, 100
  of simulated fly-overs, 173, 182
  supercomputer, 159, 190–1
Cray–2 supercomputer, 159, 190
Creation, modeling early forces of, *17*
Creativity, visualization's enhancement of, 138, 148, 150–1, 159, 168, 169
Cross, Lloyd, 75
CRT, *see* Cathode ray tube
Crystallography, X-ray diffraction, 64
Crystals, 186–7
  formation, 158
  iron, *47*
CT, *see* Computed tomography
Curves, rendering, 94–6, 98, 100–3
Cut-and-paste techniques, electronic, 86, *89*
Cytoarchitecture, in the visual system, 42

D

Data, 190
  combining observational, synthetic, and transduced, 112
  digital, transcendent quality of, 172
  elevation, 176
  human grasp of, through visual rather than verbal or numerical means, 16, 45, 132, 133, 137, 152, 162, 185
  input to computer, 194
  transduction, 47–8, 64, 72, 112, 185, 187
Data base
  amplification, 103
  centralized digital, uniting multistep or far-flung projects, 137, 148, 159, 172, 194, 198
  holograms from digital, 189
"Dataglove," 195–6, *195*
Deblurring, 13, 60, *61,* 62
Decay, 199
Demodulation, 70
Demonstration of Perspective, Dürer, *92*
Denisyuk, Y.N., 74
Density
  black hole, *161*
  within the three-dimensional geometry of bacteriophage, *186,* 187
Depth cues, 29, 77
  monocular, 29, 32–4, 171
  pictorial, 19, 32–4, *33*
Depth image, of a computer scene, 93
Depth perception, 29–39, *44,* 176
  at a distance, 123
  binocular, misunderstandings of, 30, *36*
  relying on motion, 123, 150, 151, 185
Design
  architectural, 138–49, *140, 141, 142, 143, 144, 145, 146, 147, 149,* 168, 169, 188
  computer-aided, information, to control manufacture, 138, *139,* 148
  ideas, realistic visualizations to guide experimental process to completion, 137, 138, 143, 144, 148, 150–1, 168, 169
  studio, computer as, 130
  three-dimensional record of, 188
Desktop publishing systems, 130, *130*
Diagnostics, medical
  interpreting imagery, 63–7, 77, 81
  volume visualization in, *184,* 185, *185*
  See also Images, misleading aspects of
Digital subtraction angiography, 56, *58*
Digitization, *49,* 95
Dimensionality
  two-
    animation, 124–5
    of distant view, 123
    graphics programs, desktop publishing, 130
    See also Retina
  three-, 13, 16, 34, 75
    comic books, 38
    computer world, *83*
    fly-over, 173, *174–5*
    imaging techniques, 68, 90, *91,* 93
    movies, 38
    perception of, and object recognition, 29, 34
    with polarized glasses, 38, 68, 75
    See also Stereopsis

Disorder, 199
Disparity, 74, 182
  defined, 34
  evolutionary usefulness of technique, 36
  in the mechanism of stereopsis, 37
  relative to background, 178
  and visualization, 38
Display
  computing power required, 52
  monitor, 49
  stereographic terminal, 185
Distance
  in aerial perspective, *114,* 123
  depth perception at a, 123
  determining, 76–7, 176
  of nearest surface, to viewpoint, 93
  perception of, 30, *33,* 37
  relative, 176, 182
  and self-similarity, 131
Diversity, creative, increases in, 148
Drafting, CAD, 138
Drawing, nondominant hemisphere, 14
Dual-energy radiography, 56
Dürer, Albrecht, 84, 92, 93

E

Edge enhancement, 53, *59,* 60, 186, 187
Education technology, 189
Einstein, Albert, 13, 159
Electron micrography, *47*
  rods and cones, 41
Electron microscopy, 47, 186, 187
Emanation theory, of vision, 18
Emergent, defined, 172
Empedocles, 18, 45
Energy
  kinetic, 158
  patterns of, computer's processing, 46
  wave properties, 68, *69*
Engelbart, Douglas, 127
Ensemble processing, 50, 56–8
Entropy, and life, 199
Environments, artificial, computer-generated, 46, *83,* 194–8
Epilepsy, surgically disconnected brain hemispheres, 14
Ethics, in image manipulation, 77
  See also Images, misleading aspects of
Eukaryotes, emergent qualities in, 172
Evaluation, of works in progress, 137, 144, 148
  See also Design, ideas
Evans, J.E., 76
Evolution
  emergent features, 172
  and order, 199
  usefulness of reflectance, in humans, 26
  usefulness of stereopsis, in humans, 36
Expense
  of design evaluation, 144, 148
  of holography, 70, 75
  of preparing publications, 130
  of ray-tracing, 100, 144
  of simulated fly-overs, 173, 182
  supercomputer, 159, 190–1

Experiments, 132–3
  answering aesthetic questions by, 133, 137, 169
  artistic, computer use in, 91, 194
  design, 138, 143, 144, 148, 150–1, 169
  exploring and comparing alternatives, 132–3, 138, 143, 144, 148, 150–2, 159, 160, 162, 169
  facilitation of, visualization's role, 137, 138, 144, 148
  laboratory, and computer simulations, similarities and differences, 168
  Land's color filters, 21, *22–3*
  "Mondrian," 24–5
  numerical, 152–67
  single-cell recording, 42
  thought, 16
  traditional safeguards, 152, 162
  visual, with computer graphics, 13–16, 82, 132–68
Explosion, modeling, 103, *104–5,* 116
Eye
  and brain, active creation of the visual world, 12, 18, 37, 45, 76, 132, 169
  sensitivity of, to judge algorithms, 131
  specific purpose of its design, 169
  See also Retina; Vision

F

False coloring, *47,* 52, *53–5,* 56, 76, 81, 160, *161, 176–7*
Fibrous dysplasia, volume visualization, *185*
Fisher, Robert, 150–1, *150–1*
Fisher, Scott, 195
Flight simulation, 122–3
  human/computer interface, 194
  real-time, 122, 123, 182
Floating-point operations, 159, 190
Fluid dynamics, 152, 160–3, *160,* 182, 185
  parallel computers in visualizing, 192
Fly-over techniques, 173–5, 191
  Mars, 182
  Miranda, 16, 178–82, *179–81*
Flying spot scanner, *48, 49*
Focus, poor, deblurring, *61,* 62
Form
  channel for, in the visual system, 13, 18, *43,* 44
  human perception of, 13–14, 18, 29, *36,* 42, 169
  suggestive use, in pictorial style visualization, 136
Forms
  graphic, human eye/brain's ability to recognize and compare, 132, 133, 135, 152, 185
  of great intricacy, that grow, 103, 112, 158
  wave, 60, *113*
Fourier, J.B.J., 60
Fourier analysis, 50, 60–7, *61–2,* 64, 186, 187
Fovea, 40, 41
Fractal Demo, Smith, *120–1*
Fractals, 85, *118,* 119–22, *120–1,* 131, 164–7
  algorithms, 122
  defined, 119
Frame buffers, 49, 52
Function, and structure, in molecules, 134–7

G

Gabor, Dennis, 68
Games, computer, 82
Generator, fractal, 119
Geometric processing, 50, 56, 77
  in synthetic fly-over, 173
Geometry
  analytic, in object-based systems, 90, 103
  comparing various kinds, visually, 135
  Dürer's treatise, 92
  fractal, *118,* 119–22, 164–7
  geometric affinities, in Léger's work, *85*
  hormonal, 135
  large-scale similarity to small-scale, 85
  molecular, 137
  of nature, modeling, 107–21
  of seashell, *118*
  viral, 187
Gigaflops, 159
Glowing, algorithms for, 95
GnRH, *see* Gonadotrophin-releasing hormone
Gombrich, E.H., 12, 33, 82
Gonadotrophin-releasing hormone (GnRH) antagonist,
  designing, *134–5,* 135–7
Gouraud shading, 95, *98, 114*
Grail system, 127
Graphic design, 128, 130
  See also Computer graphics
Graphics, computer, *see* Computer graphics
Graphics interface, *see* Interface, human/machine
Graphics processors, 52
Graphics tablet, 138
Grasses, particle techniques, *116*
Gravity, force of, computer modeling, 126
Gregory, Richard, 38
Grey scales, 49, 59

H

Hagler, Arnold, 135
Half-a-ray tracing, *103*
Hall, Jeff, 173
Hard copy, ways of producing, 49
Harvill, L. Young, 195
von Helmholtz, Hermann, 19
Highlights, on smooth surfaces, 95, *98,* 100, *101–3,* 171
Highly parallel computers, 190
Histogram equalization, *51*
Holograms
  color, *72,* 188
  laser-transmission, *73*
  pinhole, 70
  pulsed, 189
  reflection, *72*
  transmission, set-up for, *71*
  white light, *74*

Holographic stereogram, 75, *188*
Holography, 68–75
  combined with computer, 72, 188–9
  compared to other three-dimensional imaging techniques,
    68
  from any digital data, 189
  ideal, 188
  process, stated simply, 70
Hormones, molecules of, *134–5,* 135
Hubel, David, 42, 45, 191
Human interface research, 189
  See also Interface, human/machine
Hussey, Kevin, 173
Hydrodynamics, 160

I

Icon control, 127
Ideas
  communicating visually, as opposed to verbally or
    numerically, 16, 45, 132, 133, 135, 137, 152, 162, 169,
    185
  experimentation, with visualization to guide, 137, 138, 143,
    144, 148, 150–1, 159, 169
Illumination, 108
  vector of, 94
Illusion, search for perfect, 199
Image processing, 48–67
  algorithms for, 86, 88
  combinatory uses, in visualization, 16, 173–87
  and computer graphics, 173–82
  digitizing the image, 48, *49*
  ethics in, 77
  as extension of human vision, 13
  image storage, display, and hard copy, 49
  outside of science and medicine, 77
  techniques, 50–67, 186, 187
Images
  areas traditionally concerned with, 16
  black-and-white, and color perception, 21, *22–3,* 25, 29
  of buildings *in situ, 143–5,* 144, 148
  continuum from pictorial to symbolic, 136
  cross-sectional, 182, *183,* 185, 187
  enhancement and restoration, 50–62
  found, 12
  geometric description of, 90
  "impossible," 46, 123, 132
  misleading aspects of, 46, 152, 168, 171
  quality of, using mathematics to alter, 50
  ray-traced, 100
  simulated, confusion with reality, 46, 152, 168
  as spatial changes in brightness, 60
  stereo, in comic books, 38
  stereoscopic, in this book, *28, 30, 31, 35, 36, 38, 39, 44, 88,*
    114, 123, 176–7, 184
  technologies to make, and interpretation, 46, 76, 81
  visual thinking, 13–16, 45, 132, 133, 137, 152, 169, 185
  See also Artifacts, perceptual

Imaginary worlds, 46, *83, 113,* 123, 132, 194–8
Imaging
  ambiguity of spatial phenomena, 60, 76–7
  diagnostic, 63–7, 77, 81, 185
Imagination, and analytic solutions, 152
  See also Ideas
In-betweening, 124–5, *124*
  automating, 125
  in sculpture animation, 151
Indefinite Divisibility, Tanguy, *171*
Infinity, iteration to, in Mandelbrot set, 164, 165
Information depository, 137, 148, 194, 198
Information processing
  channels, in the visual system, 18, 42–4
  conscious and preconscious, 12–13, 45
  visual, topographic mapping in the brain, 40
Information processors
  human visual system as, 12, 18, 45, 46, 169
  parallel, versus sequential, 42, 190–3
  small cellular, in human visual system, 42, 191
Initiator, fractal, 119
Insight, substituting simulations for, 152
Integral hologram, 75
Interactive processes, 132–3, 159, 186, 187, 195–6
  complex or remote forces or entities, 137, 152, 168, 191–2
Interface, human/machine, 127, 132–3, 137, 148, 151, 159,
    162, 168, 186, 187, 194–6
  "dataglove," 195–6, *195*
  intuitive, natural, 194
  transparent, 151
  WYSIWYG ("what you see is what you get"), 130
Interference patterns, 68, *69,* 70, 74, 189
Interposition, 32
Interpretation
  problems of, 46, 76–81, 152, 168, 171
  and technique, interdependence between, 46, 76, 81
Iridescence, algorithms for, 95

J

Jansky, Karl, 48
Jobs, Steven, 127
Julesz, Bela, 30, 34, 45

K

Kay, Alan, 127, 189
Keyboard, computer, 194
Key-frames, 124–5, *124*
Kekulé, Friedrich, 13, 16
Klug, Michael, 188
Knuth, Donald, 128
Kruger, Myron, 194

L

Lambert, Johann Heinrich, 94
Lambert shading, 94, *98*
Land, Edwin, 21, *22,* 24, 26–9, 45, 58
Land's color theory, 21–9
Language
    computer understanding, of speech, 189
    programming, visual, 152, 190
    visual, 82–5, 131, 170, 171
    See also Ideas
Lascaux, caves of, 12
Lasers, 68, 70, *71,* 188–9
    to cut scale models, 148, *149*
    high-resolution printer, 130
    invention of, 70
    pulsed, 75
    smoke puff scan, 182, *183*
Lateral geniculate nucleus (LGN), processing power of, 45
Leaning Tower of Pisa illusion, 29, 76
Leaves, modeling, *108,* 109, *109*
Leith, Emmet, 70, 72, 74
LGN, *see* Lateral geniculate nucleus
Light
    algorithms to describe behavior of, 100
    brightness versus reflectance, and color, 26–9
    coherent, 68, 70, 72, 75
    and color, 19, 25
    discoveries about, and visualization schemata, 131
    dual nature of, 189
    in holography, 189
    imitating, in computer graphics, 94
    modeling, 189
    optical properties of surfaces, 100
    receptors, in retina, 40
    source, 94, 98, 171
    speed of, *20*
    and surfaces, modeling interaction of, 94–103, 144
    transduction techniques, 47–8, 64, 72
    visible, *20*
    visual system's detection of order in, 18, 76, 132, 169, 199
    wave theory of, 68, *69,* 189
Light-pen, 127, 138
Lighting studies, architectural, 144, *146–7,* 148
Lisa computer, 127
Livingstone, Margaret, 13, *14,* 43–4
Logos, spiraling, 126

M

Machines
    computer-driven, numerically controlled, 138
    macromachines, 198
Macintosh, history of, 127
Magnetic resonance imaging (MRI), 64, 67, *67*
    on the pictorial/symbolic continuum, 136
    volume visualization in, 185
Magnets
    long molecules as, 134, 135
    polarities within iron crystal, *47*
Majestic Glory, Search, *101*
Man with a Newspaper, Magritte, 39
Mandelbrot, Benoit, 119, 164
Mandelbrot set, *164, 165, 166, 167*
    cluster connections, 166, 167
    defined, 164
    subregion, *165*
Manufacture, computer-automated (CAM), 138, 148
Maple trees, modeling realistic-looking, *106,* 107–9, *107–11,* 112, 131
Mapping, topographical, 44, 173
    of foot, *43*
    real-time, animated, 191
    terrain, 185
Maps, perceptual artifacts in, 76
Mars
    canals as perceptual artifacts, 76
    fly-over, 182
Masters, Ramon, 150–1
Mathematics, theoretical, numerical experiments in, 164–7
Matter
    flow of, 168
    low-density, 160, 162
Maunder, E.W., 76
Media Lab, MIT, 189
Megaflops, 190
Memory, computer, 190
Meteorology, 160
Michie, Donald, 133
Miranda fly-over, 16, 178–82, *179–81*
Modeling
    architectural, 138–49
    biochemical problems, 134, 135, 137
    complex or remote systems, 137, 152, 153, 158, 160–2, 168
    generating artificial realities, 194–8
    to guide exploration and comparison, 132–3, 144, 148, 152, 159, 160, 162, 169
    light, 189
    with parallel computers, *192–3*
    predicting fluid dynamics, 160–3
    sculpting computer objects with "dataglove," 195–6
    unpredictable systems, *154–7,* 158
    visualization in, 132–68
Models
    analytic, 152
    automated building of, 148, 149, *151*
    ball-and-stick, versus computer visualization, 134, 137, *170, 171*
    building, visual thinking in, 13
    evolving, three-dimensional, 148
    expense of building, 144, 148
    three-dimensional, 64, 148, *149,* 151, *176–7,* 178, *182–3,* 188

Molecules
    DNA, *170,* 171
    dynamic properties of, 134, 137
    hormone, *134–5,* 135
    pigment, of visual cones, 24, 40
    simulating, 132, 134–7
Mondrian, Piet, 24
Mortensen, Bob, 173
Mother and Child, Picasso, 13, *14*
Motion
    algorithms for, 131
    in animation, 126
    parallax, 123, 150, 151, 185
    spiraling, 126
Mount Shasta, three-dimensional model, *176–7,* 178
Mountains, fractal, 120, *120–1,* 122, 131
Mouse control, 86
    defined, 127
Movement
    depth sense relying on, 123, 150, 151, 185
    of fluids, 160, 162
    hand, digitized, 195–6
    of humans, modeling, 126
    molecular, 138, 158
    perception of, and stereoscopic depth information, 42
    whole-body, computer interface with, 196
Movies
    of the future, 189
    holographic, 188
    special effects, 82, 159
    stereoptically generated, 179–81
    See also: Star Trek II
MRI, *see* Magnetic resonance imaging
Multiplex hologram, 75
Multispectral remote-sensing images, 56, *56–7*
Music, and cognition, 189

N

Nasal shifting in stereographic images, 34, *36,* 38
Natadze, R., 14, 16
National Science Foundation, supercomputing facilities, 159
Naturalism, in computer graphics, 85
Nature, geometry of, modeling, 107–21
Negative transparency, 95
Negroponte, Nicholas, 189
Nervous system, parallel organization in, 191
Neurons, 191
    processing, in the retina, 40
    "visual fields" of, 42
Neuroscience, central mystery of, 40
1984, Porter, *102*
Newton, Isaac, 19
Nudes in the Forest, Léger, *85*
Numbers, complex, Mandelbrot set, 164, 165
Numerical experiments, 152–67
    peer review of, 162
    in theoretical mathematics, 164–7
    traditional safeguards, lack of, 152, 162

O

Object beam, 70
Object recognition, 29, 34, *36*, 169
  in determining distance, 76
Objectification, as goal of visualization, 169
Objects, imaginary, 46, 93–103, *109*, 123, 132, *188*, 194–8
  interacting with, 194–8
Obscuration, 33, 34, 171
Oculation, 32
Optic chiasma, 40
Opticks, Newton, 19
Optics, formulae, algorithms based on, 189
Option menu, 127
Order, human vision, and visualization, 12, 18, 45, 76, 132, 169, 199
Organisms, nature of, 199
Output, computer, 190

P

Packard, Norman, H., 158
Page, text, as graphic form, 130
Paint systems, 86, *87–9,* 108, 109
Papert, Seymour, 189
Parallax
  binocular, *see* Disparity
  horizontal, 123, 150, 151, 185
  vertical, 74
Particles, colliding, modeling, 192
Pattern-removal techniques, *62*
Patterns, 199
  computerized texture mapping, 95
  of energy, computer processing, 46
  eye/brain's tendency to discern or create, 37, 45, 76, 132, 169
  interference, 68, *69,* 70, 74, 189
  recursive, 107, 119
  repetitive, 37, 187
  snowflake, 158
  standing, of brightness and darkness, 68–70
Peer review, 162
Perception, human visual
  of color, 18–29, 42
  of depth, 29–39
  of form, 18, 29, 42
  psychology of, and visualization, 16, 131
  research on, 189
  theories of, 18–39
Perspective
  aerial, 32, *114,* 123, 151
  CAD drawings, 138, *142–3*
  detail, 32
  Dürer on, *92,* 93
  interior, architectural, 138
  linear, 32, 34, 171
  renderings, 144, 150
PET, *see* Positron emission tomography
Phenomena, representations of, as "pictorial," 136
Phong shading, 95, *98*

Photography
  color, technical basis, 19
  digitized, *49,* 95
  questions of veracity, 77
  seamless collage, 77
  stereo, 36, 68, 188
  as transduction technique, 47
Picture, distinction from symbol, 136
Pigment molecules, of the visual cone, 24, 40
Pixels, 48, 49, *49,* 89, 100
  in a depth image, 93
Plasma, 160
Plato, 18
Plesniak, Wendy, 188
Plotter, digital, 138, *140–1*
Point-by-point processing, 50–2
Point of view, 93, 100, 124, 126, 138, 173, 178
Polaroid instant camera, 21
Population, distribution of visual ability in
  stereopsis, 30
  visual thinking, 16
Positron emission tomography (PET), 64, 66, *66,* 81
  volume visualization in, 185
Preconscious processes, engaging power of, in problem
  solving, 12–13, 42, 45, 56, 131, 133, 152–3, 185
Press, William H., 159
Pressure, black hole, *161*
Printers
  for drawings, 138
  high-resolution laser, 130
Printing
  color, technical basis, 19
  image processing in, 71
Problem solving
  making use of preconscious processes in, 12–13, 42, 45, 56, 131, 133, 152, 185
  qualitative change, with graphics interface, 137, 152, 162, 185
  when to use visualization in, 168
Procedural techniques, 103–21, *104–6, 116, 117,* 128
  animation with, 126
  graphics, 191
  two-dimensional, 128
Processes
  complex, dynamic, 138, 152, 153, 158, 160, 162, 164
  conscious and preconscious, 12–13, 45, 56, 131, 133, 152–3, 185
  design, 137, 138, 143, 144, 150–1, 168, 169
  interactive, 137, 152, 159, 168, 191–2, 195–6
  iterative, 119, 164
  tomography-like, 187
Processing
  parallel, 190–3
  retinal, 40
Programs
  challenge, of parallel computing, 190, 191
  structure of, drawing rather than typing, 152
Projection, Dürer's illustration of, *92,* 93
Prokaryotes, 172
Proof, logical, versus visualization, 167
  See also Ideas
Protein Data Bank, Brookhaven National Laboratories, 137
Pseudocoloring, *47,* 52, *53–5,* 56, 76, 81

Publishing
  desktop, 159
  electronic, 189
Pulsed hologram, 75

R

Radiation, visible and invisible, 20
Random dot stereogram (RDS), 34–7, *35, 36,* 38
Randomness
  seeking departures from, 12, 199
  in tree-growing program, 112
Raster sequence, 191
  defined, 48
Ray-tracing, 100, *101–3, 139,* 169, 189
  in architectural renderings, 139, *144–5,* 144
  real-time, 191
Real-time flight simulators, 122, 123, 182
Realism
  exaggerated, *171*
  photographic, 100, 189
  pictorial, 170
  See also Images, misleading aspects
RDS, *see* Random dot stereogram
Reber, Grote, 48
Red's Dream, 83
Reeves, William, 112, 116
Reference beam, 70
Reflectance, 26–9
  Cartesian coordinates to represent, 28
  defined, 26
  inferred from point-to-point brightness changes, 27, 29
  in multispectral scanning, 58
  of surfaces, constancy of, and color, 21, 26, 199
Reflection, 100, 103, 189
  curved surfaces, 94–5, *98,* 100, *101–3*
  hologram, *72,* 74
  mapping, *103*
Refraction, 189
Refractive index, 100
Relationships
  interactive, 132–3, 137, 148, 159, 162, 172, 191, 192
  spatial, of objects, interpreting, 77
Relativity theory, computer simulations, 159
Remote sensing, 182
Renderings, 93–4, *96–9*
  architectural, *140–7,* 144
  computer graphics, 138, 187
  large-format, 138
  ray-traced, CAD, *139, 144–5*
  realistic, to guide design process, 144, 148, 169
  sequential, 190
  wire-frame, 93, *96,* 107
Repulsion, minimizing biomolecular, 134, 135
Research, traditional safeguards, 162
Resolution, image, 49, 52

Retina, 13, 18, 29, 30, 176, 191
  brightness change analysis, 27
  in color perception, 19
  design of, 40, *41*
  processing power of, 45
  translation of two-dimensional patterns into objects, 169
  visual cones, 24, 40
Retinex theory, 21–9, *27*, 58, 199
The Rhinoceros, Dürer, *84*
Rivier, Jean, 135
Rods, visual, 26–7, 40, *41*
Roentgen, Wilhelm, 47
Rotation, mental, of figures, 14, *15*
Ruskin, John, 18, 21, 30

S

Safety codes, design experimentation and, 144, 148
Scanning microdensitometer, 48, 49
Schemata, artistic, 82, 84, 170
  algorithms as, 84
  of realism, 171
  of visualization, as discoveries about vision, 131
Schroedinger, Erwin, 199
Script, animation, 126
Sculpture
  CAD use in, 150–1, 196
  virtual, *91*
Seashell, geometry of, *118*
Sequential computing, versus parallel, 190–3
Self-Portrait, Matisse, *44*
Self-similarity, *118,* 119, *119,* 131
Shading, 108, 94–102
  algorithms for, 131
  black-and-white, and color perception, 21, *22–3,* 25, 29
  computer image, 94–103, *94, 98*
  Gouraud, 95, *98,* 114
  Lambert, 94, *98*
  Phong, 95, *98*
Shadows, 171
  and color, *44*
  as depth cue, 32, *33,* 34
Shape
  channel, brightness as perceived by, *43,* 44, 53
  high-resolution, information about, 42
  in Mandelbrot set, 166
  See also Form; Objects
Shepard, Roger, 14
Shock fronts in black holes, *161*
Side-imaging radar (SIR), *54–5,* 60, 64
Similarity, geometric, 119

Simulations, computer graphics
  architectural, during design process, 138, 143, 144, 148, 169
  flight, *122–3,* 182, 194
  human/machine interface, 127, 132–3, 137, 148, 151, 159, 162, 186, 187, 194–6
  misleading aspects, 46, 152, 168, 171
  nonscientific, thinking about variables in relation to, 168
  real-time interactive, 122, 123, 159, 182
  trial, 132–3, 144, 148, 152, 159, 160, 162, 169
  as visual experiments, 132–3, 168
Single-cell recording, 42
Sketchpad, 127
Sky exposure plane, *146–7*
Skyharp, Fisher, *150–1*
Smarr, Larry, 159, 160, 162
Smith, Alvy Ray, 103, 116, 121
Smoke, volume visualization, 182, *183*
Snowflake, pattern, simulating, 158
Soft studio, 124
Solutions, analytic, versus simulations, 16, 45, 132, 135, 137, 152, 169, 185
Sorting, algorithms for, 152, *153*
Space, undefined, on computer screen, 123, 132
Space station, visualization of, 194–8, *196–7*
Sparkling, algorithms for, 95
Spatial relationships, of objects, in image interpretation, 77
Spectrum, 20
  trivariance, 19, 24, *27,* 40
Speech, dominant hemisphere, 14
  See also Communication; Language
Speed, computational, comparisons among neuronal, sequential, and parallel processes, 191
  See also Calculations
Sperry, Dr. Roger, 14
Stability
  and potential energy, 134, 136
  visual system's creation of, 13, 18, 45
  See also Order
Standing pattern, of brightness and darkness, 68–70
Star Trek II: The Wrath of Khan, "Genesis" sequence, 103, *104–5,* 116
Stars, life cycles of, 160
Stereograms, holographic, 75
  computer-generated, 188, *188*
Stereographs, *30, 31,* 68, 75
Stereopaintings, *38, 39*
Stereopairs
  in this book, *28, 30, 31, 35, 36, 38, 39,* 114
  computer graphics production of, 38
Stereophotography, 36, 68, 188
Stereopsis
  computer, 13, 189, 191
    image processing and computer graphics, 176–82
    Mt. Shasta, *176–7, 178*
    real-time, 191
    stereographic terminal, 185
  at a distance, 123
  human visual subsense of, 18, 29–38, 42, 74, 169
    discovering depth order with, 199
    mechanism of, 36–7
    population distribution, 30
  See also Dimensionality

Stereoscope, *28*
Stresses, architectural, evaluating, 138
Structure
  Earth's inner, 64
  and function, in molecules, 134–7
  three-dimensional representation by CAD, 138
  tree, parallel processors, 191
  viral, 186–7
Structures, impact of visualization on, 138, 148
Struthers, Scott, 135
Stylus, 38, 86, 138, 150
  animation, 125
Supercomputers, 159, 163
  large-scale structures of the Universe, *17*
  versus parallel processing, 190
Superimposition, in stereopsis, 37
Superior colliculus, 40
Surface normal, 94, *94,* 95
  modified by bump-map, 108
Surfaces
  in animation, 126
  brightness versus reflectance, 26–9
  of buildings, 144
  computer-graphics objects defined as, *109,* 132
  curved, computer rendering of, 94–6, 98, 100–3
  and light, modeling interaction of, 94–103
  of micro-organisms, 182
  of mountains, 178
  optical properties of, 100
  of planets, 178–82
  See also Mapping, Shading
Surgery, computer-aided, 185
Surrealism, in visualization, 171
Sutherland, Ivan, 127
Symbol, defined, 136
Synthetic fly-over, 173–5, *174–5*
Systems
  "chaotic," 164
  complex, simulating, 152, 153, 158, 160–2
  irreducible, 152
  nervous, parallel processing in, 191
  permitting modification by degree, 169
  unpredictable, *154–7*
  See also Processes

T

Teamwork, facilitation of, with visualization, 137, 148, 159, 172, 191, 194, 198

Technologies
emergent, 16, 172–99
image, and their interpretation, 46, 76, 81
subjective considerations, 46

Television
color, technical basis, 19
commercial, image-processing techniques, *78–9*
network news, paint systems use in, 86

Template forcing, 168, 169

Temporal shifting, 36, 38

Texture
human memory for, 112
mapping, 95, *99,* 109, *114*
process of evaluating, 131

Thinking, visual, 13–16, 44, 45, 56, 131, 133, 135, 185

Tic-tac-toe, as visual versus computational example, 133, 137

Time
computation, 52, 100, 132, 135, 137, 144, 159, 161, 168, 173, 190–1
required for design evaluation, 144, 148
required by nervous system, in parallel processing, 191

Time line, illustrated, script as, 126

Tornado, simulation of, *162–3*

Touch, nondominant hemisphere, 14

Tower of Pisa illusion, 29, 76

Trajectories, of planets, 152

Transduction, of data, 47–8, 64, 72, 112
techniques, 72, 185

Transmission hologram, 70–4, *71, 73, 74*
computer-synthesized equivalent, 189

Transparency, creating effect of, 95, *99,* 100

Trees, modeling, *106,* 107–9, *107–11,* 112, *117,* 131

Trivariance, 19–21, 26, 40, 48, 49, 52, 58, 76, 94, 95, 199

Type design, 128–9

Typesetting, digital, 130

U

Universe, 160
large-scale structures of, *17,* 76

University of Illinois, supercomputing facility, 159

"Unspace," flying into, 123, 132

Upatnieks, J., 70, 72, 74

Uranus, Miranda fly-over, 178–82, *179–81*

V

Variables
distinction between dependent and independent, 168
objectifying relationship between, 169
watching influences on each other, in visualizations, 137, 152, 162, 169

Vibration
in holography, 75, 188, 189
molecular, 134, 135, 137, 158

Video, experimental techniques, 189

Viewpoint, 100
animation "camera angle," 124
artist's, 93
in CAD architectural drawings, 138
sequential, 173, 178
in three-dimensional animation, 126

Virus, visualizing, 186–7

Vision, human
analytical strategies of, 112
color (versus colorless), 24, 26, 40
organizing function of, 12, 18, 45, 76, 132, 169, 187, 199
parallel processing, 42, 191
physiological mechanisms, 40–5
preconscious processes, 12–13, 45, 131, 133, 152–3, 185
proportion of brain dedicated to, 12, 199
scotopic or low-light, 24, 26, 40
specific task, of its design, 169
subsenses, 13, 18, 42–44, *43,* 176, 185
as test of algorithms, 131
and touch, matching stimuli, 14

Vision science, and visualization, 12–14, 16, *17,* 38, 42–5, *43, 44,* 52, *53,* 56–8, *57,* 131, 169, 176, *176–7,* 178, 182, 189, 199

Visual conventions, 82, 84–5, 131, 170, 171

Visual thinking, 13–16, 44, 45, 56, 131, 133, 135, 185
distribution of, in the population, 16

Visualization
accurate data transformation/effect of technology on image, 46, 76, 81
algorithms in, 50
applications, 172, 185, 198
in architecture, 138–49
combining basic tools of, 187
communicating ideas visually, rather than verbally or numerically, 16, 45, 132, 133, 135, 137, 152, 169, 185
computational intensiveness of, 52, 100, 132, 137, 159, 161, 168, 173, 182, 190–1
of complex scientific phenomena, 124, 160–3
as a discipline, 16, 172–99
and disparity, 38
as emergent, 60, 64, 172, 187
encouraging creative diversity and experimentation, 137, 138, 144, 148, 150–1, 159, 169
to explain program function, 152, *153*
fundamental goals, 136, 169
fundamentally new techniques of, 60, 64
holography in, 72
object-based, shortcut for, 119
objectification of phenomena in, 169

order, and human vision, 45, 132, 137, 152, 168, 171, 185, 199
parallel processing in, 190–3
with a "pictorial" style, artistic judgments, 136
for prediction, in fluid dynamics, 160–3
problem-solving simplification, 135, 137, 144, 168
reason for, 45, 198, 199
schemata of, 131
shifting information processing toward preconscious processes, 12–13, 45, 56, 133, 152, 185
and supercomputing, 159
superiority to ball-and-stick modeling, 134, 137
surrealism in, 171
three-dimensional, in medical diagnostics, 64
teamwork in, 137, 148, 159, 172, 191, 194, 198
types of problems appropriate for, 168
use of visual channel information in designing, 13–14, 43–4
volume, 182–5, *183, 184,* 189

Vocabulary, visual, 82–5, 131, 171

Volume
densities within, *186,* 187
holograms, 189
visualization of, 182–5, *183, 184,* 189

W

Wavelengths, light
  defined, *20*
  distribution on Mars, 76
  independence of color perception from, 21, *22–3*, 24, *27*
  long/medium/short reflectance, and color perception, 19, 21, *22–3*, 24, *25*, *27*, 28, 29, 58, 76
Waves
  of energy, image-making properties, 68
  Fourier techniques, 60
  light, in holography, 68, *69*, 189
  water, modeling, *113*
  wave *forms*, *60*, *113*
Weather, simulating, *162–3*, 185
Weight-contrast illusion, 16
What Is Life?, Schroedinger, 199
Wiesel, Torsten, 42, 45, 191
Wiesner, Jerome, 189
Wilson, Kenneth, G., 159
Window, 127
Word processing, 86, 130, 190
Wolfram, Stephen, 154, 158
Worldwide Plaza, 138, *140–7*, 148
Writing, dominant hemisphere, 14
WYSIWYG ("what you see is what you get") interface, 130

Y

Young, Thomas, 19, 24, 69
Young-Helmholtz theory, 19, 21, 24, 26, *27*, 29

Z

Z buffer, 93
Zimmerman, Thomas G., 195
Zoning ordinances, design experimentation and, 138, 144, *146–7*, 148

credits

The authors and publisher gratefully acknowledge the companies, institutions, museums, and individuals named in the captions or in the following credits for permitting the reproduction of works and for supplying the necessary photographs. (Numbers refer to pages on which illustrations appear.)

Binding and 96–99: Copyright © 1988, Symbolics, Inc., Graphics Division, Los Angeles.

3, 5, 7, 134–35: Photographs courtesy of Scott Struthers and Arnold Hagler, Agouron Institute, La Jolla, Calif.

13: Computer-generated image, Robert Bull.

14: © SPADEM.

15: Courtesy Professor Roger Shepard, Psychology Department, Stanford University.

17 below: Research—R. Brent Tully, Institute for Astronomy, University of Hawaii; Visualization—Michelle Mercer, National Center for Supercomputing Applications, University of Illinois at Urbana-Champaign.

20–22: Computer-generated diagrams, Robert Bull.

23–25: Courtesy Edwin H. Land, The Rowland Institute of Science, Inc., Cambridge, Mass.

27: Computer-generated diagram, Robert Bull.

28: Courtesy Edwin H. Land, The Rowland Institute of Science, Inc., Cambridge, Mass.

29: Computer-generated diagram, Robert Bull.

31: International Museum of Photography, at George Eastman House, Rochester, N.Y.

35: Computer-generated diagram, Robert Bull.

36: Diagrams from Bela Julesz, *Foundations of Cyclopean Perception,* University of Chicago Press, Chicago, 1971, p. 95. © 1971 by Bell Telephone Laboratories, Inc. All rights reserved. Reprinted by permission of the publisher, The University of Chicago Press, and the author.

41: © Lennart Nilsson, *Behold Man,* Little Brown and Company, Boston.

43: Courtesy Dr. Margaret Livingstone, Harvard Medical School, Boston.

44: © SPADEM.

47: Photograph—R. Freemire and B. Young, cover of *Science,* vol. 234, October 1986; Research—R.J. Celotta and D.T. Pierce, "Magnetic Domains on a Crystal Surface," *Science,* vol. 234, October 1986, pp. 333–40. Copyright 1986 by the AAAS.

49: Computer-generated images, Robert Bull.

51: Courtesy 3M/Comtal, Altadena, Calif.

52–53: Gould Incorporated, Imaging and Graphics Division, Fremont, Calif. © 1985 Gould Electronics.

54–55: Courtesy of Jet Propulsion Laboratory, California Institute of Technology and NASA, Pasadena, Calif.

57: Available as part of the SPOT as ART™ collection. Provided Courtesy of SPOT Image Corporation, Reston, Va.

58: Siemens Medical Systems, Inc., Iselin, N.J.

59, 61: Vicom Systems, Inc., San Jose, Calif.

62: International Imaging Systems, Milpitas, Calif.

63: GE Medical Systems, Milwaukee, Wis.

65: Courtesy Skidmore, Owings & Merrill, N.Y.

66: Courtesy Drs. Michael E. Phelps and John C. Mazziotta, UCLA School of Medicine. From Dr. Michael E. Phelps et al. "Positron Emission Tomography," Fig. 4a, *Science,* Vol. 228, May 1985, pp. 799–809. Copyright 1985 by the AAAS.

67: Siemens Corporation, Iselin, N.J.

69: Computer-generated diagrams, Robert Bull.

71–74: Julie Walker, copyright MIT Media Lab 1988, Massachusetts Institute of Technology, Cambridge.

78–79: Courtesy Coca-Cola USA, Atlanta.

80: © Alyce Kaprow 1984.

87 below: Alinari (Anderson, Roma).

88–89: Charlex, Inc., New York.

90, 94: Computer-generated diagrams, Robert Bull.

101: Copyright 1987 by Patricia Search. All rights reserved.

103: Copyright © 1988, Symbolics Inc., Graphics Division, Los Angeles.

104–105: Courtesy Pixar, San Rafael, Calif.

106–108: Reprinted by permission of the creators and the Association for Computer Machinery, Inc.

109 above: Reprinted by permission of the creators and the Association for Computer Machinery, Inc.; below: Jules Bloomenthal, Xerox Palo Alto Research Center, Palo Alto, Calif.

110–11: Reprinted by permission of the creators and the Association for Computer Machinery; Inc.

115: From *Computer Graphics,* Vol. 18, Number 3, July 1984, cover. Reprinted by permission of the creator and the Association for Computer Machinery, Inc.

122–23: Courtesy Evans & Sutherland, Salt Lake City.

128: From Donald Knuth, *Computer Modern Typefaces,* © 1986, Addison-Wesley Publishing Company, Inc., Reading, Massachusetts. Pg. 306 (figure). Reprinted with permission.

129: Neenie Billawala, Stanford University.

130: Letraset Graphic Design Software, Paramus, N.J.

139: Courtesy Evans & Sutherland, Salt Lake City.

140–47: Courtesy Skidmore, Owings & Merrill, New York.

150–54: © Robert Fisher 1986.

153: Marc H. Brown and Robert Sedgewick, "A System for Algorithm Animation," *Computer Graphics,* Vol. 18, No. 3, July 1984, pp. 177–86. Reprinted by permission of the creators and the Association for Computer Machinery, Inc.

153–57: Stephan Wolfram, Center for Complex Systems Research, University of Illinois at Urbana-Champaign.

158: Norman H. Packard, Center for Complex Systems Research, University of Illinois at Urbana-Champaign.

160: © Thinking Machines Corporation, Cambridge, Mass.

161 above: Dr. Larry Smarr and Dr. John Hawley, National Center for Supercomputing Applications, University of Illinois at Urbana-Champaign; below: Dr. Larry Smarr and Dr. John Hawley, National Center for Supercomputing Applications, University of Illinois at Urbana-Champaign. Reprinted from Dr. Larry Smarr, "An Approach to Complexity: Numerical Computation," Fig. 3, *Science,* Vol. 228, April 1985, pp. 403–408. Copyright 1985 by the AAAS.

162–63: Research—Robert Wilhelmson; Visualization—Stefen Fangmeier, National Center for Supercomputing Applications, University of Illinois at Urbana-Champaign.

164–67: © 1988, Art Matrix, Cornell National Supercomputer Facility, Ithaca, N.Y.

170: Nelson Max, Lawrence Livermore National Laboratory © 1980.

174–77: Courtesy of Jet Propulsion Laboratory, California Institute of Technology, and NASA, Pasadena, Calif.

179–81: Courtesy Helen B. Mortensen, Kevin Hussey, and Jeff Hall, Jet Propulsion Laboratory, California Institute of Technology, and NASA, Pasadena, Calif.

186–87: Courtesy, IBM Scientific Centre, Madrid, from Javier Jiménez et al. "Computer Graphic Display Method for Visualizing Three-Dimensional Biological Structures," cover, and Figs., 1a, 1b, 2d, *Science,* Vol. 232, May 1986, pp. 1113–15. Copyright 1986 by the AAAS. 186 above: J.M. Carazo, J.L. Carrascosa, N. Garcia, and A. Santisteban; below: J. Jiminéz and J.M. Carazo.

188: Copyright MIT Media Lab 1988, Massachusetts Institute of Technology, Cambridge.

192–93: © Thinking Machines Corporation.

The authors acknowledge *Optical Anecdotes* by D.J. Lovell (international Society for Optical Engineering, 1981) as the source for the opening quotes used for *Images from Energy* and *Emergent Technologies.*